For years we've heard rum
Cuba. Now, for the first tii
curtain and shown us, in remarkable detail, just what God has been doing. You'll be inspired by the passion and sacrifice of these disciples of Christ and how they have emerged from years of opposition to spread the gospel, and thousands of new churches, throughout this island nation. God bless Kurt Urbanek for sharing with us this labor of love.

Dr. David Garrison,
Missionary Author, Church Planting Movements

Kurt Urbanek provides an extremely significant piece of work with implications on church planting. I first met him on a flight inside of Cuba, and was struck by his humility and love for the people there. This book is a testimony of God's mercy and sovereign power. At the center of the storm, the Church in Cuba has seen its share of affliction and heartbreak, but also many inspiring examples of personal courage, and faithfulness, as Kurt reveals. This fascinating, well-researched book will provide insight on adaptability and fortitude in the midst of enormous opposition, some of which helped to fuel the remarkable growth of the church. The reader will be inspired, challenged, and blessed!

Rick Johnson
Director, Personnel and Member Care
Assemblies of God World Missions

Cuba's Great Awakening: Church Planting Movement in Cuba is an outstanding book which masterfully documents the astounding moving of God during a crucial period in the history of this country. The author's extensive experience in ministry in Cuba, his long-term relationship with the key persons involved in this movement coupled with his disciplined and professional utilization of statistical data and keen missiological insights make this a very valuable resource for those who want to get a clear and inspiring picture of what God is doing through an unprecedented church planting movement in that part of the world. I recommend this book wholeheartedly to pastors, lay persons, professors and students.

Dr. Daniel R. Sánchez
Professor of Missions
Southwestern Baptist Theological Seminary

Kurt Urbanek's book will be required reading for all who are interested in rapid church planting movements sweeping across an entire country. A quiet revolution swept across Cuba as difficult events of the last decades created spiritual hunger among the Cuban people, and finally the evidence can be made public. Christianity is growing in Cuba faster than anywhere else in the western hemisphere. Until now no one has heralded the inspiring story of how Baptists and other evangelical Christians have lived sacrificially to share their faith and to start new churches to disciple unbelievers looking to Christ. Kurt Urbanek's study shares insights from his unique insider's perspective to document the reality of so many conversions and of so many new churches finding a way forward to serve the Lord even under difficult circumstances. Prepare to be amazed at this story of God at work!

Dr. Bob Garrett
Piper Chair of Missions
Director, MA in Global Leadership Dallas Baptist University

Cuba's Great Awakening offers a serious analysis, as much biblical as it is historical and critical, of the spiritual revival that has occurred in Cuba, beginning in the 1990s. A renewed interest of the people in the message of the Gospel of Christ has taken place. The irrefutable result has been the greatest planting of churches that has ever occurred in the history of missionary work in Cuba. The author investigates both the historical roots and the social and spiritual conditions which have provoked the surprising and extensive period of growth which has continued—for more than two decades—in Cuban churches. Besides revealing the details of a history which is unknown to many, the reading of this book will have a profound spiritual impact on those who feel the urgency to dedicate their lives to missions.

Alberto González Muñoz
President of Cuba's Western Baptist Convention from 2002 to 2007
He has served as a pastor in Cuba for close to fifty years.

Cuba's Great Awakening
Church Planting Movement in Cuba

Kurt Urbanek, Ph.D.

Cuba's Great Awakening: Church Planting Movement in Cuba

© Kurt Urbanek

Printed in the United States of America

All rights reserved. No part of this publication may be reproduced, stored in a retrieval system, or transmitted in any form or by any means—for example, electronic, photocopy, and recording— without the prior written permission of the publisher. The only exception is brief quotations in printed reviews.

Library of Congress Cataloging-in-publication Data

Kurt Urbanek 1959 -

    Cuba's Great Awakening: Church Planting Movement in Cuba

ISBN-13: 978-0692355350

ISBN-10: 0692355359

1. Missions I. Urbanek, Kurt II Title

Contents

Preface vi

Foreword vii

CHAPTER

1. UNDERSTANDING A CHURCH PLANTING MOVEMENT 1

2. ANTECEDENTS TO THE CHURCH PLANTING
   MOVEMENT AMONG CUBAN BAPTISTS 23

3. CUBAN INDEPENDENCE AND BAPTIST WORK IN CUBA 45

4. THE EFFECTS OF CUBAN REVOLUTION ON
   CHURCH GROWTH IN CUBA 65

5. THE EMERGENCE OF THE CUBAN CHURCH PLANTING
   MOVEMENT 85

6. ANALYSIS OF CHURCH GROWTH STATISTICS
   FROM 1990 TO 2010 107

7. FINDINGS AND RECOMMENDATIONS FOR THE CUBAN
   CHURCH PLANTING MOVEMENT 131

8. OBSTACLES TO OVERCOME AND CHALLENGES
   TO CONFRONT 153

9. LAST THINGS 169

Preface

While many articles have been written about Church Planting Movements, only now are we are beginning to see a few books on the subject published.

Cuba's Great Awakening unveils a Church Planting Movement that is ongoing in our own day. This CPM emerged in the mid-1990s and continues to multiply among Baptists throughout Cuba. Of great interest also is the fact that a parallel CPM emerged and is continuing to expand among the Assemblies of God churches in Cuba. I have, therefore, the pleasure of introducing you to Dr. Kurt Urbanek's first-hand report of this Church Planting Movement in Cuba.

In this work, Dr. Urbanek explores and records a summary of Christian and evangelical history, much of which has never been publically shared. It is out of this foundation that the author identifies the antecedents, phases and realities of the CPM that occurred among Cuban Baptists.

The real value of this book is not the documenting of the history or the identifying of the antecedents of the movement, nor the reality of the movement along with its fantastic growth patterns, but the struggles and issues the church leaders have dealt with, some expected and others unforeseen. The author talks about the process of how the Baptists and the traditional churches are making peace with and coming to bless the movement as God's doing.

This book should help all who pray for God to bring a revival, an awakening, or a Church Planting Movement into existence where they labor for Christ. And, you ask: how do you know so much about this Cuban CPM? My answer is that I led the missiological team that went throughout the cities and rural realms of Cuba interviewing hundreds of church members, church planters and pastors of churches. This team documented the existence and extent of the movement.

What Dr. Urbanek presents is grounded in thousands of pages of research to which I can attest that he has seen and experienced first-hand among his Cuban brethren. May God bless your journey through this book!

Dr. James B. Slack
Missiologist and Field Assessments Consultant
International Mission Board of the SBC
25 January 2012

Foreword

Positioned in the Caribbean Sea, the island nation of Cuba is often subject to the howling assaults of hurricanes. On more than one occasion, massive storms have battered the nation with devastating impact. Walking along the barren Cuban coasts after such a storm it is difficult to imagine how anything could survive. Even the Royal Palms, Cuba's national tree, stripped of their broad leaves and with jointed trunks bent low by the fierce winds, seem destined for an untimely death.

But don't be so quick to write off what remains of those once majestic sentinels of the sea. This is not the first hurricane these Royal Palms have experienced, and it will not likely be the last. The Creator's hand, in fact, has designed them to withstand such storms. With foliage designed for "quick release" and trunks designed to bend without breaking, these fragile-looking remnants will once again stand...and flourish.

Cuba's Great Awakening reveals the exciting similarity between the authentic church in Cuba and the Royal Palm. Suffering the ravaging blows of devastating political and economic storms, the church has flourished and now stands stronger than ever in that nation's history.

For decades, the attention of the evangelical world has been turned away from the small island nation. After all, it has been largely closed to outside inspection. And most of what we know has been only anecdotal, colored by the tacit assumption of persecution and hard times for believers. When the welcome mat was pulled in, the western world quickly turned its attention elsewhere.

But while the world was not looking, God was working among the believing community, "strengthening their stakes and lengthening their cords." (Isaiah 54:2) The statistics recording the growth of Christianity in Cuba are now staggering in their enormity.

As you would imagine, statistics alone can do little more than reveal the reality of the church's existence. They cannot tell the story. This is why my friend, Kurt Urbanek, has taken upon himself the enormous task of opening up the gate to Cuba's remarkable church planting movement and allowing us to walk along the path with him. The journey is breathtaking.

Cuban believers have embraced the "seminary of trials" and are showing the world the resilience and strength of genuine faith. The lessons they have to teach us must not be ignored or wasted. So it is with heartfelt gratitude to Kurt Urbanek and a growing number of evangelicals across Cuba that I urge you open the pages of this book and begin a journey that will forever change the way you look at "church."

Dr. Tom Elliff

President, International Mission Board
Southern Baptist Convention

CHAPTER 1

UNDERSTANDING A CHURCH PLANTING MOVEMENT

In the face of staggeringly difficult political, social, and economic circumstances, Cuba is experiencing an unprecedented movement of God. This inspiring movement has seen hundreds of thousands come to faith in Jesus Christ and thousands of new church starts. Congregations among Baptists alone have multiplied from 238 to 7,039 churches, missions and house churches in just 20 years. Among the Assemblies of God, the increase has soared from 89 churches in 1990 to 2,779 in 2010 and this number of congregations is augmented by 7,997 house churches. Total Assembly of God membership (including adherents) has increased from 12,000 in 1990 to over 688,931 in 2010. This spiritual awakening continues and promises even greater blessings in the days to come.

International attention has focused upon the changes occurring on the island nation. The illness of Fidel Castro, its implications for the Cuban government, and the announcement of the assumption of power by his younger brother Raúl, provoked many questions about Cuba's future. On Tuesday, February 19, 2008, Fidel Castro announced he would not accept the nomination for reelection as Cuba's president. Five days later, Raúl Castro was elected in his place.

Many observers point to the growing openness of Cuba to a tourist-market economy as a sign of change on the island. William Luis explains the circumstances surrounding the collapse of the Soviet Union and the resulting economic crisis in Cuba. He believes that Castro, in order to stay in power, restructured the Cuban economy based upon tourism.

By 2001 Cuba was already the fourth most visited country in Latin America with more than one million tourists visiting annually.[1] A release from the Ministry of Tourism states, "Cuba is expected to register a record number of 2.7 million tourists in 2011. . . Tourism is Cuba's second largest contributor of hard currency, earning 2.1 billion U.S. dollars annually. The country is expected to receive 3 million visitors in 2012."[2] These changes, along with the legalization of use of the U.S. dollar, brought millions of dollars into the Cuban

---

[1] William Luis, *Culture and Customs of Cuba* (Westport, CT: Greenwood Press, 2001), 14.

[2] Tang Danlu ed., "Cuba to Register a Record Number of Tourists in 2011. December 17, 2011; [on-line]; accessed 18 December 2011; available from http://news.xinhuanet.com/english/world/2011-12/17/c_131311909.htm; internet.

economy.³

Missing from secular news reports on the changes in Cuba is any notice of the remarkable growth of the Evangelical Churches on the island. This remarkable growth has been seen primarily among the Baptists and the Assemblies of God. While the CPM in Cuba is not limited to groups, their story is representative of the exceptional growth taking place.⁴

This book describes and analyzes the Church Planting Movement (CPM) among the Western and Eastern Baptist Conventions of Cuba from 1990-2010. There is also a brief examination of the growth of the Assemblies of God during the same time period. In order to establish a foundation for an analysis of the CPM occurring in Cuba, a description of a CPM is needed. This description will focus on a definition of the term, evaluation of CPMs, universal elements of church planting, common factors in CPMs, and the impact of CPMs. A brief introduction of the Cuban CPM and the process for assessing it will be outlined.

Description of a Church Planting Movement

The term "Church Planting Movement," or CPM, has become a key concept in mission circles today. According to the International Mission Board's (IMB) Office of Overseas Operations:

> In the midst of our search for more effective ways to reach a lost world, God has revealed some remarkable breakthroughs in evangelism and church planting that is happening in the most unexpected corners of our globe. In these situations, evangelism is resulting in rapidly multiplying churches in a phenomenal way that is vastly outstripping population-growth rates.⁵

---

³ Danielle Barav, "FAQ's about Cuba's Dual Currency System," U.S. Cuba Cooperative Security Project, April 18, 2008; [on-line]; accessed September 1, 2010. available from http://www.wsicubaproject.org/CubaDualCurrencySystem08.cfm.
In a move to bolster their struggling economy the Cuban government legalized the use of the U.S. dollar from 1993 until 2004. In 2005 the Cuban government began to require that U.S. dollar be converted to Cuban Convertible Pesos (CUC) to be spent in Cuba. On April 9, 2005, the value of the convertible peso was re-evaluated to be worth $1.08 in U.S. dollars. There was an additional 10 percent exchange fee for converting dollars to CUCs, making each dollar worth 0.82 CUC. One would have to exchange $1.22 USD to get one CUC.
⁴During the past ten years there have been reports of increasing growth among Free Methodists, Seventh-Day Adventists and several Pentecostal groups.
⁵Office of Overseas Operations, Something New Under the Sun (Richmond, VA: International Mission Board, 1999), 14.

As early as 1989, the Foreign Mission Board (FMB) was talking about the importance of fostering CPMs, especially among unreached people groups. In his February 13, 1989 report to the FMB Board of Trustees, Executive Vice President William O'Brien presented a list of items to be considered by the Board in the adoption of a Great Commission Manifesto. Included in the list was the desire, ". . . to establish a mission-minded church planting movement within every unreached people group so that the gospel is accessible to all people."[6]

On August 14, 1995, Avery Willis, Senior Vice President of the FMB, stated in his report to the Board of Trustees:

> . . . 31.5% of the world is in World A, almost one-third of the population of the world. We need a church planting movement among these peoples. We need somebody in that position to share the love of God, but beyond that we need someone there to start churches. And then beyond that, we need church planting movements so that a whole people movement can begin there.[7]

By 1995, overseas leadership of the FMB was reporting the emergence of CPMs in various World A settings. In his October 9, 1995 report to the FMB's trustees, Mike Stroope, Area Director for Cooperative Services International (CSI) shared: "Among the unreached in World A, CSI personnel reported a 52% increase in the number of new churches over the previous year. . . . a sizable number of these congregations represent church planting movements which are now well underway."[8]

According to David Garrison,[9] "In 1998, the International Mission Board's Overseas Leadership Team adopted a vision statement: *We will facilitate the lost coming to saving faith in Jesus Christ by beginning and nurturing Church Planting Movements among all peoples.*"[10]

---

[6]William R. O'Brien, "Executive Vice President Report" (Richmond, VA: Report to the Board of Trustees, Foreign Mission Board, Feb. 13, 1989).
[7]Avery Willis, "Senior Vice President Report" (Ridgecrest, NC: Report to the Board of Trustees, Foreign Mission Board, Aug. 14, 1995).
[8]Mike W. Stroope, "One Day . . . Is Today" (Richmond, VA: Cooperative Services International Area Director Report to the Board of Trustees, Foreign Mission Board, Oct. 9, 1995).
[9]Garrison has an earned Ph.D. in history from the University of Chicago, and has served as an IMB missionary in Hong Kong, Egypt, Tunisia, Europe, and India. Additionally, he served the IMB as Associate Vice President for Global Strategy, and the IMB's Regional Leader for South Asia.
[10]David Garrison, *Church Planting Movements* (Richmond, VA: International Mission Board of the Southern Baptist Convention, 2000), 7.

In the late 1990s, the IMB introduced the definition and description of the CPM phenomenon in several publications.[11] In 1999, David Garrison, speaking on behalf of the IMB, presented the definition of a CPM as a "rapid and exponential increase of indigenous churches planting churches within a given people group or population segment."[12] This is the IMB's official definition and description, as found in David Garrison's booklet *Church Planting Movements*, published in 2000. In a 2004 publication, *Church Planting Movements: How God is Redeeming a Lost World*, Garrison adjusted his definition: "A Church Planting Movement is a rapid multiplication of indigenous churches planting churches that sweep through a people group or population segment."[13] In the 2006 publication "Together to the Edge: Planting Churches Strategy Manual," Lewis Myers, James Slack, and Mark Snowden further refined the definition: "A 'Church Planting Movement' is a miraculous work of God that happens when indigenous churches begin to multiply rapidly. The churches that are started remove any barriers that could block their reproduction, so they just keep multiplying to the glory of God."[14]

For the purpose of this book, this author chose to use David Garrison's definition of a CPM as presented in his second work on the subject, *Church Planting Movements: How God is Redeeming a Lost World*. This definition states, "A Church Planting Movement is a rapid multiplication of indigenous churches planting churches that sweeps through a people group or population segment."[15] The change from Garrison's original definition is significant because it adjusts the level of expected growth from a "rapid and exponential increase of indigenous churches planting churches" to a "rapid multiplication of indigenous churches planting churches." It appears the

---

[11]The first official IMB documentation this writer found was in an in-house publication by Mark Snowden, ed., *Toward a Church Planting Movement* (Richmond: International Mission Board, 1998). The next IMB publication that included a definition of a CPM was Office of Overseas Operation's, *Something New Under the Sun* (Richmond, VA: International Mission Board, 1999). The official IMB definition was released through Garrison's, *Church Planting Movements* (Richmond, VA: International Mission Board of the Southern Baptist Convention, 2000). Additionally, this writer found the concept discussed in Rick Wood's, "A Church Planting Movement Within Every People: The Key to Reaching Every People and Every Person," *Missions Frontiers Magazine*, May-June 1995 [on-line]; accessed 20 October 2009; available from http://www.missionfrontiers.org/pdf/1995/ 0506/mj954.htm; Internet. In this article, Wood describes a CPM as a type of People Movement with a natural spontaneous reproduction of indigenous churches. Wood's identification of a CPM as a type of People Movement makes his understanding of a CPM distinct from Garrison's.

[12]Garrison, *Church Planting Movements*, 7; and see also http://www.churchplantingmovements.com; Internet.

[13]Garrison, *Redeeming a Lost World*, 21.

[14]Lewis Myers, James Slack, and Mark Snowden, "Together to the Edge: Planting Churches Strategy Manual," Tms (photocopy) (Richmond, VA: Global Research Department, Evangelism and Church Growth Section, International Mission Board of the Southern Baptist Convention, January 2006), iii.

[15]Garrison, *Redeeming a Lost World*, 21.

change was made due to the realization that the use of the term "exponential increase" was not justified in the subsequent research of the existing and emerging CPMs. James Slack explains that, "Initial CPMs that emerged among insulated and isolated unreached people groups did exhibit 'exponential' growth rates, but every one of the assessed CPMs did fit the math term 'multiplication', while not all measured up to the term 'exponential'."[16]

Garrison breaks his definition into five key ideas. First, "a Church Planting Movement reproduces rapidly. Within a very short time, newly planted churches are already starting new churches that follow the same pattern of rapid reproduction."[17] The second key word in the definition is multiplication. "Church Planting Movements do not simply add churches. Instead they multiply. Surveys of Church Planting Movements indicate that virtually every church is engaged in starting multiple new churches."[18] The third key term is indigenous. "Indigenous literally means generated from within, as opposed to started by outsiders."[19]

Garrison states, "In a Church Planting Movement the initiative and drive of the movement comes from within the people group rather than from outsiders."[20] In many of the CPMs studied, the key initiators of the CPM were individuals or organizations from outside the people group who helped in the beginning phase of the CPM, but were quickly displaced from within the CPM leadership. Within the Cuban context, the Holy Spirit initiated the CPM, and outsiders came alongside after it was initiated to fan the flames. The fourth element is that local churches are the principal players in planting the new churches. According to Garrison:

> Though church planters may start the first churches, at some point the churches themselves begin to act. When churches begin planting churches, a tipping point is reached and a movement is launched. . . . But when the momentum of reproducing churches outstrips the ability of the planters to control, a movement is underway.[21]

The final key to the definition is, ". . . Church Planting Movements occur within people groups or interrelated population segments."[22] CPMs move through networks of relationships.[23] The

---

[16] James Slack, "Church Planting Movements: Rationale, Research and Realities of Their Existence," *Journal of Evangelism and Missions* 6 (Spring 2007): 32.
[17] Garrison, *Redeeming a Lost World*, 21.
[18] Ibid., 22.
[19] Ibid.
[20] Garrison, *Church Planting Movements*, 8.
[21] Garrison, *Redeeming a Lost World*, 22-23.
[22] Ibid., 23.

homogeneous unit principle is seen clearly in the existing and emerging CPMs.[24] Cuba is a very homogeneous society; Cubans speak one language, live under the same political system, and suffer many of the same harsh economic, social, and spiritual consequences of living for decades under that system.

Evaluation of Church Planting Movements

In 2000, the executive leadership of the IMB assigned the Global Research Department the task of evaluating the validity of the existence of CPMs in various global contexts. In his article, "Church Planting Movements: Rationale, Research and Realities of Their Existence," Slack outlines the process of CPM evaluation. The process included the development of several documents which elaborated the process for CPM evaluation.[25] Using these evaluation instruments, missiologists, professors of missions, and other missiologically astute individuals were selected and trained to conduct on-site evaluations of possible CPMs. In Garrison's original publication, *Church Planting Movements*, he proposed that there were seven existing CPMs. According to Slack, "following on-site interviews, two of the seven did not prove to be actual CPMs."[26] He continues:

> At the time of the writing of this article, 12 supposed Church Planting Movements have been assessed ac-

---

[23]Garrison declares, "Unlike the predominant pattern in the West with its emphasis on evangelism and personal commitment, Church Planting Movements typically rely on a much stronger family and social connection." Garrison, *Church Planting Movements*, 37.
[24]Donald A. McGavran, *Understanding Church Growth* (Grand Rapids: Eerdmans, 1980). According to McGavran, "The homogeneous unit is simply a section of society in which all the members have some characteristic in common," 95. He defines the "Homogeneous Unit Principle as the fact that, "Men like to become Christians without crossing racial, linguistic, or class barriers," 223.
[25]The CPM assessment documents include the following: James B. Slack, "Church Planting Movements: A Clarification of the Assessment Process and CPM Definition when Compared to Historical Movements," Tms (photocopy) (Richmond, VA: Global Research Department, Evangelism and Church Growth Section, International Mission Board of the Southern Baptist Convention, 12 March 2003); James B. Slack, "Church Planting Movements Education and Assessment Process Overview," Tms (photocopy) (Richmond, VA: Global Research Department, Evangelism and Church Growth Section, International Mission Board of the Southern Baptist Convention, 17 April 2003); James B. Slack, "CPM Assessment Approach Options," Tms (photocopy) (Richmond VA: Global Research Department, Evangelism and Church Growth Section, International Mission Board of the Southern Baptist Convention, 10 August 2003); James B. Slack, "CPM Definitions and Movement Comparisons," Tms (photocopy) (Richmond, VA: Global Research Department, Evangelism and Church Growth Section, International Mission Board of the Southern Baptist Convention, 12 March 2003); James B. Slack, and colleagues, "Church Growth Audits of Church Planting Movements in Process: Assessment Criteria," TMs (photocopy) (Richmond, VA: Global Research Department, Evangelism and Church Growth Section, International Mission Board of the Southern Baptist Convention, 2001); and Slack, "Rationale, Research and Realities," 29-44.
[26]Slack, "Rationale, Research and Realities," 37-41.

cording to IMB assessment methodology. And, based upon 2005 Annual Statistical Reports and Regional Leader evaluations, at least forty-two (42) people groups were singled out and placed on the 2004-2005 Watch List of Possible CPMS. By 2007, as many as 122 people groups are on a Watch List of possible CPMs. These await field assessments.[27]

Cuba was one of the CPMs evaluated.[28]

Ten Universal Elements Present in Church Planting Movements

A CPM is characterized by a number of what Garrison calls "universal elements, observed in every CPM." They include: extraordinary prayer, abundant evangelism, intentional planting of reproducing churches, the authority of God's Word, local leadership, lay leadership, house or cell churches, churches planting churches, rapid reproduction, and healthy churches.[29] It needs to be understood that the purpose of Garrison's publications was to encourage the implementation of CPM methodologies with the hope that CPMs would emerge in other contexts as a result.[30]

---

[27]Ibid., 37-38. See James B. Slack, "Assessments of Church Planting Movements," in *Church Planting Movements in North America*, ed. Daniel R. Sánchez (Fort Worth: Church Starting Network, 2007), 265-66. Slack demonstrates the humility and the wisdom of flexibility needed when conducting research of existing or potential CPMs when he states, "We are aware, of course, that what we say about Church Planting Movements in this early stage of observation will surely be corrected and refined as more of them are observed and more carefully assessed."

[28]James Slack, Dennis Jones, Roy Cooper, and Dirce Cooper, "A Church Planting Movement Assessment of the Two Baptist Conventions: A CPM Assessment of the Eastern and Western Baptist Conventions Based Upon On-Site Interviews Conducted in 2002," 8th ed., Tms [photocopy] (Richmond, VA: Global Research Department, Evangelism and Church Growth Section, International Mission Board of the Southern Baptist Convention, 17 December 2002.

[29]Garrison, *Redeeming a Lost World*, 172. The cell church was included in the original 2000 booklet. This writer has chosen to include this element together with house churches, because it is true to the original document and both house churches and various forms of cell churches are prevalent in Cuba, and in other CPMs. No one model of church in the Cuba CPM exists, nor is the house church the only model of church found in the study of global CPMs.

[30]Garrison, *Redeeming a Lost World*, 11-12. Garrison's research seeks to understand the CPM phenomenon so as to determine how God is working through these movements, and how His people can participate in what He is doing in the world. Garrison uses the concept of "reverse engineering": if it is possible to determine what God is doing and how He is doing it, then one can understand "the Creator's designs, desires, and method of operation." This writer's belief is that Garrison and the IMB witnessed God move in such a remarkable way through CPMs that they desired to see that phenomenon spread. They felt that if they could understand the component parts of a CPM, and share the vision through publications, workshops, and changes in strategy, then those principles could be repeated in other contexts with the same results. Steve Wilkes, "Missiological Misgivings?" *Journal of Evangelism and Missions* 6 (Spring 2007):

Extraordinary Prayer

Throughout the Scripture and the history of the Church, the discipline of prayer has proved pivotal for any mighty movement of the Holy Spirit. From the prayer meetings in the Upper Room (Acts 1:1-14) and the manifestation of the Holy Spirit on the day of Pentecost, (Acts 2:41) to the daily home meetings of the early Church where believers "continued steadfastly in the apostles' doctrine and fellowship, in the breaking of bread, and in prayers," (Acts 2:44) prayer was central to the early Church. As a result of persecution in Acts 4, the church prayed, and "the place where they were assembled together was shaken; and they were all filled with the Holy Spirit, and they spoke the word of God with boldness" (Acts 4:31 NIV).

Through their fervent prayers and evangelism, the Church expanded rapidly. While it is outside the scope of this book to trace the history of prayer through the Scripture and throughout Church history, these few examples set the tone for the centrality of prayer in any movement of God. Peter Wagner declares, "The more deeply I dig beneath the surface of church growth principles, the more thoroughly convinced I become that the real battle is a spiritual battle and that our principal weapon is prayer."[31]

The CPM in Cuba was born in prayer and continues due to the sovereign grace of God and the prayers of His saints. This writer has heard countless testimonies of the years Cubans spent in tireless prayer for a divine visitation to their island nation.[32] Dr. Leoncio Veguilla Cené regards prayer as fundamental: "Without prayer, we wouldn't have been able to do what we've done."[33] Twenty-five-year-old lay missionary Dania Hernández, adds, "Baptists have always been a people on their knees."[34] In twenty years of missionary travel across the Americas and the Caribbean, this writer has never witnessed the commitment to prayer that he has seen and

---

1-2; Hoyte Lovelace, "Is Church Planting Movement Methodology Viable?: An Examination of Selected Controversies Associated with the CPM Strategy," *Journal of Evangelism and Missions* 6 (Spring 2007): 45-58; and Jeff Brawner, "An Examination of Nine Key Issues Concerning CPM," *Journal of Evangelism and Missions* 6 (Spring 2007): 3-13. These articles deal with some missiological concerns regarding CPMs. One of the major concerns is the universal application of CPM principles across the world as "the method" without considering the local field realities.

[31]C. Peter Wagner, *Church Planting for a Greater Harvest* (Ventura, CA: Regal Books, 1990), 46.

[32]Western Cuban Baptist leader Alberto González Muñoz speaks of the nightly vigils of pastor Bibiano Molina Guzmán (1906-1981), who for years would rise every night at 3 A.M. to pray for the salvation of Cuba. For this inspiring testimony of prayer, see Alberto González Muñoz, Leadership Obstacles (Barbados: Strategy Coordinator Training, 2003); available from Kurt Urbanek, 57 min., DVD.

[33]Mary E. Speidel, "A 'Drop' in the River: Cuba," *Commission Magazine*, May 1997, 10.

[34]Ibid.

experienced in Cuba. In his conclusion to the section of his book dealing with extraordinary prayer, Garrison states, "If prayer links a Church Planting Movement to God, then evangelism is its connection with the people."[35]

Abundant Evangelism

Abundant evangelism is a vital part of every CPM. Garrison uses the principle of nature to describe the relationship between the sowing of the Gospel and the harvest results: "In Church Planting Movements we find hundreds and thousands of people hear the gospel every day and out of this abundant sowing, a growing harvest begins to take place."[36] Garrison points out that both personal evangelism and mass evangelism have been a key in CPMs. An ethos develops within a CPM in which evangelism becomes the natural result of the believer's personal relationship with Christ. The proclamation of the Gospel rapidly spreads through networks of relationships.

Addressing himself to the strategy of saturation evangelism, Edward Murphy made the following observation: "Seed-sowing alone is really little more than the beginning stage of evangelism. The goal of saturation evangelism must be the multiplication of new believers and the multiplication of new churches."[37] Such efforts at evangelism constitute a major factor in church planting movements.

The result of personal evangelism in a CPM is to gather the new believers into newly formed and reproducing churches. The concept of personal evangelism is built into the DNA of the new believer that he/she is an integral part of the multiplication of disciples and churches. The ethos of the church and its members revolves around evangelism, discipleship, and the planting of reproducing churches. In the context of a CPM, the communication of the Gospel is effective, due in part to its being appropriately contextualized.

New believers understand their worldview and are the most effective at reaching into their culture to share the love of Christ with their families and relational networks. CPMs can only continue to grow as each convert continues to witness to others and bring them to faith and discipleship. Personal evangelism is critical to a Church Multiplication Movement.

---

[35]Garrison, *Redeeming a Lost World*, 177.
[36]Ibid.
[37]Edward F. Murphy, "Follow Through Evangelism in Latin America," in *Mobilizing for Saturation Evangelism*, ed. Clyde W. Taylor and Wade T. Coggins (Wheaton IL: Evangelical Information Services, 1970), 150, cited in C. Peter Wagner, *Frontiers in Missionary Strategy* (Chicago: Moody Press, 1971), 148.

Intentional Planting of Reproducing Churches

The planting of reproducing churches is at the core of the CPM evangelism and discipleship. Garrison points out:

> Intuitively one might assume that the potent combination of extraordinary prayer and abundant evangelism would naturally result in spontaneously multiplying churches. Many missionaries and church planters have held this view, and so were surprised and disappointed when multiplying new churches did not follow. What we found instead was that Church Planting Movements did not emerge without a deliberate commitment to plant reproducing churches.[38]

Garrison correctly asserts, "If you want to see churches planted, then you must set out to plant churches. . . If you want to see reproducing churches planted, then you must set out to plant reproducing churches."[39] The end goal of evangelism in a CPM context is disciples who are fully committed to evangelism and the multiplication of disciples through the multiplication of churches.[40]

Authority of God's Word

As individuals give their lives to Christ, and reproducing churches are planted, the question of doctrinal orthodoxy naturally emerges. How do these vast numbers of new believers and multiplying new churches stay doctrinally sound? The answer is the same as it was during the expansion of the early church, *absolute confidence in the authority of Scripture and trust in the leadership of the Holy Spirit*. As the Gospel is shared and disciples made, God's Word is proclaimed as the sole authority for a believer's life. In the same way, as reproducing churches are planted, they also base all that they do upon the unquestionable authority of God's Word. Obedience to God's Word and the Lordship of Jesus Christ has become the solid foundation upon which CPM evangelism and church planting takes place.[41]

---

[38]Garrison, *Redeeming a Lost World*, 181.
[39]Ibid.
[40]According to the Lausanne Covenant, "The results of evangelism include obedience to Christ, incorporation into his church and responsible service in the world." Cited in Thom S. Rainer, *The Book of Church Growth: History, Theology, and Principles* (Nashville: Broadman Press, 1993), 78. In the context of a CPM, obedience to Christ means a total commitment to fulfill the Great Commission, as read in Matt 28:19-20. The mandate of Christ is to "make disciples of all peoples."
[41]Garrison, *Redeeming a Lost World*, 183.

Local Leadership

The principle of having local leadership responsible for evangelism, discipleship, and church planting appears to be common sense; however, that has not always been the perspective of missionaries. Roland Allen, an Anglican missionary in China from 1895 to 1903, brought the importance of indigenous leadership to the forefront in his 1912 publication, *Missionary Methods: St. Paul's or Ours*,[42] and his 1927 book, *The Spontaneous Expansion of the Church: And the Causes that Hinder It*.[43] Allen clearly articulates:

> Many years ago my experience in China taught me that if our object was to establish in that country a church which might spread over the six provinces which then formed the diocese of North China, that object could only be attained if the first Christians who were converted by our labors understood clearly that they could by themselves, without any further assistance from us, not only convert their neighbors, but establish churches. That meant that the very first groups of converts must be fully equipped with all the spiritual authority that they could multiply themselves without any necessary reference to us: that, though, while we were there, they might regard us as helpful advisers, yet our removal should not at all mutilate the completeness of the church, or deprive it of anything necessary for its unlimited expansion. . . . If the first groups of native Christians are not fully equipped to multiply themselves without the assistance of a foreign bishop, they must wait upon him, and progress will depend on his power to open new stations, or provide superintending missionaries. That way lies sterility. If the first groups of native Christians are not fully organized churches which can multiply themselves, but must wait upon a bishop to move, they are in bondage.[44]

The goal of a CPM is not to pass the baton to the next generation of believers. Rather, the goal is to start with the baton already in their hands.[45] According to professor of missions Daniel R. Sánchez, "The churches that are planted utilize local means and indigenous leadership from the very beginning. This procedure en-

---

[42]Roland Allen, *Missionary Methods: St. Paul's or Ours?* (Grand Rapids: Eerdmans, 1962).
[43]Roland Allen, *The Spontaneous Expansion of the Church: And the Causes Which Hinder It* (Grand Rapids: Eerdmans, 1962; reprint, Eugene, OR: Wipf & Stock, 1997).
[44]Ibid., 1-2
[45]Garrison, *Redeeming a Lost World*, 188.

sures that the fellowship, teaching, worship, and leadership patterns that are employed are compatible with that to which the culture is already accustomed."[46] Garrison makes frequent references to missionaries and their role in the beginning and fostering of CPMs. The weakness lies in the fact that the missionary, in Garrison's viewpoint, still appears to be the focus and the prime mover of a CPM. The truth is that God is the prime mover, and if missionaries have a role, it is to encourage with focused zeal, the use of sound biblical and missiological principles.

The genius of CPMs is that the whole body of Christ is mobilized to evangelism, discipleship, and church planting, following networks of personal relationships. These same indigenous members are developed to fulfill the functions of church leadership without necessarily requiring them to become full-time professional clergy.

Lay Leadership

As a CPM produces thousands of new believers and new churches, the need is obvious for thousands of leaders for the emerging and existing churches. By its very nature, a CPM is dependent upon the development of leadership at all levels.[47] Of necessity, the majority of these leaders will be bi-vocational and come from the same ethnographic core as the local churches being planted. History has proven that a movement that is primarily dependent on full-time, seminary-trained leadership is unsustainable. The doctrine of the priesthood of all believers points to the truth that, "Every believer is fully endowed with the right and responsibility to lead the lost to salvation and maturity in Christ."[48]

Garrison argues for the importance of lay leadership.[49] A legitimate criticism of CPMs has been the emphasis on what Garrison calls "just-in-time-training." "Just-in-time" training supplies the new believer or emerging leader with only enough information or training to take the next step in their walk or the next level in their leadership development. According to critics, this concept of lay leadership thrusts *neophytes* (new believers) into local church leadership. The truth is each leader, and each context, needs to be evaluated on its own merit. Every believer, and every leader, needs to be a growing disciple of Jesus Christ. Every leader in the Church

---

[46]Daniel R. Sánchez, ed., *Church Planting Movements in North America* (Fort Worth: Church Starting Network, 2007), 38.
[46]Ibid., 1-2.
[47]For a list of the five levels of leaders and their training, see Myers and James B. Slack, "To the Edge: A Planning Process," section 6, 11.
[48]Garrison, *Redeeming a Lost World*, 189.
[49]Ibid., 189-91. Garrison groups his justification for lay leadership in this way: (1) Practical Reasons; (2) Theological Reasons; (3) Following Jesus' Model; (4) For the Purpose of Retention; (5) Reasons of Relevance; and (6) Economic Reasons.

of Jesus Christ needs access to the training necessary to lead the body of Christ. Garrison clearly says:

> For a Church Planting Movement to effectively rely upon lay leadership, two important factors must be present: First, churches must remain *small enough* to be manageable by either one or several lay leaders. . . . Second, church leaders must be *lifelong learners*. Church Planting Movement practitioners have learned to continually feed and nurture leaders and potential leaders with on-the-job training and just-in-time training. Mentoring programs, rural leadership training programs, pastoral training schools, Internet and workshops all contribute to leadership development.[50]

Garrison's idea was never to leave new believers without discipleship or lay leaders with no training. In the quotation cited above, he mentions five different delivery systems for leadership and pastoral training. *A CPM is a leadership training movement. The life of the movement depends largely on the ability to train sufficient numbers of God-called leaders.* Garrison notes that the use of lay leadership does not preclude the presence and participation of seminary-trained, ordained, professional clergymen. In some contexts, these serve as trainers for the ever-expanding number of lay leaders needed. They have a legitimate training and mentoring role to play. The challenge remains that training sufficient numbers of full-time professional leaders to sustain a CPM is impossible.

An additional challenge is that the leaders of the growing church networks need to be from the same socioeconomic, educational, and cultural level as the churches they lead. Time has proven that the majority of clergy, who are highly educated, do not remain in difficult areas. They tend to migrate to areas where the church membership is of their same socioeconomic and educational level. The majority of rural leaders or leaders among the urban poor, if taken out of their context to train in a residential seminary, have difficulty returning to that context. Charles Brock says, "In many countries a planter must be aware of what may happen if new leaders go far away to receive theological education. There are some inherent dangers, one of these is the leader may never be able to come back down to the level of the people and effectively minister to them."[51]

---

[50]Garrison, *Redeeming a Lost World*, 191.
[51]Charles Brock, *Indigenous Church Planting: A Practical Journey* (Neosho, MO: Church Growth International, 1994), 189.

Paul R. Gupta, and Sherwood G. Lingenfelter, concur saying:

> When we press evangelists and church planters into theological seminaries, we give them academic skills and make them so unlike their culture; they may no longer function in their own context. To serve effectively in the mission of making disciples, we must equip leaders in the context of their own culture, first guiding them to become disciples, and then teaching them to make disciples of those who are lost.[52]

In a CPM, leaders must be trained on-the-job and as close to their context as possible.

House or Cell Churches

CPMs depend upon the ability of churches to reproduce easily. Cell churches and house churches have been the prevalent forms for churches in the researched CPMs. According to Garrison, "the vast majority of the churches continue to be small, reproducible cell churches of 10-30 members meeting in homes and storefronts."[53] Each manifestation of church has its advantages and disadvantages. While traditional, dedicated church buildings exist in CPMs, they are more difficult to manage and are less reproducible.

Church buildings are, however, important in the Cuban CPM. These structures house government-recognized churches that function effectively as a legal umbrella of protection for the house churches. Additionally, these buildings provide an ideal location for training events, missionary training schools, and so forth.

Churches Planting Churches

As early as 1990, Peter Wagner stated, "it has been well substantiated by research over the past two or three decades: The single most effective evangelistic methodology under heaven is planting new churches."[54] If church planting is the most effective method of evangelism, one can only believe that the planting of a multitude of reproducing churches would be exponentially more effective. Within a CPM, the dominant ethos is one of churches planting churches. According to Slack, "a CPM is a movement characterized by a majority of local churches who have matured spiritually to 'own the lostness' of the people within their people group and who are themselves planting other local churches within that

---

[52]Paul R. Gupta, and Sherwood G. Lingenfelter, *Breaking Tradition to Accomplish Vision Training Leaders for a Church-Planting Movement: A Case from India* (Winona Lake, IN: BMH Books, 2006), 210.
[53]Garrison, *Church Planting Movements*, 35.
[54]Wagner, *Greater Harvest*, 11.

specific people group."⁵⁵

To qualify as a CPM, the movement does not depend upon outside missionaries, resources, or professional church planters for its growth. While, as Garrison states, "In most Church Planting Movements, the first churches were planted by missionaries or by missionary-trained church planters. At some point, however, as the movements entered an exponential phase of reproduction, the churches themselves began planting churches."⁵⁶ He emphasizes, "For this to occur, church members have to believe that reproduction is natural and that no external aids are needed to start a new church."⁵⁷

The key is not held by the missionary or the professional church planter, but lies within the local church. The missionary can encourage believers, share a CPM vision, and train those whom God is calling, but the core of the CPM is local churches planting reproducing local churches. In his chapter "Assessment of Church Planting Movements," Slack affirms, "After local churches starting other local churches reaches second and third generation status, that warrants being called a Church Planting Movement."⁵⁸

Rapid Reproduction

Another universal element within CPM is the rapid reproduction of disciples and churches. As the ethos of reproduction is built into new believers and churches, it becomes natural for them to share their faith and to plant new churches. Additionally, the inclusion of the phrase "rapid reproduction" has come under criticism.⁵⁹ While it is true that the inclusion of rapid reproduction is much different from the incremental and time-consuming process of traditional discipleship and church planting, it does not mean that the quality of discipleship or of leadership development need suffer in the process. One would also have to criticize the first-century church for spreading the Gospel too quickly and planting too many churches

---

⁵⁵Slack, "*Rationale, Research and Realities*," 32
⁵⁶Garrison, *Church Planting Movements*, 35-36
⁵⁷Ibid., 36
⁵⁸Slack, "Assessments of Church Planting Movements," 267
⁵⁹Jeff Brawner, "An Examination of Nine Key Issues Concerning CPM," *Journal of Evangelism and Missions* 6 (Spring 2007): 3-13. Brawner criticizes the push for rapid reproduction of churches and the discipling of leaders, believing this to be against the biblical pattern. He uses the fact that Jesus spent three years with the first disciples as his biblical base for his argument. However, Brawner fails to point out that the growth of the early church was rapid. New believers quickly shared their newfound faith with their family and others within their networks of relationships. The early church was characterized by the rapid growth in the number of disciples, leaders, and churches. See Lovelace, "Is Church Planting Movement Methodology Viable," 45-58. The problem Lovelace has with Garrison's "Rapidity Requirement" deal more with Garrison's analogies than anything else. He gives no sound missiological or theological objections to rapid reproduction.

among peoples of diverse religious backgrounds, who had little biblical foundation.

Discipleship is a lifelong process. It has been observed that the more quickly a person begins to share his/her faith, the more rapidly he/she will grow in that faith. The axiom is that a person who teaches learns more than his students. The fact that the new believers share their faith and co-labor in the planting of new churches means that they will, of necessity, be pushed deeper into their study of God's Word and dependence upon prayer. They will be able to exercise the gifts that God has given them rather than becoming spectators within stagnant and slow-growing churches.

Healthy Churches

Every healthy organism grows and reproduces. Ebbie Smith contends that church growth in the 21st century must include the element of "healthy growth." He writes:

> All growth is not healthy. Malignancy and obesity are growth but not healthy growth. Is it not possible that some of what we have termed growth, while it did involve increases, has not actually been healthy either for the local church or for the cause of Christ in general? In order to be totally satisfied with any Church or any congregation we must look closely at numerical growth and be certain the "growth" is not happening to the detriment of health.[60]

In his work *Natural Church Development: A Guide to Eight Essential Qualities of Healthy Churches*, Christian Schwartz calls this the "Biotic Potential." Schwartz says, "Ecologists define it as the 'inherent capacity of an organism or species to reproduce and survive.'"[61] According to Garrison,

> In Church Planting Movements maturing in Christ is a neverending process that is enhanced, rather than jeopardized, by starting new churches. In Church Planting Movements both leadership development and every-member discipleship are built into the ongoing structures of church life-along with a passion for starting churches.[62]

---

[60]Ebbie C. Smith, *Growing Healthy Churches: New Directions for Church Growth in the 21st Century* (Ft. Worth, TX: Church Starting Network, 2003), 24-25
[61]Christian A. Schwartz, *Natural Church Development: A Guide to Eight Essential Questions for Healthy Churches* (Carol Stream, IL: ChurchSmart Resources, 1996), 10.
[62]Garrison, *Redeeming a Lost World*, 191.

CPM churches demonstrate all five characteristics of healthy churches as outlined in Rick Warren's book, *The Purpose-Driven Church*: (1) Fellowship; (2) Discipleship; (3) Ministry; (4) Evangelism/Missions; and (5) Worship.[63] These characteristics are based upon Christ's teachings as found in the Great Commission and the Great Commandment, as well as the description of the early Church found in Acts 2: 40-47.[64]

Each CPM requires painstaking investigation and, within any CPM, exceptions to healthy churches can be found. The most important question and answer is found in the following statement by Garrison: "Is God's glory, his true nature as revealed in the person of Christ, evident in these movements? The answer is seen in the millions of changed lives, healed bodies and souls, passion for holiness, intolerance for sin, submission to God's word, and a vision to reach a lost world."[65]

These are clear manifestations of the healthy lives and the resulting healthy churches found in the midst of CPMs. Nothing less than healthy churches can be acceptable in a Church Multiplication Movement. An example of this healthy attitude can be seen in the Cuban musician's emphasis on *integrity of heart* and *skillfulness of hands*. They have lead by their example that Christian leaders need to be fully devoted followers of Christ first and foremost and then skillfully fulfill the calling that God has given them.

Common Factors Found in Church Planting Movements

According to Garrison, the following common factors were present in most but not all CPMs: a climate of uncertainty in society, insulation from outsiders, a high cost for following Christ, bold fearless faith, family-based conversion patterns, rapid incorporation of new believers, worship in the heart language, divine signs and wonders, on-the-job training, and missionaries suffering. This list of common factors was changed from Garrison's original 2000 list.

The original list of common factors included: worship in the heart language, evangelism has communal implications, rapid incorporation of new converts into the life and ministry of the church, passion and fearlessness, a price to pay to become a Christian, perceived leadership crisis or spiritual vacuum in society, on-the-job training for church leadership, leadership authority decentralized, outsiders keep a low profile, and missionaries suffer. The key

---

[63]Rick Warren, *The Purpose Driven Church: Growth Without Compromising Your Message & Mission* (Grand Rapids: Zondervan, 1995).
[64]Matt 28:19-20; Matt 22:37-39; and Acts 2:40-47.
[65]Garrison, *Redeeming a Lost World*, 198.

changes deal with the removal of decentralized leadership authority, outsiders keeping a low profile, the inclusion of insulation from outsiders, and the presence of divine signs and wonders.[66]

Each of these common factors can be found, to a greater or lesser degree, in the Cuban CPM.

Impact of the Church Planting Movement Paradigm

The effect of the CPM's paradigm has been felt by mission organizations, missionaries, and national church leaders around the world. According to Steve Wilkes, in Mid-America's *Journal of Evangelism and Missions*, the phenomenon of CPMs:

> . . . has widely influenced IMB work and other missions agencies around the world and in the U.S. Ralph Winter, arguably the most influential missiologist in the world today, has used glowing terms about CPM in his *Missions Frontiers* monthly magazine. Even the North American Mission Board, the North American mission agency of the Southern Baptist Convention, has used CPM thinking and terminology.[67]

In his article *"People Movements vs. Church Planting Movements,"* Mark Byrd declares: "Church Planting Movement thinking and methodology is having a profound impact on the way missions is done and analyzed by some of the leading missions agencies, including Pioneers, The U.S. Center for World Missions, and the International Mission Board, SBC."[68]

The impact of the CPM phenomenon caused the IMB to refocus its global mission efforts around the vision of facilitating CPMs among all the peoples of the world.[69] In 1997, the IMB reorganized its entire structure, from a traditional missions-sending agency, to a people-group-focused organization that is highly mobile and that exists to foster CPMs globally.[70] According to David Garrison, "In

---

[66]Ibid., 221-23.
[67]Wilkes, "Missiological Misgivings?" 1. See also, *Missions Frontiers Magazine*, April 2000 [on-line]; accessed 20 October 2009; available from http//www.missionfrontiers.org/pdf.2000/02.20000. htm; Internet.
[68]Mark Byrd, "People Movements vs. Church Planting Movements," *Journal of Evangelism and Missions* 6 (Spring 2007): 16.
[69]"Today we are again revisiting our vision and embracing a new goal. It is the goal of church-planting movements among every people group on earth." See the IMB's publication, *Something New Under the Sun*, 13.
[70]For a description of the evolution of the IMB as it relates to CPMs, see Mike Barnett and Dan Morgan, "Biblical and Historical Foundations for Church Planting Movements," in *Church Planting Movements in North America*, ed. Daniel R. Sánchez (Fort Worth: Church Starting Network, 2007), 82-90.

1998, the International Mission Board's Overseas Leadership Team adopted a vision statement: We will facilitate the lost coming to saving faith in Jesus Christ by beginning and nurturing Church Planting Movements among all peoples."[71] Further, Garrison makes the point, "This vision statement guides the work of nearly 5000 IMB missionaries serving in more than 150 countries around the world."[72]

The practical effects of the discovery and analysis of CPMs around the world have been enormous. As a direct result, various mission's agencies have reaffirmed their commitment to people group-specific strategies, and to focus the efforts of their missionaries toward church planting and the implementation of CPM-fostering strategies.

The Cuban Baptist Church Planting Movement

The Cuban CPM emerged in the early 1990s before Garrison articulated his description of CPMs in the IMB publication, *Church Planting Movements*, released in 2000. The Cuban CPM was even used in this publication as an example of an existing CPM.

Delayed Introduction of Garrison's Model in Cuba

The IMB's CPM concept, with its 10 Universal Elements, 10 Common Factors and Obstacles to a CPM, was not introduced to Cuban Baptists until 2005, and Garrison's book was not made available to them until 2006. Various circumstances contributed to the delay in communicating information about Church Planting Movements to Cuba. For example, the book, *Movimientos de Plantación de Iglesias: Cómo Dios está Redimiendo al Mundo Perdido* (Church Planting Movements: How God is Redeeming a Lost World), was introduced only because a local church in the United States contacted the IMB's Caribbean Itinerant Team and shared with them their intention to present the book to the Eastern Baptist Convention leadership in a series of conferences. The Church requested the IMB to supply the trainers for the event. As a result, IMB missionary, Jason Carlisle, traveled to Cuba, along with the IMB's Eastern Baptist Convention Strategy Coordinator, Russell Kyzar, to present the CPM principles to the Eastern Baptist Convention leadership. The outcome of the conferences was most posi-

---

[71] Garrison, Church Planting Movements, 7
[72] Ibid.

tive.[73]

The Independent Nature of the Cuban Church Planting Movement

The Cuban CPM appeared, grew, and struggled to continue without the outside imposition of this publication. That is not to say that these elements, factors, and obstacles were unknown to the Caribbean Itinerant Team of the IMB. In fact, these elements were studied in-depth and applied in the team's strategic planning and ministry. The Caribbean Itinerant Team believed the CPM in Cuba was and is a movement of God and, as such, could stand on its own without the introduction of these external concepts. The team did not want Cuban Baptists to think they necessarily needed to conform to the methods and descriptions of what God was doing in China, India, and elsewhere. The principles definitely influenced everything the IMB team did and taught, but not in such a way as to force the Cuban CPM into a foreign mold. The introduction of the CPM's book and its specific teachings has, in recent years, proven to be helpful in clarifying a number of issues. The CPM book and concepts have been found extremely helpful when they were contextualized.

Conclusion

The CPM among Cuban Baptists is occurring under the umbrella of traditional convention structures. It is important to investigate how these structures have served, in some ways, to protect the movement and to discover if and how these same structures have become an impediment to its continued health and expansion. Of crucial significance is the examination of these structures to see if they are capable of embracing the movement, making the adjustments necessary for the movement to continue, and through its testimony to influence other traditional convention contexts toward the embracing of CPM-fostering methodologies.

While the CPM among Baptists in Cuba emerged in the early 1990s, the truth is that the movement was built upon a solid foundation, the beginnings of which can be traced to the late 1880s.[74]

---

[73] During a "Best Practices Conference" held November 28-December 2, 2010, at the Baptist Camp in Yumurí, Matanzas, Eastern Cuban leaders shared the importance of their exposure to CPM concepts by Jason Carlisle and how it helped them to embrace the present CPM.

[74] Meador, "Left Side of the Graph," 59-63. In this article, Meador, the IMB's Executive Vice-President, points out that, in the majority of the mighty movements of God, historically a pattern of faithful ministry has occurred for years, maybe decades, before a movement of God ensued. The focus, it appears, is solely on the harvest period, and the foundations upon which the movement was built is underappreciated or simply ignored.

Chapters 2 and 3 present a description and analysis of the antecedents to the present Cuban CPM to determine their influence upon the development of the movement and their effect upon the movement's future. Chapter 4 discusses the effects of Cuba's revolution on church growth. Chapter 5 addresses the emergence of the movement, and Chapter 6 analyzes the growth of the movement among Cuban Baptists and Assemblies of God from 1990 to 2010. Chapter 7 deals with the findings of the research including a critical analysis of Cuba's church models. Chapter 8 addresses obstacles and challenges to the future of the movement, as well as recommendations concerning its future. Finally, Chapter 9 offers a brief conclusion to the study of the Cuban Church Planting Movement, possible topics that warrant further study, and how this book can be used to help encourage and foment Church Planting Movements in other traditional church contexts.

CHAPTER 2

ANTECEDENTS TO THE CHURCH PLANTING MOVEMENT AMONG CUBAN BAPTISTS

The ongoing CPM in Cuba has not occurred in a historical vacuum. An adequate appreciation of the unique challenges faced by Baptists during the current CPM requires a full understanding of the historical background of Baptist work in Cuba.

Cuba's first inhabitants were a tribe of pre-Ceramic Amerindians known as the *Guanahatabey*.[75] Spain laid claim to Cuba following its discovery by Christopher Columbus on October 29, 1492. Colonization, however, was not initiated until 1511 under Diego de Valázquez.[76] From the beginning of the Spanish conquest of Cuba, Roman Catholicism became the nominal religion of the majority.

The Roman Catholic Beginnings

Catholic priests and the Roman Catholic Church arrived in Cuba together with the Spanish colonizers. The effects of the Catholic Church upon the indigenous population can be clearly seen. According to Geoff Simmons, the indigenous population were read the "Proclamation of the Conquistadors," detailing the consequences of not submitting to the Spanish conquest and to the Catholic Church. This Proclamation read:

> The Lord has delegated to Peter and his successors all power over all the peoples of the earth, so that all people must obey the successors of Peter. Now one of these popes has made a gift of the newly discovered islands and countries in America and everything that they contain to the kings of Spain, so that, by virtue of this gift, their majesties are now kings and lords of these islands and the continent. You are therefore required to recognize the holy Church as mistress and ruler of the whole world and to pay homage to the Spanish king as your new lord. Otherwise, we shall, with God's help, proceed against you with violence and force you under the yoke of the Church and the king, treating you as rebellious vassals deserve to be treated. We shall take your property away from you and make your women and children slaves. At the same time, we solemnly declare that only you will be to

---

[75] Andy Gravette, *Cuba* (London: New Holland Publishers, 2000), 10.
[76] Marcos Antonio Ramos, *Protestantism and Revolution in Cuba* (Miami: Institute for Cuban American Studies, 1989), 19.

blame for the bloodshed and the disaster that will overtake you."[77]

If they refused to convert, they and their families were to be enslaved, and if killed, their blood was to be upon their own hands. The majority of the indigenous peoples chose to resist and were driven to extinction.

At the time of Columbus's arrival, the island was populated by the *Taino* and *Siboney* peoples. These groups were soon all but annihilated by forced labor and the diseases that accompanied the Spanish. Luis A Pérez, a noted Cuban scholar writes, "There were 112,000 native Cubans initially. That number was 19,000 as early as 1519, 7,000 by 1531, and fewer than 3,000 Indians twenty years later. The remaining tribal peoples were absorbed by the colonial population."[78]

The religious belief systems of the indigenous peoples were crushed under the onslaught of the forced conversions to Roman Catholicism. To some degree, these belief systems remained in the background, but no way exists to determine the extent to which they were practiced in private. One authority declares:

> We will not discuss the horrifying practices employed by the Spanish that contributed so dramatically to the demise of the Indian people or the harm it did to the mission of the church, but suffice it to say that due to Spanish aggression, disease, displacement, and the shock of occupation and suicide, the indigenous population of Cuba was virtually annihilated a short sixty years after the Europeans arrived.[79]

In short order, the Spanish began to import slaves from Africa to take the place of the dwindling native population. Miguel A. De la Torre observes:

> Many of these Africans were noble patricians and priests who had been disloyal to the new ascendency of rulers, specifically in the kingdoms of Benin, Dahomey, and the city-states of Yoruba. The vicissitudes of monarchic power struggles resulted in the enslavement of those imposing the new hegemony. Prisoners of war were routinely enslaved, but slavery was also imposed

---

[77]Geoff Simmons, *Cuba: From Conquistador to Castro* (New York: St. Martin's Press, 1996), 74; cited in Andrew Telep, "With the Blows of the Cross," *Truett Journal of Church and Mission* 3, no. 1 (2005): 67.
[78]Louis A. Pérez Jr., *Cuba: Between Reform and Revolution* (New York: Oxford Press, 1995), 30, cited in Telep, "Blows of the Cross," 70
[79]Greer, "Beginnings to 1896," 1; and see also Telep, "Blows of the Cross," 70.

as a debt payment for a period of time or as punishment for committing a crime.[80]

By the end of the sixteenth century, sugar and tobacco were the central crops in Cuba. By the seventeenth century, coffee and cacao also became important exports. Each of these was a labor-intensive crop that required further importation of slave labor. By the end of the eighteenth century, the number of slaves working in sugar production reached 500,000. Another 30,000 worked in the coffee plantations.[81]

When slaves arrived in Cuba, their owners and the Catholic Church encouraged them to become a part of a social network known as *cabildos*. Built along ethnolinguistic lines, these social organizations served as localized gathering places for the slave population. The Spanish slave-owners hoped these organizations would provide them a way to monitor the activities of the slaves and prevent them from fomenting rebellion against their control. The Catholic Church saw the *cabildos* as a place where the priests could ensure that the slaves received the proper Catholic religious instruction as to the Church's rituals and practices and to facilitate the conversion of the slaves to Catholicism.

The slaves used the *cabildos* as an opportunity to preserve their native languages and pass along their Yoruba belief system. Further, these institutions can be viewed as the precursors to what the contemporary *Santería* practitioners use as house temples.[82]

Through the use of the *cabildos*, the Catholic Church attempted to allow the slaves space to express their cultural traditions and customs within the framework of Catholicism but instead, unbeknownst to them, they provided the slaves with a vehicle by which they could preserve their native religious traditions under the veneer of Roman Catholicism.[83]

By 1884, the Spanish rulers began to view the *cabildos* as places where rebellions could be planned, and they passed the "Good Government Law," forbidding all *cabildos* from meeting or organiz-

---

[80] Miguel A. De la Torre, *Santería: The Beliefs and Rituals of a Growing Religion in America* (Grand Rapids: Eerdmans, 2004), 2.
[81] Gravette, *Cuba*, 11-13.
[82] De la Torre, *Santería*, 168-69.
[83] Ibid., xii. De la Torre describes *Santeria* in these words: "The word *Santería* itself is a pejorative term used by Catholic clerics in Cuba to denote what they considered a heretical mixture of African religious practices with the veneration of the saints. . . . Several contemporary scholars, in an attempt to break with the name imposed on the religion by white Christians, have rejected the term, preferring instead *Lucumí* (Friendship), *Regla de Ocha* (Rule of Ocha), or *Ayoba*." "The term *Lucumí* is used to refer to any characteristic of Yoruba culture, including the language. Some scholars believe that the word is derived from the Yoruba greeting *oluki mi*, which literally means 'my friend'; others believe it refers to an ancient Yoruba kingdom called Ulkumi."

ing festivals.[84]

By the time the last known slave ship landed in Cuba in 1865, one-third of the Cuban population was estimated to be of African descent, seventy-five percent of whom were African-born. The majority still practiced the religion of their ancestors.[85] The African belief system stayed fresh with the constant importation of new slaves to replace those who perished. De la Torre states:

> Slaves worked 18-hour days, six days a week. Life expectancy for a slave after arriving in Cuba was usually seven years. Slave deaths exceeded births, which necessitated new acquisitions. It was considered more cost effective to work a slave to death and purchase a new one than to expend the resources needed for adequate slave health care.[86]

As Protestants began to gain a permanent foothold in Cuba, they found an environment that was nominally Catholic with an undercurrent of African traditional religion dressed in the clothing of Catholicism. Upon cursory observation, the Cuban people appeared to be Catholic, yet all the while, the Yoruba religious system lived on in the shadows.

Beginnings and Development of Protestant Work in Cuba

From the period of the Spanish colonization in 1511, Cuba remained predominantly Catholic. The influences of native religions and the constant presence of West African traditional religions found a way of continuing to thrive under the guise of Roman Catholicism. Protestantism did not find a permanent indigenous expression until the nineteenth century. According to noted Latin American scholar Marcos Antonio Ramos, from the sixteenth to the eighteenth centuries, Protestant pirates, corsairs, and filibusters visited Cuba regularly, shuttling illegal goods to the island's residents. Ramos writes, "The natives and even the Spanish clergy indulged in contraband with them as a way of circumventing the severe economic restrictions imposed on the colony by the Spanish crown."[87] He goes on to state that many of these smugglers and pirates were Protestants (Huguenots, Dutch Reformed, and Anglicans).[88]

---

[84]De la Torre, *Santería*, 168-69.
[85] Ibid., 166.
[86]Ibid., 162.
[87]Ramos, *Protestantism and Revolution*, 20-22.
[88]Ibid.

The first Protestant services in Cuba may have been led by the French corsair Jacques de Sores. Known as a somewhat religious man, who attacked and burned Havana in 1555, de Sores then remained on the island for a time. Almost certainly other Protestant pirates, met for prayer and to read the Bible in more remote areas of the country where they sought refuge, particularly on the nearby Isle of Pines.[89] During the 1840s and 50s, British and Jamaican Protestant abolitionists, with Methodist and Baptist ties, visited Cuba with the purpose of promoting the abolition of Cuban slaves.

From the 1870s to 1890s, the Cuban economy became increasingly linked and dependent upon the United States. Trade with the United States quickly came to rival Cuba's trade with Spain. The Ten Years War (1868-1878) opened the door for change in Cuba.[90] According to Jason Yaremko,

> By the 1890s, aided by postwar economic crisis and Spanish trade concessions, North American companies invested more than $50 million in Cuba, while 94 percent of Cuban sugar production went to the U.S. market. In the aftermath of the Ten Years War, North American capital came to dominate everything from sugar and mining to the printing of Cuban currency.[91]

This writer has chosen not to detail the entry of every Protestant denomination into Cuba. He instead refers the reader to Ramos's definitive work on the subject, *Panorama del Protestantismo en Cuba* (Panorama of Protestantism in Cuba), as well as Ramos's study, *Protestantism and Revolution in Cuba*.[92]

---

[89]Ibid., 20.

[90] T.A. Sierra, "The Ten-Year War (1868-1878)," [on-line]; accessed 15 December 2010; available from http://www.historyofcuba.com/history/funfacts/tenyear.htm; Internet. The first large-scale war for Cuban independence began on October 10, 1868 with a historic speech by landowner and slave-owner *Carlos Manuel de Céspedes*. Céspedes freed his slaves and declared war on the Spain. Thirty-seven other local planters joined in, freed their slaves and donated their property. By November the rebel army had grown to 12,000 men. The war lasted ten years, but ended in a stalemate. On February 10, 1878 both sides signed the *Treaty of Zanjón* at a meeting in Zanjón, Camagüey. The agreement established that slaves who fought on either side were freed, but slavery was not abolished and Cuba remained under Spanish rule.

[91]Jason M. Yaremko, *U.S. Protestant Missions in Cuba: From Independence to Castro* (Gainesville: University Press of Florida, 2000), 2.

[92]According to Ramos, Joaquín de Palma became the first Cuban Protestant pastor with the founding of the Saint James Episcopal Church (*La Iglesia de Santiago Apóstol*) in New York, in 1866. As a predominantly Cuban congregation, many of its converts returned to Cuba following the Treaty of Zanjón, signed in 1878, ending the Ten Years War (1868-1878). Two of the churches that benefited from the converts of Joaquín de la Palma were the Faithful of Jesus (*Fieles de Jesús*) in Matanzas and Getsemaní Church in Havana. The Faithful of Jesus Church is the oldest Episcopal Anglican church

For the purpose of this book, the vital issue is that the founding of permanent Protestant work in Cuba differs from the origins of other evangelical work in Latin America. The Protestant presence and permanent ministry on the island owes its beginnings not to North American or English missionaries, but to Cuban Christians who returned to the island from abroad bringing with them the Good News of the Gospel.[93]

As Jason Yaremko describes it: "The first Cuban converts to Protestantism were among the many exiles who had immigrated to the United States as opponents of the Spanish regime and as participants in the Ten Years War. Cuban patriots like Alberto J. Díaz, J. R. O'Hallorán, H. B. Someillán and Auelio Silvera returned after the war as converted Protestants and also as pastors."[94]

Beginnings and Development of Baptist Work in Cuba (1876-1959)

Foundations (1874-1885)

Baptist ministry in Cuba began in an unusual way. In 1874, the family of Adela Fales moved from Cuba to reside in Biloxi, Mississippi. Once there, Adela and her sister, Maria Aneta, began to attend Baptist services and Sunday School with their mother. During their second year, the mother and Maria Aneta joined the Baptist church and were baptized. Though Adela desired to join the church as well, she being only seven years old was deemed too young.[95]

In 1876, the family returned to Cuba, leaving behind their relationships with Sunday School and the Baptist church. However, Adela did take with her a New Testament and copies of her favorite Sunday School literature, "Kind Words." Adela shared her Sunday School lessons with her Cuban friends and hoped one day to reconnect with the Baptist church and Sunday School and obtain more copies of "Kind Words."[96]

In 1883, the family returned to the United States and settled in Key West, Florida. While living there, the Fales family came to know the Reverend W. F. Wood, a Baptist missionary and pastor in Key West. He began an afternoon Sunday School and happened to use the "Kind Words" literature. As he distributed the literature, he was

---

still functioning in Cuba. Getsemaní Church was founded by Alberto Díaz, as an Episcopal Church in 1883, and later became a Baptist Church, in 1886.
[93]Ramos, *Protestantism and Revolution*, 20-22; and see also Yaremko, *U.S. Protestant Missions*, 109.
[94]Yaremko, *U.S. Protestant Missions*, 3.
[95]H. M. King, "Origin of Cuban Work," *Our Home Field* 1 (March 1889): 6, cited in Greer, "Beginnings to 1896," 6.
[96]Greer, "Beginnings to 1896," 7.

taken aback by the reaction of a Cuban girl in the back of the room. Una Roberts Lawrence later described the scene in the following way:

> When Mr. Wood began distributing copies of "Kind Words" in one of the afternoon sessions, a Cuban girl in the back of the room sprang to her feet and with joy on her face kissed the paper and wept over it. Mr. Wood's interested inquiries brought out the whole story of her childhood teaching, her love for the Bible and the paper that had meant so much to her young life.[97]

The Baptist church in Key West received Adela for baptism and her mother and sister for membership by transfer of their letters.[98]

Following his encounter with the Fales family and upon recognizing the need to reach the many Cubans living in Key West, Reverend Wood was moved to work with Cubans. Discovering in a cemetery the headstone of a Methodist minister engraved with the challenging words, "Don't give up Cuba"[99] motivated him further toward Cuban work.

During the 1884 Florida Baptist Convention meeting in Orlando, Rev. Wood introduced a resolution calling on the convention to facilitate the sending of the Gospel to Cuba. Following the convention, the Florida Board of Missions hired Adela Fales as a teacher and interpreter for Rev. Wood to begin an outreach to Cubans living in Key West. At the time, as many as five thousand Cubans were living in the Key West area. According to H. M. King, this constituted about one-third of the population.[100] This work among Cubans became known as the "Baby Mission."[101]

By March of 1885, Wood and Fales had already organized a Cuban Baptist Sunday School, a Cuban Baptist Aid Society, and a Cuban choir.[102] In July 1885, Wood reported that the "Baby Mission" had a total of sixteen members.[103] According to I. T. Tichenor, "Some of the converts of the 'Baby Mission' moved back to Cuba and wanted Wood to come and establish a mission there." Lloyd Corder, an official with the Home Mission Board (HMB) of the Southern Baptist Convention, describes the beginnings of Baptist

---

[97]Una Roberts Lawrence, *Cuba for Christ* (Atlanta: Home Mission Board of the Southern Baptist Convention, 1926), 143.
[98]King, "Origin of Cuban Work," 6.
[99]Lawrence, *Cuba for Christ*, 144; and see also Yaremko, *U.S. Protestant Missions*, 16. Yaremko identifies the Methodist minister as being J. E. Vanduzar.
[100]King, "Origin of Cuban Work," 6.
[101]Lawrence, *Cuba for Christ*, 77.
[102]Greer, "Beginnings to 1896," 9.
[103]"W. F. Wood to I. T. Tichenor, Key West, 22 July 1885," *Christian Index* 63 (August 6, 1885): 5, cited in ibid.

work among Cubans in the following way:

> Between the first rebellion in Cuba and the second (during the decade of 1890), Baptists assured their presence on the island through contacts with Cubans who had immigrated to American cities along the Gulf Coast: Mobile, Biloxi, Tampa, Key West. Some of the converts returned to Cuba which added to the numbers of believers on the island.[104]

Wood's contacts in Cuba sent him letters telling him about a man named Alberto Díaz who was preaching in Havana. The informants said Díaz' teachings were in agreement with Baptist doctrine, and that he would be a good resource. They went on to say that many Cubans believed his teachings and that the Catholic priests had been unable to silence him. Wood sent one of his contacts to investigate and learned that Díaz's teachings were in agreement with Baptist doctrine and that he had a large congregation meeting on Sundays. Wood reported this to the Florida Baptist Convention's Board of Missions, which decided that Wood needed to visit Cuba personally to ensure that these stories were true. During the July 1885 meeting, the Florida Baptist Convention's Board of Missions borrowed one hundred dollars from a Board member to send Wood to Havana to investigate. In September of 1885, Wood traveled to Havana to meet Díaz.[105]

Development of Baptist Work

Without doubt, Alberto Díaz, the Apostle to Cuba, became the most important figure in the beginnings of Baptist work in Cuba in general and, more specifically, in Western Cuba.[106] Díaz was born in the city of Guanabacoa, Cuba, in 1853. He studied medicine in the University of Havana where he graduated at age eighteen. Upon his graduation, he joined the Cuban military as a captain in their fight for independence from Spain during the Ten Years War, which lasted from 1868 until 1878.

During one of the battles, Díaz and some fellow soldiers were surrounded by the Spanish army near the Cuban coast. In order to

---

[104]Excerpt from letter of Wood cited in report by Tichenor, *Christian Index* 63 (July 9, 1885), 5, cited in ibid. See also Marcos Antonio Ramos, *Panorama del Protestantismo en Cuba* (Panorama of Protestantism in Cuba) (San José, Costa Rica: Editorial Caribe, 1986), 99-100. With the help of the United States, and their own fighting rebellion within the country the inhabitants of Cuba gained freedom from Spanish dictatorship, becoming the Cuban Republic in 1901 and electing Tomas Estrada Palma as president in 1902.

[105]Greer, "Beginnings to 1896," 9-10; and see also George William Lasher, *The Gospel in Cuba: The Story of Díaz a Marvel of Modern Missions* (Cincinnati: George E. Stevens, 1893), 34.

[106]Lasher's *Gospel in Cuba* is a good biography of Díaz.

escape being killed, Díaz and three of his comrades, under the cover of night, floated out to sea holding on to a wooden plank. They thought they would be able to come back to shore further down the coast and escape detection. Instead, they were swept out to sea by the prevailing currents, and after more than twenty-four hours a steam ship destined for New York City rescued them.[107]

Arriving in New York, Díaz soon found work in a cigar factory and later entered a New York Medical school to further his education in a specialty dealing with eyes and ears. Being from the Caribbean, and not accustomed to the extreme cold temperatures in New York, Díaz fell ill and was hospitalized with a severe case of pneumonia. During his stay in the hospital, he was befriended by a Christian nurse, Alice Tucker, who would read the Bible to him and pray for his recovery. During his study of the Scripture, Díaz was touched by the story of Jesus' healing of Blind Bartimaeus, and he was converted.[108]

The Ten Years War ended with the signing of the Treaty of *El Zanjón* on February 10, 1878, and with it the granting of general amnesty to the Cubans in exile who had participated in the war against Spain. Díaz took this opportunity to return to Cuba, this time with a Bible instead of a gun. He encountered stiff resistance from his predominantly Catholic family, but found others to be receptive. He began to work with university students from the University of Havana. He brought interested students together in the parlor of the Passage Hotel where he preached the Gospel and taught the Bible.[109] He soon had 100 to 150 people gathering regularly for worship. The Catholic priests became alarmed and sought various ways to pressure Díaz to abandon the work. Greer says, ". . . the priests began to persecute him by telling the people he was a heretic, a Jew, and a Protestant, and that if Díaz put his hands on them, they would die. As a result of the Catholic pressures, Díaz lost much of his income and was forced to return to New York."[110]

Soon thereafter, the entire Díaz family found it necessary to move to New York. Alberto and his older sister, Asunción (Minnie) Díaz, attended the Willoughby Baptist Church lead by Dr. R. B. Montgomery. There, Pastor Montgomery taught biblical doctrine and biblical interpretation to Alberto and Minnie. Minnie Díaz was baptized in October, of 1882, and Alberto on November 26 of the

---

[107]Greer, "Beginnings to 1896," 10.
[108]Leoncio Veguilla Cené, *Más de Cien Años de Obra Bautista en Cuba Occidental 1882-1996* (More Than One Hundred Years of Baptist Work in Western Cuba 1882-1996) (La Habana, Cuba: Oficina de Publicaciones de Seminario Teológico Bautista "R.A. Ocaña," 1997), 18. See also J. William Jones, "Sketch of Rev. A. J. Díaz, 'The Apostle of Cuba'," *Seminary Magazine* 9, April 1896, 350, cited in Greer, "Beginnings to 1896," 11.
[109]Greer, "Beginnings to 1896," 12.
[110]Ibid.

same year.[111] According to Tichenor, it was during this time that Díaz obtained his American citizenship.[112]

In 1883, Díaz accepted an offer from the American Bible Society to return to Cuba as a *colporteur*. In February 1883, he traveled to Cuba under the auspices of the American Bible Society, but with a definite desire to become a pastor.[113] From the beginning, Díaz faced opposition, but soon gathered a small group of those interested in his message. "The minds of the Cuban men were easily attracted to anything that promised rebellion against the established authority, and this hall was often crowded with a curious throng coming to hear the preacher who dared to read from the Bible and denounce the Catholic Church."[114]

Díaz rented a hall at 115 Prado, where he preached to growing crowds. A number accepted Christ and sought to organize as a church. According to Tichenor, "Díaz wrote to New York for a constitution and bylaws of a Baptist church but received the reply that the only guide should be the New Testament."[115] About this time, Díaz was visited by Rev. Wood during his exploratory visit to Cuba.

Rev. Wood reported the findings of his visit to the Southern Baptist Home Mission Board (HMB) and requested help for the ministry in Cuba. According to Greer, "He reported several hundred as being among those who composed unbaptized organizations, banded together for the worship of God. They were without anyone to administer the ordinances or to properly organize churches."[116] This report marked the beginning of the tradition in Cuba that it was necessary to have an ordained pastor to administer the ordinances and a mother church to sponsor a new church start. These concepts were brought in from the United States and came to be foundational truths for Cuban Baptists. Lasher says, ". . . as Díaz had not been ordained and not had presumed to baptize anyone, Bro. Wood undertook to supply the lack."[117] The HMB passed the report on to the Foreign Mission Board (FMB), requesting they accept the challenge of ministry in Cuba or that they allow the HMB to occupy

---

[111]R. B. Montgomery, "Letter, Brooklyn, February 23, 1893," *Our Home Field* 5 (March, 1893): 5, cited in ibid.
[112]I. T. Tichenor, "Cuba," *Our Home Field* 1 (August 1888): 2, cited in Greer, "Beginnings to 1896," 13.
[113]Veguilla Cené, *Más de Cien Años*, 7.
[114]Lawrence, *Cuba for Christ*, 146-47, cited in Greer, "1886-1916," 35; and see also Greer, "Beginnings to 1896," 13-14.
[115]Tichenor, "Cuba," 2, cited in Greer, "Beginnings to 1896," 14.
[116] Greer, "Beginnings to 1896," 14. Greer references the "Forty-First Annual Report of the Home Mission Board," *Proceedings*, 1886, ix.
[117]Lasher, *Gospel in Cuba*, 34.

Cuba as a HMB field.[118] The FMB declined to enter the Cuban field and at the same time, would not agree to allow the HMB to accept the call. Additionally, the Florida Baptist Convention appealed to the FMB for help, but was likewise turned down. The Florida Baptist Convention decided to undertake sacrificially the work in Cuba, even though they were struggling to meet their own ministry needs in the state of Florida.[119] The Florida Baptist Convention was dependent on aid from the HMB to support their work in Florida, so it was a significant step of faith for them to take on the challenge of mission work in Cuba. In their November 1885 meeting, the Florida Baptist Convention directed its mission board to establish mission work in Cuba.[120]

On December 13, 1885, Díaz was ordained as a Baptist minister at First Baptist Church in Key West, Florida.[121] That same year, the Florida Baptist Convention sent Díaz and his sister Minnie back to Cuba as missionaries.[122] On January 20, 1886, Reverend Wood, from the First Baptist Church in Key West, Florida, along with Alberto Díaz, conducted the first baptisms in Cuba that were under the auspices of the Baptists. Even though Alberto Díaz had been ordained to the ministry in December of 1885, he found it necessary to wait for the visit of Rev. Wood, the pastor of the church that had conducted Díaz's ordination, to conduct the first "Baptist baptisms" in Cuba on January 20, 1886. The practice of waiting on an ordained minister to conduct baptisms, and the mother church concept, can, therefore, be traced back to the very first Baptist baptisms and Baptist church in Cuba. According to Veguilla, the Getsemaní church had been originally organized as a Reformed Church (associated with the Episcopal Denomination) on April 10, 1883. Veguilla, being an influential leader of the Western Baptist Convention in later years, identified the Getsemaní Church at this time as more of a religious society or spiritual association than a church. The Getsemaní Church was not recognized as a church by the Baptists until "Baptist baptisms" were conducted by an ordained Baptist minister from a Baptist mother church. A total of five believers were baptized and organized into the Getsemaní Baptist church on January 26, 1886.[123] The baptisms were conducted in secret, because the law in Cuba did not permit any act of worship outside of the Roman Catholic Church.[124] Rev. Wood found the Cu-

---

[118]*Minutes, September 10, 1885, Home Mission Board of the Southern Baptist Convention* (Atlanta: Home Mission Board Files) (hereafter cited as Minutes followed by the date), cited in Greer, "Beginnings to 1896," 14.
[119]*Proceedings*, 1886, x, cited in Greer, "Beginnings to 1896," 15.
[120]King, "Origin of Cuban Work," 6, cited in Greer, "Beginnings to 1896," 10.
[121]Greer, "Beginnings to 1896," 15.
[122]Veguilla Cené, *Más de Cien Años*, 8.
[123]Greer, "Beginnings to 1896," 16.
[124]Veguilla Cené, *Más de Cien Años*, 8-9; and see also Greer, "Beginnings to 1896," 15. "Mr. Wood arrived in Havana on Tuesday, January 19, 1886, to help Díaz organize and

bans to be very receptive to the Gospel saying, "I find here, spiritually-minded people."[125] He goes on to state:

> The Baptists in Cuba had "intelligence, zeal, and spirituality." Every night the Baptists engaged in mission work in some part of the city. They helped the sick and poor as far as possible and sought out those in any way interested in the Gospel. Wood called them "Bible Baptists" because of their constant use of the Bible. The Baptists taught their children the word of God, the hymns, and to join in family worship.[126]

By March of 1886, Díaz had reported baptizing forty-five new believers, including his mother, father, and family. George Lasher, in the biography *The Story of Díaz*, describes the scene in the following way:

> "When the time for the baptism came, and he was about to go into the baptistry, his astonishment increased, as he saw his mother coming towards him. He thought at first that she must be about to upbraid him for his conduct, and tried to shun her. But she called to him saying, 'Alberto, are you not willing that your mother should be a Christian and be baptized?' The surprise was overwhelming. . . . Of course, he would baptize his mother, if she believed in Jesus as her personal savior, and repudiated the doctrines in which she had been educated."[127]

---

carry on Baptist work in Cuba. On January 20, the first Baptist baptism took place. Wood described it this way: On Wednesday night, with brother Alberta [sic], we went to meeting in Havana. At the close of the service we went by twos, and very quietly winding our way through the streets, we came to the sea, and there by the light of the moon, in an obscure place, we baptized three believers, the first fruits unto God of this mission in Havana, Cuba. Then, scattering, as we came, went to our homes. God's holy name be praised for this beginning." Taken from "Letter, Wood, Havana, January 23, 1886," *Christian Index* 64 (February 14, 1886): 4, cited in Greer, "Beginnings to 1896," 16. On Thursday night, after the services, two others were baptized in the same manner." "The law in Cuba did not tolerate any act of worship outside a building, except to the Roman Catholic religion." Taken from "Letter, Wood, Havana, January 26, 1886," *Christian Index* 64 (February 25, 1886), 4, cited in Greer, "Beginnings to 1896," 16. These baptismals [sic], therefore, had to be carried on in secret. On Friday night, when the Baptist group came near the water, they found the police. After Alberto Díaz spoke to the police, they permitted the Baptists to proceed saying, "Gentlemen could do no wrong." Thus, three others were baptized that night. Taken from: "Letter, January 23, 1886," 4, cited in Greer, "Beginnings to 1896," 16.

[125]"Letter, January 23, 1886," 4, cited in Greer, "Beginnings to 1896," 16.

[126]"Letter, January 26, 1886," 4, cited in Greer, "Beginnings to 1896," 17-18. From the beginnings of Baptist work, the Cuban Christians demonstrated a zeal for God's Word and a passion for evangelism.

[127]"Biography of Díaz," *Christian Index* 66 (December 19, 1889), 6, cited in Greer, "Beginnings to 1896," 19; and see also Lasher, *Gospel in Cuba*, 37-38.

On May 7, 1886, the Southern Baptist Convention met in Montgomery, Alabama for their annual meeting. Both Díaz and Rev. Wood addressed the convention concerning the need for mission support for the work in Cuba. The President of the convention appointed a committee to look into the possibilities of ministry on the island.[128] This committee came back with a recommendation for the HMB to be assigned the responsibility for mission work in Cuba. According to Greer, "It also recommended that the Board secure a fitting house of worship in Havana as soon as possible and maintain close ties between the Cuban work and the Florida Baptists who supported it. The report was adopted by the convention and the Home Mission Board was placed in charge of mission work in Cuba."[129]

Following the Southern Baptist Convention, Díaz traveled to Atlanta, Georgia, to dialog with the HMB about the work in Cuba. During the Board meeting on July 12, 1886, Díaz stated, "the field was inviting because of the dissatisfaction with Catholicism and the distribution of Bibles which started a spirit of inquiry. . . There were five preaching stations in Havana besides the principal one. These groups met in private residences with about one hundred people attending each."[130] That many of the original churches in Cuba were established in homes is significant. A majority of the existing historic churches originally met in private homes. Additionally, it is true that Cubans used their homes for church services during times of extraordinary growth, as well as during times of persecution.

Greer says, "At this time the HMB was already paying Díaz $1,200 a year to serve as pastor and perform other duties. They were also giving Minnie Díaz $400 for her work with women."[131] This was the beginning of the Home Mission Board's practice of paying salaries for Cuban pastors and workers.

Díaz proved to be a tireless worker. By May of 1887, the Getsemaní Baptist Church, which had been organized in January 1886, reported 301 members and had organized two churches during that same period. Further, they reported four Sunday Schools with four hundred students and two day schools with fifty-five pupils.[132] During the first fifteen months after the organization of the church,

---

[128]*Proceedings*, 1886, 13, cited in Greer, "Beginnings to 1896," 21.
[129]Ibid.
[130]Greer, "Beginnings to 1896," 21.
[131]Ibid., 20-22; 25. By January 1887, the following missionaries were under employment by the Home Mission Board: "The report listed Alberto J. Díaz and Miss Minnie Díaz in Havana, Miguel Pérez in Jesús Del Monte, Francisco P. Bueno in Vedado, José Porta in Regla, and Alfredo V. Díaz, Alberto's brother, in Matanzas."
[132]*Minutes of the Southern Baptist Convention*, 1887, App. B, XXXVIII, cited in Delgado Primitivo, "The History of Southern Baptist Missions in Cuba to 1945" (Ph.D. diss., Southern Baptist Theological Seminary, 1947), 49-50.

Díaz baptized three hundred converts.[133] The church continued to grow until reaching thirteen hundred members. Additionally, the church established other churches in Havana in Guanabacoa, Regla, El Pilar, El Cerro, and Los Puentes.[134]

Early Advances (1886-1892)

Baptist work in Cuba demonstrated some early advances in the years of 1886-1892. A major problem for the fledgling Baptist work was the fact that the Catholic Church would not allow "Non-Catholics" to be buried in their cemeteries. This prohibition became a real crisis for those who considered leaving the Catholic Church. The other issue was that the Catholic priests charged for their services to conduct marriages, funerals, and even to administer the sacraments.

The first of these issues was met by the acquisition of the Baptist cemetery. As early as July 1886, Díaz had asked for help from the HMB to purchase land for a Baptist cemetery.[135] The need for a cemetery became excruciatingly clear when a Baptist from Kentucky died while visiting in Cuba, and the Catholic priest refused to allow this "heretic" to be buried in the Catholic cemetery. Díaz was able to secure a place to bury him in a "potters' field" adjacent to the Catholic cemetery. In short order, hogs dug up the grave and desecrated the body.

When this became known, a Baptist deacon from Boston, J. S. Paine, donated two hundred dollars toward the purchase of a cemetery, and the Alabama Baptist Convention contributed another three hundred dollars.[136] On January 23, 1887, six acres of land was purchased for a Baptist cemetery.[137] For the Baptists of that epoch, it was a huge step forward in gaining legitimacy in the eyes of the Cuban people. Now those who died outside of the Catholic Church could be buried with dignity. Of interest to note is that the first person to be buried in the Baptist cemetery was Alberto Díaz's own child. According to Lasher, Díaz is quoted as saying:

> When I organized the church my mother was the first one to enter; when I organized the cemetery, my only little daughter was the first to be buried." Alberto Díaz and his wife were preparing to leave for the United States to attend the Southern Baptist Convention in Louisville, in 1887, when their daughter became ill and

---

[133]Lasher, *Gospel in Cuba*, 42.
[134]Veguilla Cené, *Más de Cien Años*, 9.
[135]Greer, "Beginnings to 1896," 23.
[136]Alfredo S. Rodríguez, *La Obra Bautista en Cuba Occidental* (The Baptist Work in Western Cuba). La Habana: Imprenta Bautista, 1930, 9-10.
[137]Lasher, *Gospel in Cuba*, 43-44; and see also Greer, "Beginnings to 1896," 23.

died. In order to make the trip, they had to leave before she was buried. Díaz's brother took care of the burial details. While speaking at the convention meeting, Díaz shared, "I was getting ready to come to this Convention, and did not have time to bury her. Friends brought flowers: my brother remained to bury my little daughter. My wife came with me here; our hearts are sad, and that is why we have not accepted invitations to ride out or to go to different places. I did not come to have a good time, but to tell you of God's work in Cuba.[138]

A further boost to Baptist ministry was the fact that, unlike the Catholic priests, the Baptist pastors did not charge for their services. This service opened innumerable doors for ministry.

In October 1887, a smallpox epidemic broke out in Havana. Baptist response to this epidemic resulted in feelings that opened people to the Gospel. Díaz reported 48 cases in his congregation alone, and within two months, 32 members and another 150 congregants had died. All of those from Díaz's church who died were buried in the Baptist cemetery. According to Greer, "One-third of the city of Havana was burying its dead in the Baptist cemetery."[139]

Díaz and many from his congregation ministered to the sick and dying. Havana reported from 120 to 200 new cases daily, with 80 to 90 of them dying. Fearing for their own safety, many of the doctors fled the city, but Díaz and his church continued to minister in the midst of the trial. Díaz, in a letter to Tichenor dated October 10, 1887, reports:

> You can't imagine how glad and pleased I am with this Baptist Cubans; they are proving they received Christ in their hearts, and leave everything for Him. While doctors, priest, high priest, lawyers and wealthy family leave the city, escaping from the epidemic, my congregation are all beside me; learned where is a new case of small-pox and as soon as they know it, some of them go and pray with the sick person, and if have not family, two brethren or sister remain there all night, assist him or her until in well. There is a Lady Association, conducted by my mother, and have about 120 ladies going house to house, carrying medicines, clothes or foods; they are doing a noble work in the

---

[138] Greer, "Beginnings to 1896," 45.
[139] Ibid., 27-29.

name of our Savior.[140]

Alfredo Rodríguez, in *La Obra Bautista*, states, "It is true that many of those believers paid with their own lives, self-denial, and a spirit of sacrifice, but the Baptist name was held in very high esteem and gained the respect of a great many people."[141]

The sacrificial ministry of Díaz and the Baptists caused the people to consider seriously the claims of Christ. Before the epidemic, the membership of the Getsemaní Baptist Church was 350, but two months later, in December, the membership had swelled to 700. According to Greer, "Personal witnessing accounted for much of this growth, with two female missionaries reporting more than 1,600 religious conversations. By this time three other churches had grown out of the church at Havana with a total of 250 members. The four churches had seventeen regular preaching stations."[142] The Cuban people responded to the compassionate ministry carried out by the Baptists. Greer says, "All the congregations were crowded wherever visitors went."[143] Tichenor reports:

> At all the services, at every station, the people fill every spot to hear the gospel. What struck us all was the deep, earnest open-eyed unflagging attention paid by all to the preaching. . . . The whole island is open to the gospel. There is not a town or city in Cuba where a congregation might not be speedily gathered and a church established.[144]

In the HMB report during the Southern Baptist Convention on May 11, 1888, there were 1,100 members among the Baptist churches and eight hundred baptisms. During that same year it was reported, "Eight thousand persons applied for membership in the Baptist churches but many of these were ignorant of the true qualifications for church membership and only desired to exchange the Catholic Church for one which they preferred."[145] This is important to note because the same trend of slow acceptance of those who voice an interest in the Gospel and church membership still prevails to this day.

---

[140]Ibid., 27-28. It is important to remember that English was not Alberto Diáz first language and therefore he struggled with English spelling and grammar.
[141]Rodriguez, *La Obra Baurtista*,
[142]Greer, "Beginnings to 1896," 27-28.
[143]Ibid., 29.
[144]Tichenor, "Visit to Cuba," *Christian Index* 65 (February 9, 1888): 2-3, cited in Greer, "Beginnings to 1896," 29-31.
[145]"Our Mission Board," Abstract of the Forty-Third Annual Report, 1888, *Christian Index* 65 (May 10, 1888): I, vi, cited in Greer, "Beginnings to 1896," 33.

Baptists realized this ministry in the face of ever-growing resistance from the Catholic Church against Protestant work, especially the work of Baptists led by Díaz. By the Spring of 1888, the Bishop of Havana was verbally attacking Díaz from the pulpit of the Havana Cathedral. During one service, he burned Díaz's photo, excommunicated all the Baptists, and sought actively to forbid the Cuban people from access to the Baptist cemetery.[146] In a circular he is quoted as writing:

> The Church of Christ is a true mother of all Christian people. When we are born she sanctifies us with baptism; she guides us in life, and teaches us the doctrine of salvation. . . . Now, why do you mix in the same place with the Baptist heretic--the apostate and the suicide with the true Roman that has received the holy sacrament, and dies in the Catholic faith? Is it because the church asks you for a few dollars to sustain the priests and cemeteries? I wish you to hear my voice today: Do not bury your dead in these heretic places, for if you do that you communicate with the heretics in spiritual things, which is not allowed by our church, and we will excommunicate you. . . . Another thing: Do you remember that we prepared those cemeteries, and that they are very expensive to us? And now you prefer the Baptist cemetery? You forget the contract you made between you and our ecclesiastical authority, and you put us in such a condition that we must abandon these holy places because we have not the means of supporting them.[147]

The priests used Spanish soldiers to disrupt funeral processions and to block the road to the Baptist cemetery, which caused an uproar among the people and sharp criticism against the Catholic Church in the local press. Tichenor gave three reasons for the positive movement among Baptists and the resulting Catholic opposition:

> One, he stressed was corruption and immorality among the priests. . . . Another reason was the strength of the Liberal Party in Cuba which opposed the existing government with which the Catholic Church was allied in all its acts of oppression. This party, composed of all native Cubans and a significant number of Spaniards, was in thorough sympathy with

---

[146] Greer, "1886-1916," 41-42.

[147] Greer, "1886-1916," 41-42. See also "Our Cuban Cemetery," *Christian Index* 65 (June 7, 1888): 1, cited in Greer, "Beginnings to 1896," 35-36. I. T. Tichenor, "A Second Visit to Cuba," *Our Home Field* 1 (December 1888): 6.

the Baptist work and principals. A third reason was the liberal position of the Havana press, which strongly opposed the existing ecclesiastical and political government and sympathized with Baptist work.[148]

Tichenor reported that one of the priests in Havana had told the Bishop, "If you do not close up that Baptist cemetery and they succeed in their efforts to get a good house of worship, we might as well gather up our effects and return to Spain. That will be the end of the Catholic Church in Cuba."[149]

The Catholic persecution during this period added to the openness of the Cuban people to Baptist teachings. The people rejected the heavy-handed tactics of the Catholic Church and also rebelled against their ties to the Spanish ruling authority.

Another stimulus to **Baptist development involved** the purchase of the Jané Church building. Tichenor, Secretary of the HMB, sought to help the growing work in Cuba.[150] The Catholic Church seemed to hold a distinct advantage, having been the predominate religion in Cuba since its settling in 1511, and due to its favor in the eyes of the Spanish government and the visibility that it enjoyed due to the large ornate cathedrals it possessed. Since Spanish law forced all Protestant worship to take place in secret, the belief was held that the Baptists and other Protestants needed to own their own church buildings in order to give the Protestant Church the sense of credibility and permanency they felt was lacking.

Tichenor, along with the Cuban Baptist leadership, believed one of the most immediate needs was for a permanent meeting place. He saw this as the only way Baptists could place a wedge between the Catholic Church and the people. He felt having a permanent place of worship would remove the Catholic argument that Baptists were a transient sect and did not have reverence for God, since they did not even bother to build a suitable place for worship, but instead met in private homes and rented halls located on back streets.[151]

---

[148]Greer, "1886-1916," 40.
[149]I. T. Tichenor, "A Second Visit to Cuba," *Our Home Field* 1 (December 1888): 6.
[150] Greer, "1886-1916," 91-92. Tichenor led the Home Mission Board to undertake and continue its mission work in Cuba. He continued in that role until his health led him to resign as the Corresponding Secretary of the HMB, in 1899. According to Greer, Tichenor was called the "Father of Cuban Missions." J. B. Lawrence, later Executive Secretary of the HMB, said of Tichenor, "No man ever faced a more difficult task than Dr. Tichenor when he became the Secretary of the HMB; no man ever triumphed more gloriously than he." F. H. Kerfoot was selected to follow Tichenor, and served the Cuban mission cause with distinction.
[151] Lawrence, *Cuba for Christ*, 82-83. See also Gertrude Joerg, "The Cuban Mission," *Christian Index* 90 (June 30, 1892): 5, cited in Greer, "Beginnings to 1896," 82-83. Miss Gertrude Joerg, an American lady who lived in Havana and attended the Baptist

In 1887, the HMB reported to the Southern Baptist Convention, "the need for a house of worship in Havana as essential to the highest success of the Baptist work in that city and on the island."[152] In November 1888, Tichenor visited Cuba with the purpose of locating such a building. Tichenor recommended that the HMB purchase the Jané Theater, which they voted to do at a cost of $65,000. The theater was originally built in 1880 for $140,000. The Jané Theater was located on the corner of Zulueta and Dragones streets in the heart of Old Havana. Located just one block from the capital building, it was a three-story stone building with a seating capacity for three thousand people. According to Tichenor, "Its purchase gave the Cuban Baptists immediate possession of a fine house of worship, still in use, and gave confidence to the people of Havana in the stability and permanence of Baptist work."[153]

Reasons for Baptist Growth

Growth among Baptists in the early years can be attributed to several factors. In his correspondence with the HMB, Tichenor gave six reasons for the growth of Baptist work in Cuba. The first was that the Cuban people found Baptist teaching and preaching to be a refreshing change from the centuries-old Catholic liturgy. The simplicity of worship, coupled with the sincere proclamation of the Gospel, was well received by Cubans searching for an alternative to the Spanish-controlled Catholic Church. Second, the teachings of the Church were shown clearly in the lives of the Baptist people. Third, the indigenous nature of Baptist work had broad appeal. That Baptist work did not depend on foreign priests or ministers, but upon the Cubans themselves, aided in the ready acceptance of the message they proclaimed. Unlike Catholics, Baptist clergy did not require payment to perform baptisms, marriages or funerals. This practice, resented by the Cuban people, had become a controlling point for the Catholic clergy. Cuban Baptist laymen and pastors were tremendous examples of sacrificial ministry.The example of ministry by the national workers, such as Alberto Díaz, José V. Cova, José R. O'Hallorán, Francisco Bueno, and Gasper de Cárdenes inspired the masses. Fourth, for Cuban Baptists, was the purchase of the Jané Theater in the center of Havana. Until this point, Baptists had been viewed as a transitory sect. The purchase

---

church, also spoke of the need for better places of worship. "All the meeting places besides the theater were not cool, comfortable, or large enough. Congregations met in small portions of the city where there was no shade or protection from the sun. The law required them to keep the doors closed or place screens before them lest the people be tempted to look in and perhaps become interested in what they saw and heard."
[152]*Minutes*, 1887, cited in Delgado, "History of Southern Baptist Missions," 51.
[153]I. T. Tichenor, "House of Worship in Havana," *Christian Index* 65 (December 6, 1888): 3, and N. N. Burrows, "The Havana Church," *Christian Index* 69 (March 31, 1892): 6, cited in Greer, "1886-1916," 43.

of this visible house of worship demonstrated in a tangible way that Baptists were there to stay. While from the beginning Baptist work was started in homes and/or rented places of worship, a strong sentiment existed that they needed to own permanent buildings to rival the visibility and heritage of the Catholic Church. Fifth, the purchase of the Baptist cemetery gave non-Catholics a dignified alternative to the high cost of Catholic burials. Sixth, Baptists exerted influence toward the freedom from political oppression. The Baptists' history of standing for their convictions in the face of government and religious persecution gave others the courage to stand up for their convictions in the face of governmental opposition. From the beginning of evangelical work in Cuba, Catholic clergy persecuted those who chose to associate with the Baptist Church. However, persecution actually served to strengthen Baptist work, as the Cuban people viewed the Catholic Church as being openly linked to Spanish rule. While the Baptist pastors' custom of not charging for the administration of the ordinances, funerals, or weddings aided the growth of the Baptist work, it simultaneously drew the ire of the Catholic clergy who began to attack Baptists openly, identifying them as heretics, excommunicating them, and barring them from burial in the Catholic cemetery.[154]

Another testimony comes through a letter from Cova stating, "The Cubans liked the simplicity of the Baptist meetings. Moreover, Baptists had a reputation of being noble and honest people that required no money to administer the ordinances and did not pretend to abuse the people, but rather did them good."[155]

First North American Missionary

A notable event in Baptist history in Cuba began with the appointment of the first North American missionary to Cuba in 1893. In a letter to Tichenor, dated April 23, 1892, Díaz expressed the need for more Christian workers, missionaries, and money to implement the work. He stated his desire that the HMB send at least two missionaries to Cuba who could speak Spanish.[156] In February 1893, the HMB appointed Reverend Pendleton Jones as its first North American missionary to Cuba. Díaz had requested a mission-

---

[154]Greer, "1886-1916," 48-49. See also "Letter, Cova, n.d.,"*Christian Index* 69 (December 8, 1892): 5, cited in Greer, "Beginnings to 1896," 81. See also *Proceedings*, 1892, 43. The report presented at the Southern Baptist Convention, in May 1892, states four reasons for the growth of Baptist work in Cuba. "One was the ability and good work of Díaz. Another was the consecration of native Christians. A third was the purchase of the Havana house of worship which had gained for the Baptists the confidence of the people, for it made them feel the Baptists had come to stay. The fourth reason was the Baptist cemetery."
[155] Greer, "1886-1916," 48-49. See also "Letter, Cova, n.d.," *Christian Index* 69 (December 8, 1892): 5, cited in Greer, "Beginnings to 1896," 81.
[156]Greer, *"Beginnings to 1896,"* 83.

ary be sent to help with the work in Havana.[157] Reverend Jones, however, only remained in Cuba from November 29 to May 1, 1894, when he returned to the United States due to health concerns. The HMB continued to financially support the work in Cuba by paying salaries for national workers, purchasing properties and building church buildings.

---

[157]Ibid., 95.

CHAPTER 3

CUBAN INDEPENDENCE AND BAPTIST WORK IN CUBA

Protestant work in general and Baptist ministries in particular developed in the years after Cuban independence. The direction of the work led to what has become known as the "Americanization of the Baptist Work in Cuba." The account of these developments is clearly seen in the years 1898-1959.

Rise of Protestantism Following the Spanish-American War[158]

The rise of Protestantism was born out of the crisis that occurred as the Spanish dominion over the island came to a close in the late 1880s. The political unrest further reinforced the people's disenchantment with Spanish rule that included disillusionment with the Catholic Church. The Protestant message was well-received, in part, due to the rise of Cuban nationalism and the openness of the people to anything non-Spanish. According to Yaremko, "Halls, hotel rooms, and homes doubled as chapels and classrooms as Protestant congregations in Cuba slowly expanded. By the time of the Cuban war of independence, Protestant affiliations included thousands of Cubans who attended church services, meetings, and Protestant schools."[159]

At the beginning of the Cuban War of Independence (Spanish-American War) on February 24, 1895, Protestant churches were growing, as was the discontent with Spanish rule. Numbers of Protestant leaders, including Baptists, were pressured into leaving Cuba in the face of growing persecution. At the beginning of the conflict, Díaz and his church members organized Red Cross stations throughout the central region of Cuba to aid the injured from both armies. Baptist women labored in these centers, witnessing and distributing tracts and Bibles to the soldiers.[160]

---

[158] On April 25, 1898 the United States declared war on Spain following the sinking of the Battleship Maine in Havana harbor on February 15, 1898. The war ended with the signing of the Treaty of Paris on December 10, 1898. As a result Spain lost its control over the remains of its overseas empire -- Cuba, Puerto Rico, the Philippines Islands, Guam, and other islands. "The World of 1898: The Spanish-American War," June 22, 2011; [on-line]; accessed 23, December 2011; available from http://www.loc.gov/rr/hispanic/1898/intro.html; Internet.

[159] Yaremko, *U.S. Protestant Missions*, 4.

[160] "The Red Cross in Cuba," *Mission Journal* 46 (November 1895): 27-28, quoted in Greer, "1886-1916," 50.

45

In January, of 1896, Díaz informed Tichenor that "he had accepted the position of commander-in-chief of the insurgent underground forces in Havana Province."[161] By 1896, Tichenor, on behalf of the HMB, made it clear that Baptist pastors were permitted to leave the country if they deemed they were in danger. They were relocated to areas in the United States where they could minister to other Cubans in exile. Protestant work in Cuba was dealt a severe blow by the accusation that Protestant pastors were involved in a conspiracy against Spain, which, according to Ramos, was most certainly true.[162]

On April 16, 1896, the HMB learned that Díaz had been arrested by Spanish authorities. Tichenor went to the United States government for help, and by April 23, Díaz had been released and, along with his family, left Cuba for Atlanta.[163] The exodus of Cuban leaders dealt a severe blow to Baptist work. Those who remained in Cuba continued to minister, but in a greatly reduced fashion. In 1896, the HMB did report seventy-five baptisms and a membership of 2,775.[164] According to Ramos:

> Many Christians were imprisoned while others took up arms. Many had to flee to the interior as the persecution grew. Hundreds remained faithful and they continued holding services as they could, in their own buildings or in ones that had been rented. . . . Eventually, to avoid suspicion of being anti-government conspirators, many preferred to meet in their homes for prayer meetings.[165]

Until the end of the war, the ministry was implemented by laymen and laywomen, many of whom were involved in the Baptist schools and medical work that had begun in the 1890s.[166]

Post-War Expansion of Baptist Work

The Spanish-American War ended with the signing of the Treaty of Paris on December 10, 1898. Following the armistice, came the United States occupation of Cuba with the provisional government.[167] As soon as peace was declared, the HMB began to repatri-

---

[161]Greer, "1886-1916," 50-51.

[162]Ramos, *Protestantism and Revolution*, 23.

[163]Greer, "1886-1916," 51-52.

[164]*Proceedings*, 1896, lvi, cited in Greer, "1886-1916," 52; and see also Ramos, *Panorama*, 121-22.

[165]Ramos, *Panorama*, 122.

[166]Primitivo, "History of Southern Baptist Missions," 52-55, 58.

[167]Lawrence, *Cuba for Christ*, 88.

ate its workers to Cuba.[168] During their exile, these workers had been very effective in reaching other Cubans who had fled to the United States during the war. Upon their arrival in Cuba, they found the work, while still functioning, to be in disarray. Although the work in Cuba had suffered, the leaders returned with a renewed passion and unquenchable hope in possibilities for the future. According to A. S. Rodríguez, the first leaders to return were Díaz and O'Hallorán, followed rapidly by M. M. Calejo and Gaspar de Cárdenas.[169]

According to Roy Acosta García, just as Díaz was the founder of Baptist work in western Cuba, O'Holloran was the pioneer of Baptist work in eastern Cuba.[170] O'Hallorán traveled to Santiago de Cuba, where he organized two churches in a space of two months and baptized 150 people.[171] Further, he opened work in Guantánamo in eastern Cuba. A letter written from Guantánamo says,

> In the first meeting that Parker and O'Hallorán held, twenty-one professed faith in Christ and sixteen were baptized in the next meeting. These sixteen were organized into a church, a preacher was ordained, and the Lord's Supper administered. Twenty-seven others were received for baptism while O'Hallorán was there, and regular meetings were set up for Parker and the new preacher to lead.[172]

While the letter does not say who the newly ordained pastor was, it does reveal, at least under O'Hallorán's ministry, that during the second meeting of the new group, new believers were baptized. The church was organized with these new believers and the new pastor was ordained at the same meeting. This practice did not appear to be the norm for the rest of the Cuban Baptists.

Díaz returned to Havana in September 1898 and continued his ministry at the Getsemaní Church. Soon after his return, however, he came into conflict with the HMB over financial irregularities in his

---

[168]Rodríguez, *La Obra Bautista*, 21-23.

[169]Roy Acosta García, *Historia y Teología de la Convención Bautista de Cuba Oriental 1898-1960* (History and Theology of the Eastern Baptist Convention of Cuba 1898-1960), vol. 1 (Santiago de Cuba: privately printed, 2000), 12. O'Hallorán was one of the first people baptized by Wood and Alberto Díaz in Havana on January 26, 1885.

[170]Acosta García, *1898-1960*, 11-12. Acosta states, "No evidence exists that Jamaican Baptists had begun a missionary work in Santiago de Cuba, nor had Rev. Wood, working with Miss Adela Fales visited Santiago de Cuba during their time in Cien Fuegos. There is also no evidence that Dr. Alberto Díaz had any opportunity to work in Santiago. The beginning point for Baptist work in Santiago de Cuba is the work of Rev. José Ramón O'Hallorán."

[171]Delgado, "History of Southern Baptist Missions," 60.

[172]"Letter, Parker, Guantánamo, November 2, 1898," *Christian Index* 78 (November 24, 1898): 1, cited in Greer, "1886-1916," 62.

ministry. Additionally, Greer commented that the HMB was not pleased with Díaz's constant political activism.[173]

The particular circumstances surrounding the dispute are beyond the scope of this book, but the conflict continued until Díaz and the Getsemaní Church were expelled from the Jané property, and Díaz was lost to Baptist work. He filed a lawsuit against the HMB, which eventually rose to Cuba's Supreme Court, where the court ruled definitively in favor of the HMB. Important to note is that, despite the difficult circumstances surrounding Díaz's leaving HMB employment, and his eventual departure from Baptist work altogether, his contribution to the cause of Christ cannot be underestimated or devalued.

Cova moved to Matanzas where he organized a church. Calejo, who was not at the time working for the HMB, traveled to Jovellanos as an English teacher and, at the same time, worked with Cova to open work in the homes of those interested in the Gospel. Gaspar de Cárdenes was sent to Pinar del Rio where he began the first Baptist church in the area.[174] Francis Bueno went to Cienfuegos, where he preached, drawing large crowds who had never heard the Gospel.[175]

With the American occupation, came a lifting of the anti-evangelical restrictions so long imposed by the Catholic-supported Spanish government. According to Una Roberts Lawrence, "The people, restless in their new situation, were eager to listen to any doctrine that savored of freedom from the old conditions, and old oppressors. While the difficulties were many, still there were golden opportunities."[176] An opportunity for change had arisen.

The Americanization of Baptist Work

During the United States occupation, which lasted from 1898 until 1902, United States Protestant denominations began sending their missionaries to Cuba. The missionaries that arrived during this time came from the traditional United States denominations including Southern Methodists, Northern and Southern Baptists, Lutherans, Episcopalians, Presbyterians, and the American Friends. Without question, the arrival of these missionaries contributed to

---

[173]*Minutes* 1899, cited in Primitivo Delgado, "History of Southern Baptist Missions," 60; and see also Greer, "1886-1916," 64-82; 105. See also Delgado, "History of Southern Baptist Missions," 62-65. Delgado gives the account of the events from the perspective of the HMB from its own archives. Ramos says, "Díaz, after having a difference of opinion and personality conflicts with North American missionaries . . . left Baptist work in 1903. He had resigned from the Home Mission Board in 1901."
[174]Rodríguez, *La Obra Bautista*, 23; and see also Ramos, *Protestantism and Revolution*, 24-26.
[175]Lawrence, *Cuba for Christ*, 90.
[176]Ibid., 88-89.

the "Americanization" of Protestant Work in Cuba, including Baptist ministries.[177] According to Ramos:

> After 1898, new names began to dominate the Protestant horizon in Cuba. Bishop Warren Chandler of the Methodist Church of Florida and brother of the owner of the Coca Cola Company became the architect of Methodism in Cuba, and the denomination spread across the island. Moises Natanael McCall extended the work of the Western Baptist Convention of Cuba--organized in 1905 with the support of the Southern Baptists. In the Eastern part of the island, a Cuban named J. R. O'Hallorán, at the request of Alberto J. Díaz, had founded a Baptist church in 1898. After the missionary work in Cuba was divided up between the Northern and Southern Conventions (1898), eastern Cuba was assigned to the Northern Baptist Board, and its envoy, missionary Hartwell Robert Moseley, played a decisive role in the first stage of the work.[178]

Ramos further states, "In Cuba Protestantism was Cuban until 1898. That year missionary boards that had previously limited themselves to cooperating economically with the local efforts took over. The Cubans who had led the movement thus far were relegated to secondary positions."[179] Theron Corse says:

> . . . U. S. missionaries were highly reluctant to hand over control of the church institutions they were building to Cubans, whom they generally viewed as too culturally immature to run their own organizations. Instead the missionaries copied U.S. institutions and theologies wholesale, seeking to create a microcosm of America in Cuba as a model for Cuban society to follow.[180]

According to Yaremko, "Many Cuban pastors and *laicos* (lay workers) did not easily accept their displacement; however, most chose to work within the new order of things. Later there would be a movement toward re-Cubanization within the ranks of national Protestantism, which resulted in friction between missionaries and national workers."[181]

---

[177]Yaremko, *U.S. Protestant Missions*, 5.
[178] Ramos, *Protestantism and Revolution*, 26.
[179] Ibid., 23.
[180]Theron Corse, *Protestants, Revolution and the Cuba-U.S. Bond*. Gainesville, University Press of Florida, 2007, 2.
[181]Yaremko, *U.S. Protestant Missions*, 6; and see also Ramos, *Protestantism and Revolution*, 25.

Western Convention leader, Nilo Domínguez, identifies the substitution of Dr. Charles David Daniel for Dr. Alberto Díaz as being the first major crisis in Baptist work in Cuba. This was the beginning of the "Americanization" of Cuban mission work in general and Baptist work in particular.[182] Domínguez states:

> From his arrival in Cuba in 1882 until the situation in 1904, he (Alberto Díaz) was the key man in Western Baptist work. His substitution was the beginning of the first great crisis. Alberto J. Díaz had a very strong personality. He was a man who operated independently and as a rule was not open to receiving orders from anyone. Consequently with this type of personality, when the HMB tried to impose certain requirements upon him and his work, he opposed. His stubbornness and inflexibility caused and escalated the crisis. The HMB was accustomed to its orders being obeyed. What the HMB was asking of Díaz was not anything that should have brought on the resulting crisis."[183]

As will be seen later, Baptist work remained under the control of the United States' missions boards until the missionaries had to abandon the country in the years following the Fidel Castro-led Revolution.

The Western Cuban Baptist work was begun by Cubans with limited economic support from the Florida Baptist Convention, the Home Mission Board, along with numbers of local United States associations, churches, and interested individuals. Upon the entry of American missionaries, the control of the finances and the direction of the ministry passed from Cuban hands to North American control. The Northern Baptists (later American Baptists) entered eastern Cuba in a controlling position. From the beginning of the relationship, Moseley was established as the Superintendent of Northern Baptist work in eastern Cuba.

Ramos goes on to note that after 1898 the missionaries ran the work. The vast majority of the new converts, however, were reached by national workers and the number of Cuban pastors quickly surpassed that of the North Americans.[184] Ramos states:

> True the Cuban pastors and leaders had some influence over the North American missionaries, but the missionaries always had the last word. The Baptist

---

[182]Nilo Domínguez, "Las Crisis de Nuestra Obra," ("The Crises Within Our Work") Tms (photocopy). La Habana, Cuba: Editorial Bautista, 1982.
[183] Ibid.
[184] Ramos, *Protestantism and Revolution*, 26; and see also Nilo Domínguez, "Las Crisis."

work had begun to produce leaders who carried a certain degree of weight such as Abelardo Béquer, but the presence of an appreciable number of Cuban pastors and evangelists by no means indicates that the Cubans were in control of the Baptist denomination.[185]

American Baptist and Southern Baptist Comity Agreement

As these missionaries from North America spread out across Cuba, agreements were sought between denominations and between mission agencies that would preclude them from establishing new work in the areas where other denominations were already working. Such arrangements are known as comity agreements in missionary circles and have been in use in various parts of the world. In 1898, an agreement was established between Southern and American Baptists that affected the manner in which Baptist missions were conducted in Cuba. Ramos writes:

> On November 23, 1898, in a meeting held in Washington, the HMB of the Southern Baptist Convention came to an agreement with the American Baptist Home Mission Society (ABHMS), dividing the work so that the Western portion (Pinar del Rio, La Habana, Matanzas, and Las Villas) remained under the Southern Baptists, and the Eastern (Camagüey and East) was to pass into the hands of the American Baptists.[186]

First North American Superintendents

On February 3, 1899, Dr. Hartwell Robert Moseley arrived in Santiago de Cuba to serve as the Superintendent of the Northern Baptist Mission Board's efforts in eastern Cuba.[187] Upon his entrance into Cuba, J. R. O'Hallarón, because he related to the Southern Baptist HMB, exited the work he had started in Santiago de Cuba and Guantánamo and returned to work in western Cuba.[188]

---

[185]Ibid., 29; and see also Nilo Domínguez, "Las Crisis."
[186]Ramos, *Panorama*; and see also Ramos, *Protestantism and Revolution*, 26; Veguilla Cené, *Más de Cien Años*, 12-13; Rodríguez, *La Obra Bautista*, 23; and Greer, "1886-1916," 76.
[187]Ibid., 209-10; see also Veguilla Cené, *Más de Cien Años*, 14; and Greer, "1886-1916," 83.
[188]*Minutes*, January 17, 1899, Home Mission Board of the Southern Baptist Convention (hereafter cited as *Minutes* followed by the date), cited in Greer, "1886-1916," 84. See also Acosta García, *1898-1960*, 13. Upon leaving Santiago de Cuba, Rev. O'Hallarón went to work in Santa Clara, Cienfuegos, Sagua la Grande, and Ranchuelo. By 1905, O'Hallarón was again working in pioneer mission work in eastern Cuba in Nuevitas and

The HMB named Charles David Daniel to be the superintendent of its work in Western Cuba, a role he faithfully implemented from January 1901 until 1905 when he returned to the United States due to his family's poor health. Daniel had previously served as a missionary with the Foreign Mission Board of the Southern Baptist Convention in Mexico and Brazil. He was called by the Cubans the "Hombre de Oro" (The Golden Man), because of his enthusiasm for the work and his rich experience. Soon after his arrival in Cuba, he founded the Calvary Baptist Church, an English speaking congregation, which also met in the Jané Theater.[189]

Daniel was known for his total commitment to the ministry. Even when his wife was forced to return to Texas due to severe health concerns, Daniel stayed and worked until his own health was compromised, forcing his return also.

Daniel added stability to the Cuban work in the aftermath of the Spanish-American War. He is credited with sharing a large vision for the future, based on the training of Cuban pastors who would be central in the expansion of ministry on the island. Additionally, he helped in the building of chapels so that the fledgling churches would have adequate places to meet. The Home Mission Board became very interested in 1904 in buying lots on which to build churches in towns where it had work. Daniel gave five reasons why the Board should buy lots for permanent centers as soon as possible.

The first reason was the economy. The mission rents averaged twenty-five dollars per month each. Chapels could be erected at an average of five thousand dollars each. Second, the people could not easily be induced to attend religious services constantly in rented halls connected to private dwellings. The Baptists in the summer of 1904 were preaching to about one thousand persons weekly. Daniel felt that the number would increase to two thousand if there were suitable chapels. A third reason was that owning property gave an appearance of permanency inspiring confidence in Baptists. Fourth, Cuba was making great strides as a republic and with this progress the value of property would advance. Finally, some unforeseen national calamity might befall the United States as the Civil War had earlier and the mission work would have to cease. The Cuban work might then disappear as the Cuban churches could not possibly pay rents and press their work. But with chapels of their own they could perpetuate the work without assistance from Baptists in the United States. *Daniel felt that no unhoused church could be*

Palma Soriano. O'Hallorán continued to work in eastern Cuba until his death in July, of 1920, in the city of Ciego de Avila.
[189]Rodríguez, *La Obra Bautista*, 25-26. See also Veguilla Cené, *Más de Cien Años*, 13; and Greer, "1886-1916," 106-09.

regarded as a permanent institution (italics added by this writer).[190]

Daniel was able to stay in Cuba long enough to give orientation to his replacement, Moses Nathaniel McCall, who arrived in Havana on February 15, 1905. McCall served in Cuba for more than forty-two years.[191]

During the United States intervention and the years following, U.S. denominations demonstrated an increased interest in buying strategic properties and constructing church buildings. Una Roberts Lawrence explains the felt need for buildings saying:

> When one remembers that for generations, religion and worship has been accompanied by such beauty, it is easy to understand the difficulty the missionary faces in securing a hearing for his religion when he must preach in an unattractive rented hall on a back street. . . When contact has been made, the Word of God is enough, but the difficulty is in making the contact. The Cuban argues that we must think very little of our religion or we would not house it so meanly and unattractively. This is the basis for the very serious need of our mission stations in Latin-American countries for attractive church buildings.[192]

Yaremko describes these events showing that Missionary groups appeared to compete with their business compatriots in the flurry of property acquisitions. He further indicated that this spirit of property acquisition characterized both eastern and western Cuba in the postwar period of U.S. military government. Further,

> The American Baptists then vigorously acquired more property for churches, schools, and offices, and, by 1905, had accumulated forty-five properties in at least sixteen cities and towns throughout Camagüey and Oriente. Fifty percent of these early sites were 'acquired by gift' from North American companies or leased at token rates from local municipalities."[193]

Numbers of properties were acquired to build churches and schools. The repercussions of this methodology were both positive and negative. The plan will be analyzed in a later chapter.

---

[190]Delgado, "History of Southern Baptist Missions," 66-69. See Charles David Daniel, "Church Buildings for Cuba," *Christian Index* 84 (July 21, 1904): 2, cited in Greer, "1886-1916," 192-93.
[191]M. N. McCall, *A Baptist Generation in Cuba* (Atlanta: Home Mission Board of the Southern Baptist Convention, 1942), 9.
[192]Lawrence, *Cuba for Christ*, 97-98.
[193]Yaremko, *U.S. Protestant Missions*, 6, 11.

Founding of the Western and Eastern Baptist Conventions

Both the Western and the Eastern Baptist Conventions were established in 1905. On February 6, 1905, during a meeting of Baptist churches from western Cuba, the Western Baptist Convention (La Convención Bautista de Cuba Occidental) was organized. The meeting was held in the city of Havana and representatives attended from all the churches with the exception of Sagua la Grande, which was represented by a letter. The meetings became a rallying point for the churches represented. They elected Daniel as the first president and Cova as secretary. The Convention organized upon a simple cooperative structure, which allowed each church representation and participation.[194] According to Primitivo Delgado:

> The Western Convention was established on the basis of the principle that "in union there is strength." A convention uniting the Baptists into one larger body would make them conscious of themselves and of one another, thus diminishing the discouragement that so often preys on minority groups. It also would give direction to their united efforts by providing channels whereby their Christian energy might be expressed, thus aiding in the development of their inner vitality as a denomination.[195]

The Convention became a rallying point and a place for mutual encouragement, training, and vision casting.

Beginning in 1902, a number of Northern Baptist missionaries joined Moseley in the work in eastern Cuba. As was stated previously, Moseley became the first general missionary of the Northern Baptists to eastern Cuba.[196]

While Baptist churches started by O'Hallorán already existed when Moseley arrived in eastern Cuba, it was under his direction that the churches met and formed the Association of Baptist Churches of the East and Camagüey *(Asociación de Iglesias Bautis-*

---

[194]Veguilla Cené, *Más de Cien Años*, 18; and Ramos, *Panorama*, 240. The eight churches that made up the Western Baptist Convention included the churches of Pinar del Rio, La Habana, Guanabacoa, Matanzas, Santa Clara, Colón, Cienfuegos, and Sagua la Grande.

[195]Delgado, "History of Southern Baptist Missions," 72.

[196]Acosta García, *1898-1960*, 15-30. In these pages, Acosta García lists the different missionaries during these early years and their particular contributions to Baptist work in eastern Cuba. See also Ramos, *Panorama*, 240. Beginning in 1902, a number of Northern Baptist missionaries joined Moseley in the work in eastern Cuba. Among these missionaries were: A. B. Howell, E. G. Goven, David Wilson, B. L. Boyenton, Miss Merrium, J. McCarty, and Fred J. Peters.

tas de Oriente y Camagüey) on February 7, 1905. The name was later changed to the Baptist Convention of Eastern Cuba (*Convención Bautista de Cuba Oriental*).[197] Moseley continued as the Superintendent for the American Baptist Home Mission Society (ABHMS) until his retirement in 1914. He continued living in Guáimaro, Camagüey, until he was forced to return to the United States due to poor health. Moseley passed away on October 7, 1926. His wife, Etna Moseley, due to her passion for the work in Cuba, returned to western Cuba where she worked with the HMB and Western Cuban Baptists until she retired from the HMB, in 1946.[198]

Influence of Moses Nathaniel McCall[199]

Moses Nathaniel McCall arrived in Cuba on February 15, 1905.[200] He became undoubtedly the most influential missionary in the history of the development of the Western Baptist Convention. According to Delgado, "It is he [McCall] who has shaped Baptist policy and work in Cuba more than anyone else."[201] Of McCall's influence, Delgado writes:

> The result of his more than forty years of service in laying the foundations and strengthening the Baptist cause in Cuba, along with the Cuban Baptists, most of them whom he himself developed into leaders of the denomination, will stand as a memorial to his devotion, insight and love for the Banner of the Cross in this beautiful island.[202]

McCall's original assignment in Cuba was as an educator. Once he finished his first tour of the island, including his participation in the Havana meetings where the foundation was laid for the formation of the Western Baptist Convention, he learned of the plans Daniel had for him. McCall had been preaching the English services at the Calvary Baptist Church since his arrival in February.

---

[197] Ramos, *Panorama*, 240-41. The twelve churches that made up the Eastern Baptist Convention were: Ciego de Avila, San Luis, Victoria de las Tunas, Camagüey, Santiago de Cuba, Bayamo, Manzanillo, Baire, Boniato, Alto Songo, El Cristo, and Dos Caminos de San Luis.
[198] Acosta García, *1898-1960*, 15-30.
[199] To undertake all of the contributions made by Moses Nathaniel McCall to Baptist work in Western Cuba is outside the scope of this book. For further study into the life and ministry of this heroic missionary, see McCall, *Baptist Generation*; Rodríguez, *La Obra Bautista* (Baptist Work); Delgado, "History of Southern Baptist Missions"; Greer, "1886-1916"; and Lawrence, *Cuba for Christ*.
[200] Greer, "1886-1916," 208.
[201] Delgado, "History of Southern Baptist Missions," 68.
[202] Ibid

In April 1905, Daniel recommended McCall to become the pastor of the Spanish congregation of the Calvary Baptist Church, which also met in the Jané Theater. McCall at first opposed the idea, because he was only beginning his Spanish language studies. Daniel insisted saying, "Our few Cuban preachers are good, but they are not perfect, and I am afraid of the jealousies and rivalries if any one of them is asked to be pastor."[203] That the missionary chose a non-Spanish-speaking North American over a Cuban national and native-Spanish speaker, because the latter might not be "perfect" is noteworthy.

The pattern continued to develop in the years to come that a Cuban national had to attain a certain level, arbitrarily set by the missionary or convention leaders, before he was allowed to pastor. In the beginning, it was necessary for McCall to speak through an interpreter. What is interesting about this is that McCall preached the Sunday morning English service and then allowed an aspiring young Cuban preacher to preach the Spanish service, while he sat in the front and listened.[204] Although Cubans began Baptist work in Cuba, and controlled all the ministries until 1898, with the arrival of a permanent North American missionary presence on the island, the national workers were not seen as being capable or mature enough to assume the main leadership positions in the pastorate, the seminary, or the convention.

McCall was elected president of the Western Baptist Convention during its second meeting in January, of 1906, and every year thereafter until his death in 1947. During these years, he was crucial in laying the foundations for the Baptist work in Western Cuba. He held all of the major convention positions, including superintendent of the HMB, treasurer of the HMB, president of the Western Baptist Convention, pastor of the Calvary Baptist Church in Havana, president of the three Western Convention Boards (Cuban Missions, Education, and Publications), rector of the Western Baptist Convention Seminary, internal director of the seminary, professor in the seminary, preacher for the radio program *La Hora Bautista* (the Baptist Hour), director of the convention publication *La Voz Bautista* (The Baptist Voice), and president of the Baptist Men's Society.[205]

While in practice, McCall was in total control of the work in the West, he did mentor the majority of the Cuban leadership and

---

[203]Greer, "1886-1916," 212.

[204]Ibid., 212-13. "McCall describes their arrangement as follows: 'I preached in English while he held down a chair in the morning. He preached in Spanish while I held down a chair at night'."

[205]Veguilla Cené, *Más de Cien Años*, 18-19. See also Alberto González Muñoz, *Y Vimos Su Gloria: Documento Histórico de la Convención Bautista de Cuba Occidental 1959-2006* (And We Saw His Glory: Historical Document of the Western Baptist Convention 1959-2006) (La Habana, Cuba: Editorial Bautista, 2007), 33.

taught sound principles of empowering leadership. McCall built the ministry in the Western Baptist Convention around the following three fundamental principles:

> (1) . . . no country can be evangelized by forces from without. The foreigner can plan, initiate, lead and of course do much work, but no board can send men enough to enter all the fields. It would seem reasonable then that we major on the native-born preacher.
>
> (2) . . . the idea must be instilled that the forces from without are auxiliary, and the burden must be principally on the native-born preacher and the Christians who have been won and gathered into churches.
>
> (3). . . from the beginning we have told Cuban Baptists that the HMB is not a corporation that seeks to strengthen itself in Cuba, but a fraternal agency that has come to hold up their hands as they evangelize their own people, until they are able to get along without help from elsewhere. It must be a Cuban responsibility to carry the Gospel to all parts of Cuba. . . . we resolve that fraternal relations should be just as frank and sincere between missionary and the Cuban brethren as they would be if we were of the same nation and tongue.[206]

McCall sought to build the ministry around these principles. First, if Cuba was to be won to Christ, it would be won by Cubans. Second, if Cuba was to be won to Christ, the effort would be led by Cubans. Third, if Cuba was to be won to Christ, the effort should be financed by Cubans.

Acosta, from the perspective of the Eastern Baptist Convention, makes the same point. "The missionaries of the ABHMS, with their leader being the superintendent, also considered evangelization as primarily the work of the local church, and even though the missionaries were involved in evangelistic activities, they promoted that the evangelization of Cuba be done by Cubans."[207] Acosta points out that Routledge pushed for the Eastern Baptist Convention to take ever-increasing responsibility for convention and pasto-

---

[206]McCall, *Baptist Generation*, 33-34; Veguilla Cené, *Más de Cien Años*, 21-22; and Lloyd Corder, "Baptists in Cuba," in *Encyclopedia of Southern Baptists*, ed. Norman Wade Cox (Nashville: Broadman, 1958): 339-42.

[207]Acosta García, *1898-1960*, 107. Robert Routledge, the ABHMS superintendent, is quoted as saying, "The ABHMS acts as counselor in the planning of the work, and helps materially when possible, but the work of evangelization is carried entirely by the Cubans." Robert Routledge, *Annual Report of the Board*, 1921, cited in Acosta García, *1898-1960*, 107.

ral self-support.[208]

The first principle recognizes that Cuba would never be won to Christ by relying solely on outsiders (missionaries) and, therefore, it was logical that national convention leaders, pastors, evangelists, and empowered laymen needed to be trained. To accomplish this, the western seminary opened in 1906 with the first six students. Three more joined the classes a year later.[209]

The second principle states that Cuban Baptist work need not depend on outside agencies to evangelize their country. To deal with that issue, they established the cooperative convention structure so that Cubans could work together toward the evangelization of their people.

The third principle deals with the issue of stewardship. If the Cuban Church was to win their country effectively, they needed to build a cooperative system of stewardship, whereby they could sustain the work without undue dependence on outside resources. McCall led the newly formed convention to establish a series of offerings, whereby they could sustain the convention's ministries, including the seminary.[210]

Additionally, McCall felt that Cuban Baptists were not receiving the respect they deserved, because they were seen as a passing fad by their fellow countrymen. This was due to the fact that the Baptists did not house their churches in fine buildings as did the Catholics and some of the other evangelical denominations. Ramos relates McCall's feelings in the following way:

> Quickly it dawned on McCall that the Baptists could not continue to be considered as being 'migratory birds' in some of the locations where they had work, especially because of the lack of having their own buildings. In the beginning they only had the temple located on the corner of *Zulueta* and *Dragones* and a number of rented buildings. In the years following 1907 the situation changed and they built several buildings and temples, many of them very costly, others were more modest

---

[208]Acosta García, *1898-1960*, 105-06.
[209]Veguilla Cené, *Más de Cien Años*, 19. The first three professors were M. N. McCall, L. T. Hayes and W. W. Barnes, who later was to serve with distinction as a professor at Southwestern Baptist Theological Seminary in Fort Worth, Texas.
[210]Veguilla shared these principles and their application with the International Mission Board of Trustees in closed session of the Board in Lansing, Michigan, on March 22, 1999. Eventually, the offering included the Woman's Missionary Union supporting the Seminary, the Men's Brotherhood organization supporting the Retirement Home, and the Youth organization's offerings supporting the Baptist Camp in Yumurí, Matanzas.

chapels.[211]

The Baptist work in Western Cuba expanded throughout the region, at times using tents, and afterwards renting buildings and building chapels.[212]

Development of the Western and Eastern Baptist Conventions

From the founding of the conventions in 1905 until 1965, HMB missionaries worked with the Western Cuban Baptist Convention, and the American Baptist Home Mission Society (ABHMS) missionaries cooperated with the Eastern Baptist Convention to start churches, train leaders, and establish and strengthen the convention's structures. The date 1965 is used because HMB missionary Herbert Caudill remained as the Superintendent of the Western Baptist Convention until his imprisonment on April 8, 1965. Though Caudill and fellow HMB missionary David Fite did not leave Cuba until their release, in 1969, their control over the Western Convention strategy and activities effectively ended with their incarcerations.[213]

A series of dedicated Southern Baptist HMB missionaries and American Baptist ABHMS missionaries, along with faithful Cuban Baptist leaders, invested their lives laying the solid foundation upon which the current CPM is built.[214]

---

[211]Ramos, *Panorama*, 289.
[212]Ibid.
[213]Acosta García, *1898-1960*, 146. According to Acosta, ". . . the presence of Dr. Rodríguez as the head of the Cuban Mission (in eastern Cuba) became unsustainable, causing him to leave the country in August of 1958." Oscar Rodríguez Quiles was a Puerto Rican national who, in 1948, traveled to Cuba as the Superintendent of the ABHMS.
[214]Veguilla Cené, *Más de Cien Años*, 92. Veguilla supplies a complete list of the Southern Baptist home missionaries from 1893-1969, including their names and years of service. Fifty-four North American missionaries are listed, with years of service ranging from one to forty-six years. This list includes twenty-seven single women and thirty-seven men, most of who were married. Also interesting to note is that during these years, the Western Convention's Cuban national pastors were counted by the HMB as HMB missionaries. See González Muñoz, *Y Vimos Su Gloria*, 36. The HMB sent fifty-four missionaries to Cuba between 1886 and the leaving of Caudill and his family in 1969. Among them, a little less than half served in Cuba only one to three years. A fourth served between four and ten years. Another group served a little more than ten years. Katheryn Sewel served twenty-nine years, and Mildred Mathews served thirty-five. Those who served more than forty years included Moisés N. McCall, Hebert Caudill, and the missionary Cristina Garnett, who lived more years in Cuba than any other missionary. Miss Garnett served in Cuba for forty-six years, arriving in 1918, and leaving against her will at the end of 1964. See also Acosta García, *1898-1960*, who, in his book, includes a list of ABHMS missionaries and their contributions to the development of the Eastern Baptist Convention.

Inevitably, many of the structures, traditions, and practices of both the Western and Eastern Baptist Conventions were shaped and solidified under the leadership of the missionaries from Southern Baptist and American Baptist backgrounds. Some of these traditions and practices helped to keep these conventions grounded doctrinally and structurally during very difficult years. As will be seen later in this book other traditions and practices, while they helped the conventions during times of trials and persecution, have not served them as well in the present climate of unprecedented growth.

Influence of Missionary Schools

Much of the contribution made by the North American missionaries over the years came in the area of education. Ramos states:

> The main mark of the North American missionaries upon Cuban Protestantism was the one that they left in the schools. The principal Protestant schools in Cuba were started during the first years of this century: Candler College (Methodist) in Havana, Trene Toland (Methodist) in Matanzas, La Progresiva (Presbyterian) in Cardenas, Elisa Bowman (Methodist) in Cienfuegos, Pinson (Methodist) in Camagüey, the International Colleges of El Cristo, Oriente (Northern Baptist) and los Amigos (Quakers) in Holguín and other cities of the Oriente Province. . . . The Cuban-American High School started by Southern Baptists in Havana soon became known as the Baptist High School. All told, there came to be more than 100 Protestant schools in Cuba, which had a combined enrollment of several thousand students.[215]

Yaremko concurs saying, "Education became the principal instrument in missions efforts to combat and replace what missionaries believed were the benumbing influences of Spanish colonial policy and of Rome's ecclesiastical system."[216]

Both the Eastern and Western Baptist Conventions regarded education as a primary means for evangelism. They felt that the centuries of Roman Catholic teaching could only be thwarted through the systematic education and indoctrination that could be implemented through educational programs of all types. The Sunday School became, and remains, a key tool for both conventions. Additionally, they opened day schools and colleges to attract those

---

[215]Ramos, *Protestantism and Revolution*, 26.
[216]Yaremko, *U.S. Protestant Missions*, 6.

interested in receiving a North American-type education.[217]

The missions and conventions saw these schools as an open door, as Yaremko puts it, to ". . . attract those Cubans for whom traditional preaching had no appeal. 'New ideas' would be 'patiently implanted' by mission teachers within the walls of these institutions."[218] González says, "Wherever there were evangelical schools the work prospered because the schools ministered intentionally to the students and their families. Many schools functioned inside the local church buildings using the same rooms as the Sunday School."[219]

Many Cubans clamored for entrance into these schools, seeing it as an opportunity to learn English and to prepare for the growing business ties with North American companies.

Influence of the Economic Crisis (1920s-1930s)

Important to note is that during the 1920s and the beginning of the 1930s, Cuba suffered from the same economic crisis that afflicted other nations during that epoch, particularly the United States, a country upon which Cuba depended both economically and politically. As a result, the Eastern and Western Baptist Conventions faced a severe decline in financial support from the United States. By 1928, the United States economic depression had devastating effects in Cuba. The Eastern and Western Conventions were both affected, but the degree of privation differed due to missiological and circumstantial distinctions between the conventions and their supporting denominations from the United States.

By way of clarification, as early as 1917, an attempt had been made on the part of both conventions to unite as one. In 1918, the Eastern Baptist Convention decided to suspend the process for the following two reasons. First, the Eastern Baptist Convention was more ecumenical in its relations, and that reality continued as a source of friction between the two conventions. The second reason dealt with the ecclesiastical issue of self-support. The Eastern Baptist Convention was moving forward in efforts to become self-supporting, while the West remained very dependent on HMB finances. González Muñoz concludes, "The HMB always made it clear that Cuba should be won to Christ by Cubans and that they were only there to help, which did not stop them from at times operating paternalistically, assuming the role of directing the work for more

---

[217]González Muñoz, Y Vimos Su Gloria, 26.
[218]Yaremko, U.S. Protestant Missions, 19.
[219] González Muñoz, Y Vimos Su Gloria, 26

time than was logical or needed."[220]

In 1918, the ABHMS made some clear and forward-thinking missiological decisions. First, they began to send their funding directly to the Eastern Convention, which allowed the convention to make decisions as to its distribution. While the Eastern Convention continued the practice of pastoral support, they, and not the ABHMS missionaries, made the decisions. Further, the ABHMS decided that their missionaries would no longer serve as local church pastors, but instead would serve as encouragers, counselors, and partners in the ministry.[221]

While their workers suffered privations due to the economic crisis, as did those in the West, their attitude of self-determination aided their ability to weather the storm. Ramos shows how they responded in his recounting of events during the 1927 Eastern Baptist Convention annual meeting: ". . . there was great enthusiasm among eastern Baptists, even though they were in the midst of a period of economic crisis. In 1927, during the convention meeting celebrated in San Luis, a large number of men offered themselves for missionary service and the women gave their jewelry to be sold in support of the missionary efforts."[222] Due to their ability to face the economic crisis head-on and even expand the work in spite of the crisis, the Eastern Convention began the 1930s with a tremendous sense of enthusiasm.

Meanwhile, the crisis in the Western Convention was exacerbated by internal HMB problems in the United States. Ramos notes:

> The economic depression gravely affected Cuba and other developing countries. But what most affected the work was the embezzlement of funds by the treasurer of the HMB in the United States. This person had speculated with mission funds and brought the Board to the gates of total ruin. . . . In Cuba the salaries were reduced to a minimum, the same for the Cubans and the North Americans. Many pastors were forced to take on secular employment.[223]

Ramos extols the efforts of B. D. Grey, who was the secretary of the HMB, along with McCall in Cuba, for doing all they could to reduce the damage in Cuba, and to head off the growing discontent among Cuban workers. Additionally, he points out that the Western Convention leaders and members also made great sacrifices so that the work could continue. He points out:

---

[220]González Muñoz, *Y Vimos Su Gloria*, 37."
[221]Ramos, *Panorama*, 291-92.
[222]Ibid., 293.
[223]Ibid., 290.

McCall was able to reduce to a minimum the discontent and was able to carry out, in spite of the factors mentioned, an extraordinary amount of work which was shown by the resultant idealism among almost all of the Cuban workers. In the midst of this situation, the epoch of economic and political crisis in Cuba, Cuban Baptists sent two missionaries to begin Baptist work in the Republic of Columbia.[224]

Ramos concludes saying, "The Western Cuban Baptists . . . were able to overcome their initial problems and learn to confront others with an appreciable level of maturity. Their denomination came out of the crisis strengthened."[225] These events did much to prepare the conventions to confront future crises that were to hit the island.

Influence of a Renewal of Evangelistic Passion

In the late 1940s and early 1950s, a renewal of evangelistic passion arose in the churches. Veguilla calls it a "Period of Great Growth."[226] Ramos identifies it as a "Renewal among historical churches," stating:

> A renewal began amongst the historical churches and the way was opened for new leaders. More missionaries arrived and, beginning in the forties, the Cubans assumed positions of responsibility. McCall died in 1947, and Baptist work faced profound changes and the responsibilities of that remarkable missionary passed into the hands of missionaries like Herbert Caudill and Cubans like José M. Sánchez and Domingo Fernandez. The work in the East made great strides towards becoming self-supporting and towards nationalizing its leadership.[227]

The growth experienced during the 1950s was not limited to Baptists. J. Edwin Orr declares in his book, *A Re-Study of Revival and Revivalism*, "In 1950, 'a mighty wave of revival' began to sweep all over Cuba touching all evangelical denominations although predominantly Pentecostal in manifestation. This phase end-

---

[224]Ibid.
[225]Ibid.
[226]Veguilla Cené, *Más de Cien Años*, 1882-1996.
[227]Ramos, *Protestantism and Revolution*, 31-32.

ed with Castro's dictatorship."[228]

By the time of the triumph of the Castro Revolution, the work of both the Western and Eastern Baptist Conventions had strengthened considerably. In 1960, the Eastern Convention reported 125 churches, and 103 missions with a total of 6,537 members. Additionally, they reported 645 professions of faith during the year, but did not report the number of baptisms. There were 264 Sunday Schools with a matriculation of 15,536 students, and 17 day schools with a daily attendance of 2,342.[229]

The Eastern Convention had a strong program structure that included a seminary, a Mission Board, Education Board, a Board for Evangelism and Stewardship, and a Board for Evangelism and Social Concern, as well as highly developed Sunday School and day school ministries. Further, the convention had societies for men and women, as well as youth and children. The Eastern Convention had its own convention publication, *El Mensajero* (The Messenger).[230]

In 1960, the Western Baptist Convention reported 85 churches and 196 missions, with a membership of 8,775, with 611 persons baptized during the year. There were 412 Sunday Schools with a weekly attendance of 15,020. Further, they had a highly structured convention with a seminary, a mission board, organized departments of Sunday School, evangelism, Christian education, and stewardship. In addition, the Western Convention operated a Baptist camp, a Baptist clinic, a bookstore, a radio ministry called *La Hora Bautista* (The Baptist Hour), and a retirement home. The Western Convention's publication was *La Voz Bautista* (The Baptist Voice).[231]

During this period, strong traditions were established, many of which were very positive, but other practices were introduced and fostered that would potentially become a danger to the health of the future movement. These traditions and practices included extrabiblical requirements for ordination and baptism, as well as the slow assimilation of new converts into the life of the church. Other traditions included the mother-church concept, as well as issues of dependency on outside funds for pastors' salaries, buildings, and so forth. These issues will be addressed in detail later.

---

[228]J. Edwin Orr, *The Re-study of Revival and Revivalism* (Pasadena, CA: School of World Mission, 1981), 59.
[229]Acosta García, *1898-1960*, 12-13. Acosta states that twenty-two churches did not report, due to the disruption caused by the ongoing Castro rebellion. This means that the actual numbers were higher, just not reported.
[230]Ibid.

[231]Veguilla Cené, *Más de Cien Años*, 39-49.

CHAPTER 4

EFFECTS OF THE REVOLUTION ON CHURCH GROWTH

Few historical events have exerted a larger influence on Baptist work in any country than the Communist Revolution in Cuba. The period 1959 to 1990 was marked by extreme pressure from the revolution and the continued influence of the generations old methods of doing ministry in Cuba. This chapter traces the events of these pivotal years and the responses of Cuban Baptist to them.

Early Period (1959-1962)

Castro and Communism

Following the revolutionary takeover by the forces of Fidel Castro on New Year's Day, 1959, the national Baptist conventions, churches and foreign missionaries began making adjustments to the realities brought on by the revolution. Most of the Protestant denominations were glad to see the Batista regime fall. While these denominations were not active participants in the Castro rebellion, Eastern Cuban Baptists seemed to have had a broader level of involvement. Corse says:

> Between them, the Eastern Baptists and the Presbyterians seem to have provided the largest number of active players in the rebellion, although some pastors in other denominations took part as well. . . . Eastern Baptist pastors provided leadership for the Civil Resistance Movement and provided services to the rebels. Lay Eastern Baptists became involved as well, spreading rebel propaganda and in some cases joining the rebellion.[232]

Missionaries and nationals praised the Castro government's decrees against gambling, prostitution, and its attempts to put an end to the Batista regime's corrupt ties to United States racketeers.[233]

They hoped the new government would put an end to the abuses of the Batista era, and at the same time, further the

---

[232]Corse, *Cuba-U.S. Bond*, 10-11.
[233]Ibid., 14-15. "Hubert Hurt, a Southern Baptist missionary, praised the new government's attack on gambling. . . . Marjorie Caudill concurred, praising Fidel Castro for forbidding gambling, drinking, and 'immorality,' while also blaming 'the big gamblers and other cohorts of Batista' for spreading false propaganda about the new government." The quote from Marjorie Caudill, cited in Corse's book, was taken from Marjorie Caudill, "Cuba's Crucial Hour" (late January 1959), 1.

Church's agenda of social reform. During the early days of the Revolution, Fidel Castro stated repeatedly that he was not establishing a Communist government, but as time passed, it became evident he was moving Cuba in that direction. Johannes Verkuyl indicates that Castro introduced a new ingredient into Latin America, namely, the Cuban form of Communism. He states, "Castro finally came to power on January 1, 1959, and he swung around and headed in the Communist direction, finding the organizational framework of the Cuban Communist party most useful for his purposes." According to Verkuyl, Castro had "at first tried to carry out the Socialist revolution without communism, but now he had come to see that it was a necessary point of orientation and reference."[234]

The Communist and atheistic direction of the Revolution greatly troubled the majority of Christians and church leaders. While many Baptists had initially agreed with and participated in the Revolution,[235] as time passed, they became disillusioned with its direction. "Most church leaders had backed agrarian reform, the literacy campaign and promised to eradicate administrative corruption, but they were unwilling to go so far as to exchange the socio-political structure of liberal democracy for that of socialism. In 1961 the Cuban Revolution declared itself socialist, and by the end of that year, the government announced its intentions to implant a Marxist-Leninist system."[236]

In October of 1960, the revolutionary government instituted a series of actions to nationalize the large companies in the country. According to Acosta, "This placed in the hands of the government all of the businesses that had more than twenty-five employees."[237]

He goes on to say:

> Although modern historians recognize that the Revolution exhibited socialist characteristics as early as Octo-

---

[234]Johannes Verkuyl, *Contemporary Missiology: An Introduction*, trans and ed. Dale Cooper (Grand Rapids: William B. Eerdmans Publishing Co., 1978), 379-80.

[235]Roy Acosta García, *Historia y Teología de la Convención Bautista de Cuba Oriental* (History and Theology of the Eastern Baptist Convention of Cuba) (Santiago de Cuba: privately printed, 2005), 3:5. According to Acosta, "Even though the Eastern Baptist Convention did not participate officially in the Revolution, in various ways many laymen and pastors gave themselves to the revolutionary struggle. . . . Some of the youth became martyrs of the Revolution, such as Frank and José País, Marcelo Saldo, Oscar Lucero, Rubén Casaus and Joel Jordán. . . . the Cuban Baptist Church, as well as other evangelical groups in the country, repudiated with all their strength the dictatorial government headed by Batista and his generals, and enthusiastically supported the new order established on the first of January 1959. In cities and throughout the countryside men and women from the churches, including pastors, dressed in militia uniforms, and with great enthusiasm occupied political positions, understanding that God had called them through the cruel insurrection to serve their country during the new birth of the nation."

[236]Ramos, *Protestantism and Revolution*, 70.

[237]Acosta García, *Oriental*, 3:16.

ber 1960, it was not until April of 1961 that the Commander Fidel Castro proclaimed officially the socialist character of the Revolution, thus initiating the second stage of the Cuban Revolution, or in other words, the *Construction of Socialism*.[238]

Finally, on October 3, 1965, the movement adopted the name the "Cuban Communist Party."[239] Corse says, "On April 16, 1961,...Castro openly declared the socialist character of the Revolution in response to the Bay of Pigs invasion."[240]

The defining blow for the churches came on June 6, 1961, when the "Law for the Nationalization of Teaching" was enacted. According to Acosta, "This law put an end to every form of private education in the country, and directly impacted the conventions, not only economically but also functionally."[241] This provoked conflicts not only with the evangelicals who ran private religious schools, but with the Catholic Church as well.

Dialectical materialism became the centerpiece of the public education system. As materialistic atheism began to be taught to all children, Christians and their church leaders scrambled trying to discover how to confront a system that attempted to eradicate their beliefs in favor of an entirely secular worldview. Up until this moment, the religious schools had taught Bible classes as a part of their curriculum. Now, religious teaching was relegated to the church and to the home.

Conflict ensued! Children of believers were taught about faith in their homes and in their churches. They were, however, taught the exact opposite in the schools, where they studied atheism and were taught that their religious convictions were wrong, even counter-revolutionary. The children of Christians, and children who were themselves Christians, became subjected to constant belittlement and open ridicule. They were banned from certain areas of study and at times faced harships and threats if it was discovered that they were sharing their faith.

With Marxism and its accompanying atheistic teachings being propagated by every means of mass communication, pastors and convention leaders sought ways to counter these teachings. Pastors began to focus their preaching on apologetics, defending the existence of God. They used the only forum of mass communication available to them, their pulpits. Baptist leadership with focused energy began to teach apologetics and Christian evidences at every

---

[238]Ibid., 2:16-17
[239]Ibid.
[240] Corse, *Cuba-U.S. Bond*, 50.
[241]Acosta García, *Oriental*, 3:17.

training retreat and every camp activity. According to González, "It was rare that a sermon or teaching did not touch on these themes." Veguilla describes the situation in the following way:

> In 1962 a special preparation course was taught to pastors and lay leaders titled, "Training Course in Preparation for the Ideological Offensive." Among the themes covered were Philosophy, Psychology, Analysis of Scholarly Texts, Sermons, Testimonies, etc. Everything dealt with the revolutionary offensive with its direction towards Marxism. Many pastors held a right wing conservative position; the members of their churches who were committed to the Revolution left their churches. Others were moved in favor of the Revolution. This added to the division. No one was indifferent. One group planned to leave the country. The churches were aflame with activity. Everything was done on a massive scale: congresses, conventions, fraternal meetings, retreats at the camp, increased church attendance. The churches were a refuge for many. At times there were those who abandoned the simple preaching of the gospel and preached instead strongly against the Revolution.[242]

The Churches and Communism

The churches saw the principles and teachings of Communism as propagated by the State to be an assault on their beliefs. As the State sought more and more control over every facet of peoples' lives, that feeling intensified. At the same time, the State viewed the Church and its teachings to be in direct opposition to the interests of the State. The new government viewed the conventions as a threat, because they had seen the churches mobilized on the side of the revolution.[243] They knew the churches and conventions could prove themselves dangerous adversaries if allowed to mobilize against the Communist regime for the Christian churches were very well organized.

In order to control their influence, the State proceeded to make life and ministry for Christians increasingly problematic. González recounts:

> It was difficult, when believers were confronted by these situations, with the teachings against the exist-

---

[242]Veguilla Cené, *Más de Cien Años*, 53.
[243]Acosta García, *Oriental*, 2:5. According to Acosta, "many laymen and pastors fully participated in the Revloution." If they could be mobilized in favor of the revolution they could also be mobilized against it.

ence of God, the ridicule of God, the blaspheming or the denial of His existence, which were believed by the church to be vicious attacks against humble believers who believe in Him and love Him. . . . These were times when we were constantly being told that religion was the opiate of the people and we were taught that it was not necessary to attack the churches or religion, because they would in time disappear as the people were taught and learned the truth concerning the scientific concept of the universe.[244]

These are interesting comments in the light of Lenin's teachings. A. D. Sujov describes the reaction of Socialism and Communism to religion in the following way:

We should fight against religion--says Lenin. . . The only formation at the social roots of religion that weakens it notably and later completely destroys it is communism. But in socialism, as you know, religion continues to exist, and the motivation for its existence has not totally as yet been eliminated. However, it will slowly disappear at the same pace as the society advances through the path of socialism and communism. The strengthening of communism on all fronts will create the conditions for it to finally and definitively conquer the ideology of religion.[245]

Sujov goes on to say:

In the Soviet Union one sees the gradual conquering of religion through the implementation of active scientific and atheistic propaganda that opposed the scientific assertions of religious dogmas. The deeper and more multifaceted the fight against religious prejudices, the quicker the society would cut their ties to the religious ideology.[246]

To look back in time and see that the Church and the teachings of Christ did not disappear is easy. In fact, many in the churches grew stronger in their faith as a result of their conflicts with the atheistic State. But at that moment in history, they did not know what was going to happen. All they knew was that the newly formed government actively sought ways to undermine and eventually eradicate the Church and its teachings. They felt they were

---

[244]González Muñoz, *Y Vimos Su Gloria*, 44.
[245]A.D. Sujov. *Las Raíces de la Religión* (The Roots of Religion), Editorial de Ciencias Sociales. La Habana, 1972, 103. Quoted in González Muñoz, *Y Vimos Su Gloria*, 44.
[246]Ibid.

the last line of defense to protect future generations from the onslaught of atheistic Communism.

The Hard Period (1962-1969)

The Governmental Tightening

Sensing the church's opposition, the State began to find ways to tighten control over churches and their members.[247] According to Theron Corse:

> Castro accused 'imperialists' of switching from using the Catholic Church as a front for counterrevolutionary activities to using instead certain Protestant groups, which he characterized not only as security threats but also as obstacles to modernization and nationalism."[248]

Corse continues:

> The broader restrictions on Protestant groups shortly after the March speech seemed to have derived from the state's desire to marginalize the churches and to ensure they could not become centers for counterrevolutionary activity. Primarily the measures did two things: they restricted religious activities to religious buildings and required the registration of all Protestant groups, buildings, and pastors. They eliminated outdoor services. It also became illegal to host religious meetings in private homes.[249]

As living conditions in Cuba became increasingly untenable, a number of Southern Baptist HMB missionaries, as well as other Protestant missionaries began to leave the country. Ramos shows, "Starting in 1960, but especially in 1961 and 1962, nearly all the foreign Protestant missionaries abandoned the country. . . . In any event, several hundred missionaries left Cuba between 1960 and 1962."[250] The last American Baptist missionary left Cuba in August of 1958.[251] As Communism took hold in Cuba, life in general and Christian ministry in particular, became increasingly difficult.

---

[247]Corse, *Cuba-U.S. Bond*, 73. Corse states, "More serious than harassment were the reports of arrests and detentions of Protestant pastors between 1961-1963."
[248]Ibid., 73-74, 76.
[249]Ibid.
[250]Veguilla Cené, *Más de Cien Años*, 54; and see also Ramos, *Protestantism and Revolution*, 71-72.
[251]Acosta García, *1898-1960*, 146. According to Acosta, ". . . the presence of Dr. Rodríguez as the head of the Cuban Mission (in eastern Cuba) became unsustainable, causing him to leave the country in August of 1958."

During the years of 1960-1964, an exodus occurred of church leaders and members alike.[252] In the Western Convention alone, ninety of the one hundred and three pastors were lost to the work through retirement, death, or immigration.[253] At least one-third of the members of the Western Baptist Convention's churches (over 3000 members) immigrated to the United States.[254]

The Eastern Convention witnessed a similar exodus of leaders and members. Many felt that their only recourse to save their children from State control was to flee the country. The pressure increased with the nationalization of public radio and the discontinuation of evangelical programing in 1961 as well as growing limitations to freedom of assembly for worship. According to Acosta:

> The majority of the churches shut down in this period were house-churches, or *casas cultos*, where the congregation met in private homes of either pastors or parishioners. . . . Forcing congregations to meet only in formal buildings made surveillance easier.[255]

The Imprisonment of Pastors and Missionaries

A powerful blow struck the Western Baptist Convention when, in April of 1965, about fifty-five Western Convention leaders were jailed, along with HMB missionaries Herbert Caudill and David Fite.[256] In his book, *Y Vimos Su Gloria: Documento Histórico de la*

---

[252]While the United States Government was encouraging missionaries to leave Cuba, some chose to stay, seeing the need to minister in the midst of the radical changes they were witnessing. See Margaret Fite to Lloyd Corder, October 4, 1960, file 3, box "Caudill, Herbert," Herbert Caudill Collection, Home Mission Board of the Southern Baptist Convention Collection, cited in Corse, *Cuba-U.S. Bond*, 52. "Margaret Fite, Herbert Caudill's daughter, wrote to the Southern Baptist Home Mission Board to declare that Communism was a reason to stay, not leave: 'If Communism is an ideal, and the only thing that can combat it effectively is a strong, sure, positive presentation of Christianity. And who will do this job if we leave? I am sure that our Cuban co-workers would continue but our leaving when there is no real danger would have a demoralizing effect'."
[253]Veguilla Cené, *Más de Cien Años*, 54.
[254]Ibid. Veguilla says, "The leaving of pastors and members (3000 is a very conservative number) was a severe blow due to the loss in the economic, personal and leadership areas."
[255]Corse, *Cuba-U.S. Bond*, 77.
[256]For a detailed account of the imprisonment and eventual liberation of these two missionaries, see *On Freedom's Edge*. See also Clifton Edgar Fite, *In Castro's Clutches* (Chicago: Moody Press, 1969). Herbert Caudill and David Fite were arrested on April 8, 1965. Caudill was sentenced to ten years in prison and Fite to six. Due to his failing eyesight, Caudill was released from prison into the custody of his wife on November 25, 1966. He remained under house arrest until his departure from Cuba. Fite was held until December 16, 1968. On February 7, 1969, both the Caudills and the Fites left Cuba.

Convención Bautista de Cuba Occidental 1959-2006 (And We Saw His Glory: Historical Document of the Western Baptist Convention 1959-2006), Alberto González provides an invaluable service as he relates in excruciating detail the arrest of the pastors and their subsequent trials and imprisonments. González lists the charges as follows:

> (1) Conspiracy against the security and integrity of the nation, saying that Caudill was the leader of a band of spies, made up of pastors and lady missionaries; (2) Collaboration with the Central Intelligence Agency (CIA); (3) Helping persons leave the country illegally; (4) Ideological diversion; (5) Covering up the activities of others; and (6) Illegal currency exchange.[257]

Caudill testified at his trial:

> I insisted that there was absolutely no basis for charges 1, 2, 3 and 5. About the charge of ideological diversion, I argued that we simply continued to preach and teach the gospel as we had done before the coming of communism. The government under which we lived had changed. With respect to number 6, the Cuban government permits no currency to leave the country. It is illegal to possess money of other nations. If persons have permission to leave the country and want to buy tickets, they must have on deposit with the government money of value in international exchange. Cuban money has no value on the world market at present. When people left the country, they sometimes gave us Cuban currency for use in our work. No money from Cuba left the country. What was given to us was used in Cuba.[258]

According to González, the charges of illegal money exchange against some of the Western Baptist pastors were true. It is the contention of many that, while a level of impropriety existed on the part of some pastors, it did not warrant the sanctions of between two and thirty years imposed by the revolutionary court. These charges were excessive, and were used as an excuse to attempt to shut down the Baptist work, which the government viewed as counterrevolutionary due to its historic ties to the United States churches and denominations.

---

[257] González Muñoz, *Y Vimos Su Gloria*, 42.

[258] Herbert Caudill, *On Freedom's Edge: Ten Years Under Communism in Cuba* (Atlanta: Home Mission Board of the Southern Baptist Convention, 1975; reprint, Atlanta: Home Mission Board of the Southern Baptist Convention, 1984), 66-67.

The Military Work Brigades for Aiding Production [UMAP]

While the work was still reeling from the arrest and imprisonment of pastors and missionaries, a second blow followed on its heels. Just six months later, sixteen students from the Havana Seminary were called to special military service in "Las Unidades Militares de Ayuda a la Producción (Military Work Brigade for Aiding Production [UMAP])," along with youth leaders from almost all the churches.[259]

This loss of members and leaders was a hard blow for the Baptist work, which was forced to continue with most of the trained leadership behind bars or held in agricultural camps. For the next five years, the ministry of local churches remained in the hands of the few pastors who had not been imprisoned, laymen, and pastors' wives, who worked diligently and sacrificially to see that the ministry of the church continued.[260]

Although the Eastern Baptist Convention leadership did not suffer the same extreme prison experiences that struck the Western Convention, they were affected by UMAP.[261] Nine Eastern Convention pastors, including the convention's president Orlando Colás, were sent to UMAP. In addition, a number of laymen and seminary students suffered the same fate. Acosta says:

> There were traumatic results from the unexpected way in which the immense majority of those recruited were, in the blink of an eye, taken to distant fenced work camps where they and their families did not know where they were or why they had been taken. The purpose of these 'concentration camps', was to gather the anti-socials together in one place. In the same camps there were homosexuals, common criminals, and all types of vagabonds, together with pastors, priests, seminary students and other young people

---

[259]Veguilla Cené, *Más de Cien Años*, 55-56. See Ramos, *Protestantism and Revolution*, 76. In 1965, the so-called Military Work Brigade for Aiding Production (UMAP) was introduced. Many ministers and seminarians were called into active duty or drafted into the brigades. See also Alberto González Muñoz, *Dios No Entra en Mi Oficina* (God Does Not Enter My Office) (La Habana, Cuba: Editorial Bautista, 2003); and idem, *Y Vimos Su Gloria* (And We Saw His Glory). González gives a detailed reporting of the arrests, trials, and prison experiences of the Baptist leaders, as well as his personal experiences as a seminary student, placed by the government in the service of UMAP.

[260]González Muñoz, *Y Vimos Su Gloria*. González describes the trials and tribulations of the pastors' wives and families in excruciating detail. Further, he shares about the tireless ministry that was carried out by pastors who were not imprisoned. They carried unimaginable loads as they sought to maintain a semblance of calm in the midst of an escalating hostile state intrusion into the life and ministry of the Church.

[261]Acosta García, *Oriental*, 2:33.

that the government did not trust.[262]

Those held in UMAP, from both the Eastern and Western Conventions, were all released by June 30, 1968.

By 1968, a majority of the pastors had been released from prison.[263] Over the succeeding years, the Church experienced slow growth and strengthened, in spite of its isolation and the immigration of members and leaders. It appeard as if the government sought to remove the leadership of the local churches and conventions, thinking that the body of the Church would wither and die. However, the final result of all the trials they suffered (social changes, imprisonment of pastors, the internment of seminary students and leaders in work camps as well as the emigration of members and leaders) caused the Church to unify in order to survive. This writer's observation has been that the existing convention's structures, polity, and long history aided its ability to withstand the ideological and practical assault of Communism upon the churches, leaders and members.

The effects of the imprisonments were widespread. González outlines in detail ten consequences that Baptists suffered as a result of the imprisonment of the pastors and missionaries in 1965. They include:

> (1) The loss of liberty by the accused; (2) The separation suffered by couples and families; (3) The general destabilizing of the work and the resulting economic crisis; (4) The spiritual crisis and the psychological trauma suffered; (5) The immigration of pastors, leaders, and members from the churches to other countries; (6) The heightening of tensions between the church and the state; (7) The loss of young people aspiring for vocational ministry; (8) The radicalization of political positions inside the conventions; (9) The reaffirmation of the feeling of persecution felt by Christians and churches; (10) The church's abandonment of a sense of social consciousness.[264]

Effects of the Government Strategy To Remove Church Leaders Through Imprisonment and UMAP

This strategy of removing the church leaders did work in many denominations, including the Roman Catholic Church. For example,

---

[262]Ibid.
[263]Veguilla Cené, *Más de Cien Años*, 63.
[264]González Muñoz, *Y Vimos Su Gloria*.

after the foreign Catholic priests were exiled, the number of Catholic churches dropped from 893 in 1965, to 472 in 1970.[265] Many other denominations suffered similar consequences.

While many Catholic churches appear to have closed because of the lack of priests, the Baptist churches continued to function. According to Catholic polity, where no priest exists, you cannot celebrate the Mass or the Church ordinances. Therefore, by expelling the foreign priests from Cuba, the government greatly reduced the number of available priests and, thus, the number of places where Mass could be celebrated and the ordinances offered to the Catholic parishioners. The basic idea was that where no priest is present, no ordinances exist, and where no ordinances exist, no Catholic Church exists.

The Baptist story is different because of its church polity. In-depth conversations with both Eastern and Western Baptist Convention leaders show that the Baptist's strong emphasis on the Priesthood of Believers saved them from the severe decline suffered by Roman Catholicism. The Baptist doctrine of the Priesthood of every Believer means that a Baptist church does not cease to be a church in the absence of an ordained pastor. The ordinances of baptism and the Lord's Supper are the ordinances of the Church and not of the Church's ordained leadership. While many Catholic churches closed due to a lack of priests, the Baptist churches continued to function because of the faithful ministries of the non-imprisoned pastors, wives of imprisoned pastors, and local church laymen. Baptist churches did not cease to function in the absence of the ordained leadership. Faithful saints continued the ministry of the local churches, while the majority of the pastors were in prison or serving in UMAP.

For the next thirty years, the Baptist conventions slowly rebuilt and, by 1991, returned to two-thirds the size they were at the beginning of the revolution.[266] They continued to sow the seed of the Gospel faithfully during very difficult circumstances. In spite of their

---

[265]James B. Slack, "Churches and Denominations in Cuba from 1960-1995," PowerPoint presentation at the Church Growth Conference, McCall Baptist Church, Baptist World Alliance meeting, Havana, Cuba, July 3-8, 2000. The conference was attended by pastors and denominational leaders from the Eastern, Western, and Freewill Baptist Conventions.

[266]Alberto González Muñoz, "50 [sic] Años en la Convención Bautista de Cuba Occidental: Estudio de Estadísticas (50 [sic] Years in the Western Baptist Convention: Statistical Study)," PowerPoint, 2001. This presentation was a part of an analysis of the growth of the Western Baptist Convention from 1950-2000, presented as a PowerPoint presentation at a conference of a select group of Eastern and Western Cuban Baptist leaders, along with selected IMB personnel at the Boca Raton Conference Center in Boca Raton, Florida, April 1-6, 2001. See also González Muñoz, *Y Vimos Su Gloria*, 210. The Western Convention shows a net loss of 2,659 members from 1960 to 1991, indicating that, in spite of evangelism efforts during these years, the immigration of members outweighed the conversion growth.

faithful witness, evangelistic results remained sparse. Christians were only allowed to hold services within the existing church buildings, and were not allowed to hold services in homes or to conduct evangelistic activities outside the buildings.[267] Open discrimination occurred in the community, places of work, and in the schools. To profess the name of Christ bore a cost. The Baptist conventions remained solid, and the seminaries continued to prepare pastors for the existing churches, along with the few churches that were started during this period. The Soviet influence continued to dominate the economic and political landscape of Cuba until the break-up of the Soviet block and its economic and military support failed.

The Defining Period (1970-1994)

Western Baptist Internal Conflicts

Even though the Baptist Conventions remained strong, it was not without a price. Each convention had internal conflicts that affected the work. The Western Convention experienced some excruciating conflicts during the 1970s and 1980s, culminating in the expulsion of three pastors and three churches from the fellowship of the Western Baptist Convention.[268] The details and personalities of this conflict fall outside the scope of this book, but to have a general understanding of the conflict and the Western Convention's method for its resolution is important.[269]

In essence, the conflict dealt with misunderstandings and divisions among the pastoral and convention leadership concerning the perception that there were among them pastors and churches who had aligned themselves with the Cuban Revolution and its purposes.[270]

---

[267] One example is a personal story shared with this writer about how a church family's birthday party was raided by government officials, because they thought that it was a clandestine church meeting.

[268] Internal conflicts, which arose among the Western Baptist Convention leadership during these years, led to the expulsion of the First Baptist Church in Matanzas, the Ebenezer Baptist Church in Colón, and Baptist Church in Reparto Mañana in the city of Havana, along with their pastors. While those conflicts existed, the continued faithful ministry of the local churches was not threatened. See González Muñoz, *Y Vimos Su Gloria*, 95-96.

[269] González Muñoz, *Y Vimos Su Gloria*, 75-104. González explains the details of the conflicts and the parties involved in chapter 5, titled, "*Luchas Internas: Radicalización y División* (Internal Fighting: Radicalization and Division).

[270] There were those in the Western Convention who began the organization, *Obreros Estudiantil Bautista de Cuba COEBAC* (Baptist Student Workers of Cuba), which met to discuss political and theological themes, as well as to participate in work brigades with militants from the Communist Party and the Communist organization, *La Unión de Jóvenes Comunistas* (The Communist Student Union). The conservative Baptist pastors and convention leaders rejected the idea that Baptist youth should work with, and hold meetings for dialog, with atheistic communists.

Due to the crisis of 1965 with the imprisonment of the pastors, the UMAP work camp experiences, and the ongoing government discrimination against the Baptist work, any person or group who worked too closely with the government became suspect. Suspicion fell on others, due to a new openness for foreign travel that the government afforded some Baptist leaders and not to others.[271] The convention had no control over the government's harassment, limitations, and impositions, but they did feel a certain sense of control over their own members and leaders. Whereas the convention could not sanction the Cuban government for perceived persecution and obvious discrimination, they could sanction those of their convention whom they perceived as collaborating with or informing their persecutors.

Ever-growing tensions between convention leadership and the Cuban government exacerbated the internal convention conflicts. During the years of 1983-1985, the Western Baptist Convention had not been allowed to celebrate their annual convention meetings due to lack of government permissions. The government imposed a limitation of 350 delegates on the Western and Eastern Conventions for their perspective annual meetings, and neither convention would agree to limit the delegates' participation. Therefore, both conventions decided not to hold the meetings rather than submit to government restrictions.[272]

In 1980, the Mariel Boatlift increased the conflicts as many church members and leaders fled Cuba. Further, in 1980, the Cuban government renewed pressure on the churches by sending government inspectors from the *Registro de Asociaciones* (Associational Inspectors) to solicit lists of church members from the local churches.[273] In 1982, two convention leaders were arrested and interrogated for a four-day period. They were never charged with a crime, but these types of detentions alarmed the Baptist leaders.[274]

According to González, "We had begun a very difficult period, marked by growing misunderstandings, with brothers rejecting each other because of their political and theological opinions. It was a long period of intense fighting, discussions, mistrust, discrepan-

---

[271]Permission for pastors to travel outside of Cuba was a rare thing. As the government began allowing pastors to travel, it afforded these pastors the opportunity, not only to see the outside world, but to earn enough money through speaking engagements and offerings to sustain their families and invest in their ministries. This created a situation where some had outside contacts and, thus, access to resources others did not have. Some took advantage of these opportunities, while others became jealous, and even suspicious, because they were not allowed to travel.

[272]Ibid., 86-87.

[273]Ibid., 88.

[274]Ibid., 89. Those detained included pastor Ernesto Alfonso Díaz, pastor of the San José de las Lajas Church, and one of the youth from his church, Joel Díaz.

cies, marginalization and polarization."[275] Additionally he says, "We experienced external problems with the growth of atheism and the discrimination that believers felt in every sphere of society."[276] The external discrimination and perceived persecution further drove a wedge between those in the convention who did not trust the government and those who felt they could garner further benefits by embracing the revolutionary government or at least trying to make peace with it.

The conflict in the Western Baptist Convention came to a head on February 27, 1987, during the convention's annual meeting. The convention voted, for the first time in their history to expel three of its churches.[277] The pastors of these churches had previously been expelled from the Ministerial Department (*Departamento Ministerial*).[278] These pastors and their respective churches formed a separate Baptist convention on September 8, 1989. This organization, *La Fraternidad de Iglesias Bautistas de Cuba* (FIBAC) (Fraternity of Cuban Baptist Churches), has been a constant point of conflict with the Western Convention. A major point of contention has been that, upon leaving the Western Convention, the FIBAC took possession of the church buildings where they were meeting. The land for these buildings was purchased, and the buildings erected with funds from the HMB. These buildings belonged to the Western Baptist Convention, but have been under the control of the Fraternity of Baptists since 1989.

Eastern Baptist Internal Conflicts

In the Eastern Baptist Convention, the internal conflicts dealt with a clash between "liberals" and "conservatives" in the 1970s, and the participation of some pastors and their churches in the charismatic movement in the 1980s. According to Acosta, conflicts arose in the early years of the Revolution, as some within the convention sympathized with the social concerns of the Revolution, and others sought to emphasize the evangelistic mandate of the Church.[279] By 1968, the division rose to the level that the Eastern

---

[275]Ibid., 81.
[276]Ibid., 82.
[277]Ibid., 95. The churches that were expelled were the First Baptist Church in Matanzas, the Ebenezer Baptist Church in Colón, and Baptist Church in Reparto Mañana in the city of Havana.
[278]Roy Acosta García, private e-mail to this writer, 7 November 2009. Following the expulsion of the Western churches, Reverend Víctor Mercedo met with the Eastern Baptist Convention's Executive Committee, in the San Juan Hotel in Santiago, Cuba, requesting that these churches be accepted into the fellowship of the Eastern Baptist Convention. The Executive Committee rejected this appeal, feeling that it would be unethical to consider such a request.
[279]Acosta García, e-mail, 7 November 2009. In this e-mail communication, Acosta states, "Due to the continuing conflicts with the State as a result of the laws concerning 'Obligatory Military Service', and the UMAP experience that traumatized the pas-

Convention ceased its participation in the Cuban Council of Churches, due to its perceived ties and alliances with the Communist government. As the government limitations concerning the free exercise of religion grew a further polarizing of relationships in the convention developed. Acosta states:

> The majority of the pastors and laymen, who were conservative, strengthened their ties with the conservative wing of the Western Baptist Convention while the liberal wing of the Eastern Convention began to relate closely with the small group within the Western Convention that held the same position. This relation gave rise in 1974 to the *Coordinación Obrero Estudiantil Bautista* (COEBAC) (Baptist Student Workers of Cuba), which can be considered the antecedent to the Fraternity of Baptists, where pastors and leaders from both conventions aligned themselves with the fulfilling of the socialist aims.[280]

Further, according to Acosta:

> Following a meeting of pastors and leaders, which became known as '*La Cumbre*' (the summit), both groups came to clearly understand each other's position. The Executive Committee decided the convention needed to concentrate its efforts on missionary and evangelistic work and not be distracted by internal conflicts, and with time the confrontation was averted. No pastors were expelled, and each church kept the pastor they desired. At the peak of the conflict, the Executive Committee, with the support of the immense majority of the churches, reaffirmed the Convention's conservative missionary and evangelistic direction. Therefore, the liberal group was isolated, and many of the youth who followed them felt defrauded due to ethical problems. Some of these pastors left the work, due to sick-

---

tors and seminarians caused an intensified ideological conflict in the church, that ultimately led to the convention breaking its ties with the Cuban Council of Churches, in 1968. During this period, two opposing factions existed in the convention, namely "liberals" and "conservatives."

[280]Acosta García, e-mail, 7 November 2009; and see also González Muñoz, *Y Vimos Su Gloria*, 84-85. González dates the creation of COEBAC in 1973. He describes the organization in the following way: "The organization of the Coordination of Baptist Student Work (CBEBAC), was created, in 1973, to offer a place for theological reflection to the brothers interested in social action from a Christian perspective. Pastors and laymen from both conventions met together and strengthened their relationships. They met monthly and held an annual camp meeting concerning 'Christian social responsibility.' Some pastors organized work teams that would labor for fifteen days a year along side Communist party militants and the Communist Youth Union (*Unión de Jóvenes Comunistas*)."

ness, death, or by joining a different denomination. Even though we fought to hide the political nature of the conflict, the truth is that behind the liberal movement, there was a militant political faction linked to the government and the conservatives refused to make those compromises with the government.[281]

By dedicating themselves to the common goal of evangelism and missions, the Eastern Baptist Convention was able to ride out the storm of the "liberal" versus "conservative" controversy. They trusted that the convention's unified effort in these areas would overcome the social agenda of the liberal faction. This strategy proved to be effective.

In the early 1980s, the Eastern Baptist Convention faced a second internal conflict. This time it was a "conservative" versus "charismatic" conflict. According to Acosta, the charismatic movement was introduced into Cuba by Christian visitors who entered from other countries bringing this influence with them.[282] Acosta avows that, as early as 1985, several members of the convention's Executive Committee resigned over their involvement in this movement. Further, the Executive Committee requested that the pastoral body undertake a serious study of the charismatic phenomenon.[283]

In his annual report during the Eastern Baptist Convention's annual meeting in 1988, the convention's president, Víctor Ruiz Victores, expressed his concerns about this area of convention life saying:

> We would not be honest if we did not express our concern over the form of worship that some of our pastors and churches of our convention have adopted. Our concern is founded in the divisions that we have witnessed in our pastoral body and that exist in the congregations that practice this type of worship. This assembly should call for a point of order and determine if we are a Baptist convention or if we want to change our form of worship.[284]

Acosta takes a longer historical view saying:

> In the following years this tension between "conservatives" and "charismatics" became increasingly intense. Strong conservatives within the convention leadership stood on one side, faced on the other by the new gen-

---

[281]Ibid.
[282]Ibid.
[283]Acosta García, *Oriental*, 3:80.
[284]Ibid., 81.

erations who entered the seminary identifying with a more open style of worship . . .[285]

By 1994, the polarization between the charismatics and the conservatives reached a crisis point. The convention believed that if something were not done, a rupture of fellowship would occur in the convention. Roy Acosta García served as president of the Eastern Baptist Convention at that time. In his report to the convention in February 1995, he sought again to deflect the controversy by calling the convention to join together in a common purpose. In his report Acosta says:

> . . . our unity in Christ serves as our one constant for the people of God. Every member of the Executive Committee has focused our attention on maintaining unity in Christ in our thoughts as well as our actions. It is necessary that we continue working together united by the purpose of the Convention in the edification of the Kingdom of God in our midst.[286]

Again, the crisis was overcome by seeking common ground in the purposes of the Kingdom instead of focusing in on the division. The convention adopted as its theme for the year, "United in Christ for an hour such as this."[287]

Results of the Conflicts

Over the years, this writer has observed, in the Eastern Convention, a healthy pattern of dealing with divergent beliefs in their midst. Instead of ostracizing or expelling the divergent group, the Eastern Convention leadership allowed these groups enough room for their practices to run their course. In the case of the younger leaders and their charismatic forms of worship, the convention leadership wisely stayed in contact with them and kept an open dialogue even though they did not agree with their form of worship.[288]

In the end, a majority of these "charismatic" leaders were assimilated back into the mainstream of convention life, bringing with them the fire of their passion for worship without the charismatic idiosyncrasies. Acosta does recall:

---

[285]Ibid.
[286] Ibid.
[287]Ibid.
[288]Acosta García, e-mail, 7 November 2009. Acosta does say that meetings were held to reach mutual "understanding." Rules were established for convention meetings, retreats, and so forth, to control the external manifestations such as screaming and applauding.

The movement did serve to attract a lot of people, and these churches did begin to really grow. We began holding conferences so the pastors could discuss the themes and practices, but we tried to ensure that the movement did not fall into the excesses of what we called "charismania" in order to differentiate it from the biblical concept of *charisma*. When talking about this epoch we prefer to talk in terms of "revival" or "churches revived."[289]

The Western Baptist Convention, on the other hand, has taken a stronger approach to squelch any practices that diverge from the accepted norm.[290] The Western Convention prizes a spirit of unity almost above anything else. However, its interpretation of unity borders on the requirement of uniformity rather than unity.

The Western Convention has chosen a different approach when dealing with churches choosing to align with the Fraternity of Baptists. In open assembly, the convention decided to affirm as the true church those within the congregation that choose to remain affiliated with the Western Convention, and have virtually ignored those who choose to leave and affiliate with the Fraternity. By doing this they hoped to reduce the possibility that the defecting group could justify the taking of the Convention owned property. They have taken this approach in an attempt to retain the church buildings occupied by the group seeking to align with the Fraternity.[291]

During the years of conflict in the 1980s, church growth among Western Cuban Baptists was affected adversely. According to González, "At the end of the long conflict...the Baptist work reached its lowest level since the triumph of the Revolution. They had 3,000 less members, had not organized a church in seven years and had lost three."[292] During the presidency of Antonio Pérez Rabelo (1987-1990), things began to turn around. "The numbers continued to

---

[289]Acosta García, e-mail, 7 November 2009.
[290]Several cases occurred where students from the Western Baptist Convention Seminary were expelled for holding views not consistent with the Western Convention's theology.
[291]This writer observed this process during the Western Baptist Convention's annual meeting in February of 1998. The convention affirmed the true William Carey Baptist Church as being comprised of those who chose to remain in the Western Convention. Unfortunately, the property where the William Carey Church met is, to this day, under the control of the William Carey Church that chose to leave the Western Baptist Convention and to affiliate with the Fraternity of Baptists. This property is still in the name of the Home Mission Board of the Southern Baptist Convention. The Western Convention makes annual pleas for the recuperation of this property. They have been able to recuperate some of the apartments on the property, one of which now houses the offices of the Western Baptist Convention's Home and Foreign Mission Board.
[292]González Muñoz, *Y Vimos Su Gloria*, 121.

decline in 1988, but in 1989 there was a growth in baptisms, especially in 1990." In 1987, they baptized 272 people. In 1988, they baptized 324. In 1989, they baptized 306 and, in 1990, they baptized 421. In 1991, the number of baptisms jumped to 747. González says, "These were historic and very special circumstances because they marked the beginning stages of the longest period of sustained growth in history."[293]

The rich history of Cuban Baptists positioned them to experience an unprecedented movement of the Spirit of God. This legacy provided a solid doctrinal and organizational foundation upon which to build the future of Baptist work in Cuba. As Cuban Baptists approached the 1990s, they were unaware of the blessings the Lord was about to pour out upon his Church. They had faithfully proclaimed the Gospel for decades with limited results. They continued to pray that the Lord would pour out His Spirit on the people of Cuba. Their prayers were about to be answered.

Conclusion

Cuban Baptists continued to sow the seed of the Gospel faithfully during very difficult circumstances. In spite of their faithful witness, evangelistic results were sparse. The Baptist conventions remained solid, and the seminaries continued to prepare pastors for the existing churches and for the few churches that were started during this period. Cuban Christians poured out their hearts before the Lord in intercessory prayer. They called upon Him to rend the heavens and come down to fulfill the Cuban Christians' dream of "Cuba for Christ."

Cuban Baptists, therefore, approached the 1990s with a sense of trepidation and expectation. With the fall of the Soviet support system, the Cuban people fell on hard times economically, socially, and spiritually. Little did Baptists know that their faithfulness in sowing the Gospel during decades of abuse and discrimination was about to yield an unprecedented harvest.

---

[293]Ibid., 124.

CHAPTER 5

THE EMERGENCE OF THE CUBAN CHURCH PLANTING MOVEMENT

As seen previously, Cubans have exhibited receptivity to the Gospel from the time of Christianity's introduction to the island in the late 1800s. A number of times mass turnings of the Cuban people to Christ appeared to be on the horizon. Divergent circumstances, however, prevented the emergence of a CPM prior to the 1990s. In the fullness of His time, God has visited Cuba with an unprecedented movement of the Holy Spirit.

At the beginning of the 1990s, many changes marked the Cuban landscape. A number of world events and the Cuban government's reaction to them left the Cuban economy and society in a state of chaos and uncertainty. This unrest helped to open the door for the CPM to emerge.

This chapter highlights and describes some of the major events that served as catalysts for evangelical growth, primarily among Baptists and Assemblies of God, from the early 1990s until today. The following will be an analysis of Cuban Baptist church growth from the time the CPM began to appear until 2010. This account will serve to describe the growth dynamics of the CPM, helping as well to identify its strengths and weaknesses.

During the first thirty years of the Revolution, in the face of government and societal pressures, the Church struggled to maintain some sense of control over its circumstances. The government restricted the Church's evangelistic outreach and worship services to their existing church buildings. They were not allowed to "proselytize" outside of these structures.

Though they continued the faithful proclamation of the Gospel during this restrictive period, they became accustomed to sparse results. Further, the consequences of a continual migration of leaders and members left the work in a constant state of flux. Not only were the evangelistic results sparse, but the church planting efforts yielded little fruit. From 1960 to 1990, the Eastern and Western Baptist Conventions, combined, started only twenty-eight new churches.[294]

The conventions wrestled with governmental restrictions which did not allow them to evangelize openly nor to repair their existing buildings, much less build new ones. The emerging CPM of the 1990s took Cuban Baptists by surprise. Leaders were pleasantly

---

[294]See Graph 1: Traditional Churches 1905-2010 page 113.

surprised with the significant increase in the number of people flocking to their churches and missions and what those churches, at that time, only understood to be home Bible studies or home worship services.

Understandably, the Cuban Baptist leaders did not recognize that a CPM was emerging, nor could they recognize the magnitude of the movement. The leaders were cognizant that attendance in their churches, missions, and outreach groups was growing rapidly, and knew that churches were being started at an unprecedented rate, but they viewed that growth through the eyes of their highly traditional structure. They did realize that in only three years, from 1990 through 1993, they had established the same number of new churches (twenty-eight) that had previously taken the denomination thirty years to accomplish.[295]

At the same time, it is important to notice, these same leaders did not understand the significance of the *casas culto* (house church) phenomenon. What they did notice and rejoiced over was the total number of traditional churches that grew from 238, in 1990, to 792 in 2010. In church growth analysis terms, this was a steady, incremental increase.

While the growth was very healthy, this numerical increase alone did not reach the level of CPM status. The leaders of the Baptist Conventions are to be applauded for remaining faithful evangelists and church planters in the face of government restrictions, which resulted in the planting of 564 churches in twenty years. This level of growth had never been witnessed in the history of Cuba. These statistics, however, only provide the reader with an introduction to the story. The actual growth in "churches" was much more than could be seen on the surface.

Historically, the method of planting a church had been for a seminary student or a faithful layman from a local mother church to begin outreach in a new area and to establish a "mission." Over time, that mission would grow and conform to the image of the mother church, which included Sunday School and other organizational structures that the conventions required. The mission could mature to become a recognized church, only at the rate that ordained leadership could be provided. Every new convention-recognized church was, and is, required to have a convention-recognized, ordained pastor responsible for that church.

During the mid to late 1990s, both conventions experienced explosive growth in the number of mission starts. From 1995 to

---

[295]See Graph 1: "Traditional Churches 1905-2010," page 113 and Graph 2: "Traditional Churches 1990-2010 page 114."

2010, Cuban Baptists saw the beginning of 993 missions.[296] The 564 missions that had been recognized as convention churches during this period must also be considered and added to that number. This translates into the planting of 1,557 new works during the years 1995-2010.

In order to put this into context, it needs to be understood that the vast majority of these missions, apart from the conventions' educational requirements for pastors, met all the biblical characteristics of New Testament churches. At the same time, due to government restrictions and convention polity issues, the Cuban Baptist leaders did not think these missions were autonomous local churches. This level of growth was well beyond the ability of the conventions to provide a sufficient number of seminary-trained, ordained pastors. They were at a loss about how to address this level of growth. Again, more was happening at the grass roots level than was immediately apparent.

From 1992 to the present, lay leaders began the spontaneous opening of their homes, apartments, patios, roofs, yards, and so forth, for the beginning of house churches (*casas culto*). In 1993, after noting the rapid growth of churches meeting in homes, now called *casas culto*, the government began to implement a process requiring them to officially register. The government imposed certain conditions on the house churches that the conventions interpreted as restrictions. In the face of this pressure, the conventions simply changed the nomenclature from *casas culto* to houses of prayer (*casas de oración*) and continued to multiply.

These groups were evolving and later their distinct characteristics became clearly recognizable. From 1992 to 1995, Cuban Baptists planted 1,369 house churches and houses of prayer. During the next fifteen years, from 1995 to 2010, they started an additional 3,532, reaching a total of 4,901.[297]

Baptist leadership knew these new works were being started but had no mechanism, under their traditional denominational structure and polity, coupled with governmental restrictions, to recognize them as churches. When asked, they would say the majority of these groups met the characteristics of New Testament churches, but they did not necessarily meet the conventions' traditional expectations of owning land, a building, and having the necessary convention departments, and an ordained pastor.

The leadership of the conventions continues to struggle with these issues until the present day. How can all of these new churches be recognized without feeling the government's pressure

---

[296]See Graph 3: "Missions 1995-2010," page 115.
[297]See Graph 4: "House Churches and Houses of Prayer 1995-2010, 31," 118.

on one side, and destroying the conventions' traditional structure on the other? The remainder of this book will address these concerns.

Contributing Factors to the Emergence of the Cuban CPM

Political and Economic Factors

Changes in Church-State Relations

A number of political factors produced an atmosphere ripe for the emergence of the CPM in Cuba. In the 1970s, Church-State relations began to improve slowly. In 1971, the first changes in attitude followed Fidel Castro's visit to Chile. During his meetings with Salvador Allende and Cardinal Raúl Silva, Castro intimated that Marxism and Christianity shared common ethical goals and could form a strategic alliance for social justice and liberation in Latin America.[298] In 1975, the Revolutionary government held the first Communist Party Congress. The result of that congress was the production of a Cuban Constitution, which officially declared freedom of religion in Cuba.[299]

In 1977, Fidel Castro participated in a meeting of Protestant leaders in Jamaica, in which he emphasized the revolutionary nature of Christ.[300] With the visit of Rev. Jesse Jackson to Cuba, in 1984, changes began to accelerate. During Jackson's stay, Castro made his first visit to a Protestant church. The Jackson meeting was the first in a series of meetings that Castro held with foreign and Cuban religious leaders over the next year and a half, something he had not done since the early days of the Revolution and a sign that his comments about cooperation and dialogue were finally being backed up with action.[301]

The publication of *Fidel y la Religión: Conversaciones con Frei Betto* (Fidel and Religion: Conversations with Frei Betto), in January 1985, provoked many questions and discussions about the future of Church-State relations in Cuba. The publication, primarily a transcript of interviews conducted by Frei Betto, a Brazilian priest, shed light into Castro's education in Catholic Schools, his opinions concerning Church-State relations, and liberation theology. The first

---

[298]John Kirk, *Between God and Party: Religion and Politics in Revolutionary Cuba* (Tampa: University of South Florida Press, 1989), 131-34.

[299]Corse, *Protestants, Revolution and the Cuba-U.S. Bond*, 136. According to Corse, this is ironic, because "1975 was also the year when, after extensive harassment, the government officially banned the Jehovah's Witnesses."

[300]Ibid.

[301]Ibid., 136-37.

printing of 200,000 copies sold out in just a few days. According to Corse:

> With the book's publication, discussion of religion became more open in Cuba, not just on the level of leadership, but on the street as well. In the immediate aftermath of the publication, the government allowed a shipment of 20,000 Bibles into the country, a dramatic shift in a longstanding policy of restricting Bible imports.[302]

As the world's socio-political landscape began to change, Cuba was being slowly prepared for a spiritual revolution.

Changes in Soviet Policy and the Special Period

The Soviet Union's policies of *perestroika* (a restructuring of the Soviet economy) and *glasnost* (literally meaning "publicity," which came to signify an openness and transparency in the discussion of news, social discussion, and so forth) brought about the fracturing of the old Soviet Union, and ushered in tremendous economic and political reform.[303] Beginning on November 9, 1989, the fall of the Berlin Wall shocked much of the world and represented unprecedented change.

Against Cuba's wishes, in September of 1991, Soviet troops began withdrawing from Cuba. The Cuban government was concerned that a complete withdrawal of the Soviet military would leave the island vulnerable to U.S. aggression. By December 21, 1991, the Soviet Union had imploded, leaving its global partners without its military or economic support. The cold war ended, and Cuba found herself alone and isolated, without political friends or military allies.

The Cuban economy was almost totally dependent upon outside assistance. With the breakup of the Soviet Union, Cuba ceased to receive the generous subsidies to which it had grown accustomed. In 1989, for example, the country received aid valued at five billion dollars.[304] The old Socialist block ties amounted to 85 percent of Cuba's trade. Now, the island found itself increasingly unable to import the goods it consumed, and without markets to export what it produced.

---

[302]Ibid., 137.
[303]"Russia," *Encyclopedia Britannica Online* (2007) [on-line]; accessed 21 August 2007; available from http://www.britannica.com/eb.article-38564; Internet.
[304]Efrén Córdava, "The Situation of the Cuban Worker During the 'Special Period in Peacetime'," Association for the Study of the Cuban Economy [ASCE], Sixth Annual Meeting, University of Miami, James L. Knight Center, Hyatt Hotel, August 8-10, 1996, 358.

These drastic political and economic changes took the Cuban people by surprise. For the first time in decades, Cuba was forced to rely upon its own resources, and discovered very quickly that it could not sustain itself without some drastic changes. The government was entering a time where it needed to maximize its own resources and build new commercial ties.

In March of 1990, the Cuban government introduced the "Special Period in a Time of Peace." Alberto González Muñoz provides a stark description of the period:

> Very few Cubans could imagine what was going to happen following the fall of the Soviet Union and the consequences that this event would bring to Cuba's economy. Cubans, who for years were accustomed to shortages, failed to grasp the magnitude of the crisis they were to experience in the coming years. We were beginning the infamous "Special Period" that drove the country into a time of absolute shortages of every type of resource. It virtually paralyzed the country in the areas of industrial production, transportation and economic development. The streets were totally emptied of vehicles, and the markets of food. The very health of the Cuban people deteriorated as signified by the spread of polyneuritis that attacked a large part of the population, brought on by a vitamin deficiency. There was a dearth of medicines with which to treat the people. Also, there was a tightening of the North American economic blockade due to the Torricelli and Helms-Burton Acts, making it increasingly difficult for the country to obtain what it needed.
>
> From a faith perspective, conscious of the sovereignty and providence of God, we are able to see that the stage was being set for the arrival of a spiritual awakening to the country. On one side, the terrible economic situation affected everyone where the only hope was to just survive . . . what happened though was that it provoked in the country an existential crisis.[305]

The Torricelli Act, passed in 1992, strengthened the U.S. blockade on Cuba. President George Bush signed it into law just before the presidential election. The Torricelli Act prevented food and medicine from being shipped to Cuba, the only exception being humanitarian aid. The Helms-Burton Act, enacted in 1996, further strengthened the U.S. embargo against Cuba for the purpose of

---

[305]González Muñoz, *Y Vimos Su Gloria*, 127.

forcing the island nation to move toward democratic reforms. The legislation received the push it needed to pass from Cuba's shooting down of two Miami-based planes operated by Brothers to the Rescue on February 24, 1996.[306]

Though the Cuban government declared the "Special Period" to be temporary, it dragged on for years with increased suffering. Unemployment rates skyrocketed, reaching an estimated 51 percent. Sugarcane workers were forced to work fifteen hours a day, seven days a week, but cane production in 1994-95 fell to its lowest point in sixty years; 3.3 million tons.[307] According to Efrén Córdova, "Seventy-five percent of the people were concentrated in the urban areas; food supplies were insufficient, and the threat of starvation was looming on the horizon."[308] Córdova recounts:

> Nutrition deficiencies and poor sanitation were responsible for the appearance of epidemics of beriberi, optical neuritis, and leptospirosis. In 1993 the rate of suicides amounted to 21.7 per one hundred thousand inhabitants; the next year it reached 20.7 and both figures were the highest in Latin America. . . . Sharp increases in the number of abortions (8 for each 10 births), the consumption of alcohol and the crime rate were also salient features of the special period.[309]

Not surprisingly, he concludes, "Small wonder that it was during these years that the number of rafters and boat people reached incredible figures (35,375 in 1994, for instance)."[310] The Cuban people were in a state of real physical, mental, and emotional crisis.

Changes in the Cuban Government

One of the most radical changes in Cuba during this period occurred within the Cuban Communist Party (PCC) itself. In 1965, the PCC was established upon a Marxist-Leninist materialist, philosophic base, and for over thirty years, the entire Cuban system propagated an atheistic philosophy that denied the existence of God, persecuting and discriminating against those who dared to believe. Christians were viewed as having at best a mixed allegiance, and at worst--due to their beliefs--a counter-revolutionary ideology.

---

[306]Ibid.
[307]Córdava, "Situation of the Cuban Worker," 359.
[308]Ibid., 361.
[309]Ibid., 364.
[310]Ibid.

In October, of 1991, the PCC made a significant change in their membership rules. For the first time in almost thirty years, the door opened for Christians to become members of the PCC.[311] As one can imagine, this came as a shock to the conventions, churches, and their members. This agreement was as controversial for the churches as it was for the Communist party. How could Christian believers become members of the atheist Communist Party that had abused them for so many years? An additional question arose; if the PCC was willing to accept Christians into its ranks, would the churches be willing to accept PCC members into their churches?[312]

The real effect of this shifting situation opened the churches' eyes to the fact that change was in the wind. They had lived so many years with a "bunker mentality," just trying to survive the constant onslaught of atheistic Communism. One Cuban leader shared with this writer an illustration of the "Bunker Mentality" that dominated the church's perspective:

> A prime example of our bunker mentality can be found in our interpretation of Matthew 16:18 which says, "And I tell you that you are Peter, and on this rock I will build my church, and the gates of Hades will not overcome it." To Cuban Baptists, due to the government regulations, that were strictly enforced, requiring that all religious activities take place within the walls of the existing church buildings, this meant that the "gates of Hades" signified the Communist government, and that they would not prevail against or overcome the existing church in its buildings. Once the atmosphere in the country began to change, and more openness existed, Cuban Baptists realized that the Church, the body of Christ, was to storm the gates of Hades, the lost of Cuba, and overcome their hatred with the love of Christ.[313]

In the beginning, the churches were disoriented due to the extreme economic privations, coupled with this radical deviation from the Communist Party's usual attitude toward the Church. A continual lack of trust existed concerning anything that had to do with the government.

---

[311]Acosta García, *Historia y Teología*, 3:86.
[312]González Muñoz, *Y Vimos Su Gloria*, 129-30.
[313]The writer met with this Cuban leader was held at the writer's home in Weston, Florida on November 3, 2009. For a separate confirmation of how Matthew 16:18 was interpreted in Cuba, see: Mary Speidel, Wally Poor, and Betty Poor, "Walking in Victory," *Commission Magazine*, May 1997, 16.

Changes to the Cuban Constitution in 1992

While the Cuban Church sought to understand the change in posture of the Communist Party, they were again shocked by the decision of the National Assembly of Popular Power to modify the Cuban Constitution. On July 12, 1992, the National Assembly of Popular Power (*La Asamblea Nacional del Poder Popular*) modified the February 24, 1976 version of the Socialist Constitution of Cuba (*La Constitución Socialista de la República de Cuba*). According to Article 8 of the revision, "The State recognizes, respects, and guarantees religious liberty. In the Republic of Cuba, the religious institutions are separate from the state. The differing beliefs and religions enjoy equal consideration."[314] In Chapter V of the Constitution, under the title "Equality," Article 43 states:

> The State consecrates the rights won by the Revolution that all citizens, without distinction of race, skin color, sex, religious beliefs, national origin and other areas prejudicial against their human dignity: Have access, according to their merits and capacities, to all positions and jobs of the State, of the Public Administration, production, and service positions; are able to be promoted to any level in the revolutionary army hierarchy, state security and the department of the interior, according to their merits and abilities; will receive equal pay for equal work; enjoy studying in any of the educational institutions in the country, from grade school through the universities, that are the same for all; they will receive help in all the institutions of health; housing in any sector, zone or neighborhood in the cities and stay in whatever hotel; they will be served in all restaurants and other service-oriented public establishments; be able to use, without segregation, sea-going vessels, trains, airlines and automobiles; enjoy all resorts, beaches, parks, social circles and other cultural centers, sports, recreation and rest.[315]

---

[314]"Constitution of the Republic of Cuba, 1992" [on-line]; accessed 7 December 2006; available from http://www.cubanet.org/ref/dis/const_92_e.htm; Internet.
[315]Ibid. For an in-depth discussion of the changes made to the Cuban Constitution on July 12, 1992, and the implications for the Church, see: González Muñoz, *Y Vimos Su Gloria*, 133-38. Additionally, González references an important publication on the subject: Hugo Azcuy, "Los cambios de la constitución cubana (The Changes to the Cuban Constitution)" in *Cuadernos de Nuestra América* (Notebooks from Our America), no. 20, La Habana, 1993.

Another significant change in the constitution appears in Article 55 of Chapter VII titled "Rights, Responsibilities and Fundamental Guarantees":

> The State, that recognizes, respects and guarantees the freedom of conscience and of religion, recognizes respects and guarantees at the same time the freedom of each citizen to change their religious beliefs or to not have any, and to profess, within respect for the law, the religion of their preference. The law regulates the relationship of the State with that of religious institutions.[316]

These articles effectively declared the illegality of any discrimination against a person for his or her religious beliefs. Additionally, this allowed a person the ability to profess his/her faith as long as that faith did not threaten the State. According to González, while it was positive to hear that believers were now constitutionally protected and had all the rights and privileges of other Cuban citizens, other realities became obvious to all Cuban believers:

> Nevertheless, it is still true that due to the many years where being "a religious person" prohibited a person from attempting certain professions in the universities, from working in certain places, and from ascending to a certain levels of leadership, in some jobs and in some parts of society, there still persists a remnant of these discriminatory attitudes; and as a result regrettable acts still occur.[317]

González continues, ". . . it would be naive to hope that this mention of the illegitimacy of religious discrimination in the Constitution would completely put an end to these types of discriminatory acts. It requires the passage of time for a new mentality to take hold."[318] In other words, the law provided rights, but the application of the law varied.

One must remember these constitutional changes came at a very difficult period in Cuban history. The conditions in the country deteriorated to the point that the government, of necessity, had to make some fundamental changes to survive. One such change was the attempt to transform the global community's perception of Cuba as an atheistic state that persecuted and/or discriminated openly against Christians, and acted aggressively against the Church. As the regime began to build business ties with other countries to

---
[316]"Constitution of the Republic of Cuba, 1992," cited in González Muñoz, *Y Vimos Su Gloria*, 136.
[317]González Muñoz, *Y Vimos Su Gloria*, 135.
[318]Ibid., 136.

strengthen tourism, and so forth, it needed to improve its global image.

Furthermore, in 1992, the government declared Cuba to be a secular state versus an atheistic one.[319] Now reaching adulthood, an entire generation raised under an atheistic Communist ideology, began to question its past and make inquiries about its future. The Cuban government had sought for decades to eradicate God from the consciousness of the people, replacing it with dialectical materialism and a faith in the State. The government had attempted to establish a personality cult around the person of Fidel Castro, known in Cuba as *Fidelismo* (Fidelism).

After more than thirty years, Cuban society was in turmoil. People were starving. The country was paralyzed. The government had, in a sense, removed God from the consciousness of the people, but had failed to put any better alternative in its place. Due to these factors, Cuba was poised for a mighty movement of the Holy Spirit.

Religious Factors

From the Home Mission Board to the Foreign Mission Board

In 1988, the responsibility for the work with Western Cuban Baptists passed from the Home Mission Board to the Foreign Mission Board of the Southern Baptist Convention. During a very difficult time in Cuban history, FMB leadership was able to relate to Cuban Baptists in helpful ways. According to González, the transfer of the relationship from the HMB to the FMB was significant:

> It was a historic decision. . . . The relationship with the FMB and the Convention was from the very beginning an example of cooperation for the strengthening of the Lord's work in our country. Offering each year a large amount of economic assistance, these brothers have respectfully served us as consultants, encouragers, and catalyzers. They quickly began to help us to develop leaders and in every area of the work, always offering ideas and resources, but leaving the final decisions in the hands of Cuban leadership.

The passing of the work from the HMB to the FMB was not only providential, it was also timely. Many feared

---

[319]"Constitution of the Republic of Cuba, 1992,"Internet; see also "Open Doors International: Country Profiles: Cuba" [on-line]; accessed 2 April 2002; available from www.opendoors/countryprofiles/ cuba.htm; Internet.

the new mission board would not be able to achieve the degree of understanding and work with the level of love that the HMB had attained in Cuba after having served there so many years. In reality the opposite was true. The change placed Cuban Baptists in relationship with persons, who with their vision and understanding of global missions, were in a better position to help us confront the circumstances that were about to hit in the near future.[320]

The initial coordinator for the work in Cuba relating to the Western Baptist Convention was Dr. Ron Wilson. He was replaced by Mark Smith who served from 1991-1997. Smith did a masterful job of building strong relationships with convention leaders and acting as a stabilizing factor during the tumultuous years of the "Special Period." In 1997, this writer followed Mark Smith as coordinator. This writer's role was completely distinct from that of Wilson and Smith. He was to function as a Strategy Leader with the objective of helping the Western Convention to maximize the growth they were experiencing. Further, in 1998, this writer had the privilege of opening an official relationship between the IMB and the Eastern Baptist Convention, serving as the Strategy Coordinator for that convention until the arrival of Howard Atkinson, in 2000.

The HMB had cared for and nurtured the work for generations. The FMB leadership was able to relate to the Western Baptist Convention in ways that helped the convention recognize and take advantage of ever-growing opportunities. The FMB, now the International Mission Board (IMB), has had the blessing of walking alongside Cuban Baptists during these years of unprecedented growth.

The Beginning of the Harvest

Continued government pressure, as well as economic and social instability, led to an atmosphere ripe for an extraordinary increase in the number of new believers as well as new church starts.[321] As the social, economic, and political conditions deteriorated, the Cuban people began to awaken to their spiritual needs. Neither the conventions, nor the local churches, were prepared for the surge in attendance. They continued to celebrate evangelistic meetings and other worship activities, but for the first time in decades, a multitude of people began to attend. Church buildings that had been, at most, half full were now full to overflowing.

---

[320]González Muñoz, *Y Vimos Su Gloria*, 126.
[321]Acosta García, *Historia y Teología*, 3:86.

Two types of people now visited the churches. The first were those who at one time had a relationship with the Church, but because of the influence of the Revolution, fear of persecution, or other reasons had ceased to attend. The second were young people reared under the Revolution who were spiritually illiterate. The first group returned to the Church, because they had known it as a place of refuge, the second group came for the first time seeking spiritual answers in the midst of societal chaos.

The churches scrambled to accommodate the crowds. Some were overwhelmed with thanksgiving, and witnessed the outpouring of the Holy Spirit as an answer to their prayers. Others became uncomfortable, because the newcomers outnumbered the regulars and they were afraid of the changes they might bring. Many were concerned about the danger of government infiltrators being among the newcomers. Some had grown accustomed to their quiet reverent worship and their small intimate fellowship. There were those who saw the flood of visitors as an invasion.

The churches had grown accustomed to virtual emptiness, with the same faithful few attending week after week. They built strong relationships from having suffered through the same societal rejection and discrimination. González writes, "Even though they prayed constantly for an awakening, they felt secure among their small group of brothers, in the midst of a society that rejected them."[322]

The new believers brought to the church a heightened level of spiritual fervor and excitement. González further explains, "Since the growth arrived unexpectedly and did not happen as a result of a developed and detailed strategy, the new conditions began to upset the established customs and securities. The new converts arrived with a contagious enthusiasm."[323]

Along with the growing numbers that began to attend church meetings, a crisis emerged, brought about by the lack of transportation. Due to the economic crisis, the roads were virtually empty of public taxis or buses. Church members found it increasingly difficult to travel to local churches that were any distance from their homes. The churches and the Christians constantly struggled with these new realities.

A Fundamental Change in Strategy

Because the existing church buildings were packed beyond capacity and members constantly complained about their inability to travel to the existing church buildings due to the transportation crisis, the conventions appealed to the Department of Religious

---

[322]González Muñoz, *Y Vimos Su Gloria*, 142.
[323]Ibid., 143.

Affairs of the Communist Party for intervention. The convention leaders declared in meeting after meeting the need to build additional church buildings and to repair the existing buildings that had fallen into disrepair due to government restrictions.

During this time, a providential meeting was held with Dr. José Felipe Carneado, the Chief of the Office of Attention to Religious Affairs of the Cuban Communist Party. According to the testimony of those present, Carneado stated, "Why don't you hold meetings in your houses like the Pentecostals? Near to where I live is one of these houses and they hardly let us get any sleep. But for now we cannot authorize the construction of any new buildings."[324]

Even though Carneado later said his comments were not intended to be used as an official authorization for the planting of *casas culto* (House Churches), Baptists and others understood it as such and never looked back. The first year that the Western Convention recorded *casas culto* was 1993, at which time, 237 had been planted. In 1994, 278 existed, and by 1995, there were 563. The Eastern Convention did not report *casas culto* in their statistical report until 1995, and by then they had planted 806. From 1992-95, following Carneado's suggestion, the two Baptist conventions started 1,369 *casas culto*, in addition to the 297 existing traditional or historic churches and 353 missions that the conventions recorded in 1995.

The *casas culto* were a key element in the beginning and expansion of the CPM in Cuba. According to Roy Acosta, "In an unexpected manner the government began to make official and legalize these house meetings which were baptized with the name 'casas culto.' A new period in the development and growth of the Church had begun in our country."[325] The new missions and *casas culto* took the Gospel outside the walls of the traditional church to where the people lived.

Due to extreme privation, many people did not own clothing suitable to wear to a church service. Many, due to the years of atheist indoctrination, still harbored a fear of being seen entering an evangelical church. Where they may have feared attending a traditional church service, no such obstacles existed to attending an informal service in a private home or apartment. Members of the *casa culto* would visit with their neighbors and ask how they could pray for their family. Many came to the *casas culto,* and to Christ, through the testimony of answered prayer.

The concept of the *casa culto* was not totally foreign to the Cuban population. Prior to the Revolution, they had been called "*cul-*

---

[324]Ibid., 149.
[325]Acosta García, *Historia y Teología*, 3:86.

tos de barrio" (neighborhood worship services). As the Revolution took hold, these neighborhood services were banned, along with any missions that did not have their own building. Beginning also in the 1960s, church services were only allowed inside a government-recognized church building. Over the years, the traditional church began to develop a bunker mentality and poured all of its efforts into the program held within the local church building. Now, through the *casas culto* the church was freed from its buildings to go back to the neighborhoods and into the people's homes.[326]

The Cubans view this as nothing less than a sovereign act of God. According to González:

> This was not the result of a specific strategy on our part nor was it the application of some plan from another country. No one came to tell us to do this or that. It emerged spontaneously, as the logical result of a special moment and following a renewed spiritual interest on the part of the Cuban people. Paradoxically, if anyone could be said to be the author, the inventor of the idea, it was a leader of the Cuban Communist Party. What amazing ways God fulfills his purposes! Is there anything impossible for Him?[327]

Only God could release the Church from its captivity and provide the boldness to move out in such a powerful way. Only God could plant it in the heart of a long-time Communist official to suggest the best way for Cuba to be won to Christ.

Visit of Pope John Paul II to Cuba and the Subsequent Evangelical Celebrations

Much has been made of Pope John Paul II's visit to Cuba on January 21-25, 1998. This visit was the Pope's first to the island nation since the triumph of the Castro-led Revolution in 1959. Much anticipation was present, since his Papal visit to his native Poland, in 1979, gave impetus to the Solidarity movement that ultimately

---

[326] González Muñoz, *Y Vimos Su Gloria*, 149.

[327] Ibid. In this chapter, Gonález identifies the Western Convention President, Nilo Dominguez, as being a key person for "inaugurating a new vision with respect to the organization of new churches," ibid., 148. González says that Dominguez "used his platform as president and began to promote the organization of new churches breaking the traditional forms that they had used for many years," ibid., 139. While it is true that many of the churches organized during this time had been missions for many years, a huge paradigm shift for the convention and its traditional churches was needed to begin to recognize the churches they had planted. According to González, during his presidency "he had organized thirty-five new churches in five years. As a comparison, it is good to mention that to organize the same number of churches, before this time, it had taken the Convention nothing less than fifty-four years!" (ibid., 141).

produced the fall of the Communist government and contributed to the eventual crumbling of the Soviet Union.[328] During his visit, the Pope celebrated four open air masses: in Santa Clara, Camagüey, Santiago de Cuba, and in Havana's Revolution Plaza. In his speeches, the Pope criticized the U.S. Embargo, as well as spoke on issues such as the breakdown of family values and abortion, and called for the release of some imprisoned Cuban dissidents.[329]

Many expected the Pope's visit to bring about a change in U.S. policy concerning the decades-old embargo. Others hoped that Cuba would change its restrictive practices and allow the church and the peoples of Cuba expanded freedoms. While an increased openness to evangelism and Scripture distribution occurred during the Pope's visit, as well as the Cuban government allowing Christmas to be celebrated openly for the first time since the Revolution, the major changes people expected did not materialize.

The Pope's visit was, however, a major public relations success for Fidel Castro and the Cuban government. In a sense, the Pope validated the Cuban government by his visit. From that moment forward, an increased openness to the Castro government has existed in the Caribbean and in Latin America.[330]

Did the Pope's visit assist the emergence of the CPM in Cuba? There are mixed opinions. An initial, albeit short-lived, surge of attendance occurred in the Catholic churches. The CPM, which had begun in the early 1990s, would have continued whether or not the Pope's visit had taken place. However, one important fruit of the Pope's visit was the Evangelical Celebrations allowed by the Cuban government from May 30-June 20, 1999.

In response to the Pope's visit to Cuba, the Cuban government granted Protestants permission to conduct a series of outdoor events. During the "Cuban Evangelical Celebration," eighteen open air meetings were held across the island, culminating in the June 20th mass gathering in Havana's Revolution Plaza, which attracted over 500,000 people.[331] The Cuban Council of Churches, along with the majority of Evangelical denominations, participated in the

---

[328]Jack Wintz, "The Pope in Cuba: A Call for Freedom" [on-line article]; accessed 24 December 2009; available from
http://www.americancatholic.org/Messenger/Apr1998/feature1.asp; Internet.
[329]Steve Wilkerson, "The Pope's Visit to Cuba" [on-line article]; accessed 21 December 2009; available on line from http://www.poptel.org.uk/cuba-solidarity.CubaSi-January.PopesVisit.html; Internet.
[330]Ibid., The Pope called "for Cuba to open itself up to the world, and for the world to open itself up to Cuba." In the U.S., this renewed the dialogue concerning the validity of the embargo, as well as opened the minds of countries, that were predominantly Catholic, to the legitimacy of the Cuban government.
[331]"Evangelicals Come Up for Air," *Christianity Today*, June 1999 [on-line]; accessed 24 December 2009; available from
http://www.christianitytoday.com/ct/1999/june14/9t723a.html; Internet.

meetings. Evangelicals took advantage of the event to do mass door-to-door evangelism and Scripture distribution. Many of the events were shown on national television and covered by the national press.

While the government did not change as a result of these events, and though the U.S. Embargo was not lifted, benefits resulted from these gatherings. For the first time in more than forty years, religious meetings were broadcasted over Cuban television and radio--locally, as well as internationally. It was shown openly that the churches in Cuba, both Catholic and Protestant, had not died, nor were they crippled by the generations of atheistic teaching. According to González:

> For the first time the world was a direct witness that, after many years, Christianity, in its Catholic version as well as Evangelical, had not only survived more that forty years of official atheism, but was alive and growing. . . . The people saw the President of their nation, along with high officials of the Central Committee of the PCC, participate respectfully in the activities. They witnessed them listen attentively during the meetings and afterward greet respectfully the priests and pastors, conversing with them openly and comfortably.[332]

For decades, Christians had been portrayed by the State as a marginal group who, in many ways, were perceived as being unfaithful to the State. Now, as González puts it, "who could criticize those who had suffered so many years of ostracism and discrimination? . . . They had now been able to demonstrate publically and in full color, the life that they had for many years lived in the shadows."[333] Many of those who attended and participated were young people. A sense of hope prevailed that the future of evangelical work was in the capable hands of a new generation of evangelical leaders.

Baptist World Alliance Meeting in Havana

In 2000, the Baptist World Alliance held its first international conference on Cuban soil. A great deal of excitement surrounded the meeting, because it was the first conference of its type allowed by the Cuban government. During the meetings, held July 3-8, the IMB hosted a Church Growth Conference at the McCall Baptist Church in Havana.

---

[332]González Muñoz, *Y Vimos Su Gloria*, 158-60.
[333]Ibid., 159.

In preparation for this conference, this writer constructed a church growth matrix using the data collected from the Eastern, Western, and Freewill Baptist Conventions. James Slack of the Evangelism and Church Growth Section of the IMB, using the church growth matrix data, made presentations covering the church growth of all denominations in Cuba from 1965-1995, as well as a study of the growth in the Western, Eastern, and Freewill Baptist Conventions from 1990-2000.[334]

This event marked the first time all of the Cuban Baptist leadership was exposed to the level of growth taking place in Cuba.[335] A great deal of enthusiasm surrounded the conference, as they began to realize the magnitude of the church growth.

A Local Example of the Emerging Church Planting Movement

The following is the testimony of how God was able to break down the barriers in a community through the use of *casas culto*. The full story can be found in González's book, *Y Vimos Su Gloria* (And We Saw His Glory), in which he shares the testimony of how Christ's Church was planted in an area dedicated to the Revolution. González recounts:

> A particular case worth mentioning, for its significance, repercussion and multiplication after its organization, is the First Baptist Church of Alamar, in the city of Havana, which was organized as a church on November 28, 1992, sponsored by the *Aposento Alto* (Upper Room) Baptist Church in the center of Havana.
>
> Located in the Municipality of East Havana, the neighborhood Alamar was built by the Revolution in answer to the need for housing in the city of Havana and was made up of a multitude of apartment buildings. The construction of the neighborhood purposely prevented the possibility of church buildings or churches, because the building of the neighborhood was linked to the ideological battle and the affirmation of the Marxist-Leninist Revolution. Its first inhabitants were very politically integrated in the Revolution and had no religious affiliation. However, as the community grew, little by little Christian families came to live in the

---

[334] James Slack, "Church Growth Statistics," PowerPoint presentation.
[335] In 1998 and 1999, annual consultations were held for senior convention leadership. The convention's statistics were presented at these consultations, but this was the first time that all of the pastors of the three Baptist groups were able to see the growth of all denominations in general, and of Baptists, in particular.

neighborhood. They had to travel long distances to attend their respective churches in the city of Havana.

The story is thrilling. At the petition of Sister Carmen Lorenzo, a member of the *Aposento Alto* Baptist Church, and resident of Alamar, her pastor Roberto Hernández Aguilar began the work. During the end of the decade of the 1980s, he would travel by bicycle, accompanied by some youth from the church, and every Sunday he would hold a service in the house of a sister of Carmen, Maria Elena Lorenzo, who was a member of the Guanabacoa Baptist Church. This group holds the distinction of being the first evangelical group to meet in Alamar. Some years later, on November 28, 1992, the First Baptist Church in Alamar was organized with forty-one members, but in the apartment of brother Job Matos and his wife, where there were other members of the Aposento Alto meeting. The work grew quickly. The church expressed great enthusiasm and over two hundred people began to gather in the living room of the small apartment, the kitchen, the bathroom and in the two bedrooms. They celebrated Sunday School by using rooms in their neighbor's apartments, whose owners would lend them to the church for meetings.

Brother Job and his wife knocked out the wall of one room that divided the living room from the entry way to have more room. The authorities insisted that there were too many people gathered in such a small apartment and insisted several times that the church services be closed. Fortunately the brothers did not back down. There were several meetings between the authorities and the church leaders. In the end they came up with a good solution, insisting that it would be impossible for that large number of people to meet in a small apartment and the bother they were to their neighbors, even though the neighbors helped by providing furniture and rooms for Sunday School classes to meet. The government official suggested that the solution to the problem was that the church needed to find another two houses and divide the group into three. And that is what they did! In no time at all they were meeting in three different zones of the city and thus able to reach many more people. They began to put into practice, empirically, the concept of cell church, even though at this time no literature concerning these types of methods had found its way into the country. As it was impossible to meet more than one time a week in a single apartment, and so as to not overly disrupt the life of the host family, the church started more than fifty *casas de oracíon* (houses of prayer), where they would meet during the week and in the three worship centers, that were the apartments where the brothers would meet on Sundays in the different zones. Periodically the entire group would meet on the coast, for worship and to celebrate baptisms. They developed many leaders and won many people to Christ. Today, in the neighborhood of Alamar there are five recognized Baptist churches as well as churches from other denominations. It is inspiring to see all of these believers in a city that was conceived by people who did not think they needed any churches.

In the same way, they organized new churches in areas where no Baptist work existed, all of them in the humble houses of brothers, in the living room, in the doorway or on their patios or under trees. For those of us who have lived this experience and seen it repeated over and over again, it has been like returning to New Testament times![336]

Here, one can see an example of how, through the use of traditional churches, *casas culto* and *casas de oración*, a community can be saturated with the Gospel. It is interesting that, once again, the idea for church multiplication came from government authorities, and not from the church leaders. This pattern has been repeated across Cuba.

In April 2005, the *Registro de Associaciones* (Registry of Accociations) passed a law forbidding a *casa culto* from being located within two kilometers of an existing church, mission, or other *casa culto*. The government required house churches to provide a clear proof of ownership for the house where the meetings take place, the names and ages of all those who lived in the house, the number of worshipers who would attend, the days and times that the services were held. In the same way, the authorities stated that they did not want foreigners to visit house churches and did not want them to visit the poorer rural areas of the country[337].

At the same time, the restraint did not apply to *casas de oración*, since they tended to be small. The government dictated

---

[336]González Muñoz, *Y Vimos Su Gloria*, 148-49 (used by permission).
[337]Lena López, "Cuba: Draconian New Restrictions on 'Home Religious Meetings,'" *Christian Solidarity Worldwide*, September 15, 2005 [on-line]; accessed 28 December 2009; available from http://dynamic.CSW.org.uk/article.asp?t=report&id=21; Internet.

that the *casas de oración* needed to be no larger than ten to twelve people.[338] It was almost as if the government authorities took classes in cell group methodology. In spite of some of the harsh tactics of the authorities they, perhaps unwittingly, became the source of some great church growth strategies in Cuba.

---

[338]Ibid.

CHAPTER 6

ANALYSIS OF CHURCH GROWTH STATISTICS FROM 1990 TO 2010

Upon entry into Cuba, in August 1997, as the Southern Baptist IMB representative to Cuba's Western Baptist Convention, this writer quickly recognized the extraordinary movement of the Holy Spirit that was taking place. The testimonies about the growth and spiritual fervor of Cuban Baptists paled in comparison to the actual experience of walking with Cuban Baptists during this time of unprecedented harvest. Early on, this writer began to compile all available church growth data. He collected all of the existing Western Baptist Convention's annual statistical reports, participated in regular meetings with Baptist Convention leadership, traveled frequently across the island, visiting churches, missions, and house churches to confirm the validity of the data.

In 1998, this writer traveled to eastern Cuba to discuss the possibility of opening an official working relationship with the Eastern Baptist Convention. At the Eastern Convention's invitation, the IMB began to relate to them much in the same way that it had historically related to the Western Baptist Convention. Again, this writer began to compile the church growth statistics as a tool to measure the health of the work, and to discover ways to encourage the conventions to gain additional levels of growth.

Church Planting Movement Assessment of the Two Baptist Conventions

Upon the invitation of Cuba's IMB Field Strategy Leader, a CPM assessment team traveled to Cuba during the first quarter of 2002 to conduct an analysis of the two Cuban Baptist conventions, in order to determine whether a CPM existed among Baptists in Cuba.[339] A four-person team participated in the assessment.[340] The

---

[339]Following the introduction of the *Church Planting Movements* book by the IMB, many questions arose concerning the validity of the CPM concept and the validity of the CPMs described in the book. According to James Slack, many of the misconceptions were due to fundamental misunderstandings as to what a CPM was. In 2000, IMB leadership (Jerry Rankin, Avery Willis, and David Garrison) assigned the Research Department of the IMB's Overseas Division the task of developing a process by which it would be possible to evaluate and track existing CPMs, as well as possible CPMs. An evaluation process was developed, whereby missiologists, seminary missions professors, and other trained individuals could personally assess the validity and/or status of a given CPM. By 2007, at least twelve such assessments have been conducted on three continents. For a detailed description of the process, see: Slack, "Church Planting Movements," 29-44.

team traveled across the island from the extreme western province of Pinar del Rio, to the extreme eastern province of Guantanamo. They conducted interviews with 215 individuals in a variety of settings. They reviewed this writer's missiological church growth research as a part of the investigative process. The results of the findings were presented first to the IMB Field Strategy Leader, then to the IMB Regional Leadership, and finally to the IMB executive leadership in Richmond Virginia.[341]

The results of the CPM research project revealed, as of the first quarter of 2002, an active CPM was taking place among Eastern and Western Cuban Baptists. They described the magnitude as "staggering."[342] In their confidential report, the researchers concluded:

> It was verified by on-site interviews and other kinds of research during the first quarter of 2002 that a Church Planting Movement began to emerge in the Eastern Baptist Convention by 1994 and within the Western Baptist Convention by 1993. The Church Planting Movement had emerged to become a full-fledged reality in 1997. From 1997 to the time of the in-country interviews in 2002, the Church Planting Movement continued to multiply in classical CPM fashion.[343]

Further, the researchers concluded, "Compared to other CPMs that have been observed recently, the spiritual, functional and doctrinal foundations are fairly sound and healthy."[344] However, the assessment team did note real concerns about several polity issues. They stated that if these issues were not addressed, "the movement will likely stall, decline, fragment or filter and flow into other groups that have similar vitality."[345]

---

[340] Team members included Dr. James Slack (Missiologist and Researcher with the Global Research Office of the IMB), Dr. Roy Cooper and his wife Dirce (the Coopers are IMB missionaries and leadership developers for the Caribbean Itinerant Team in Cuba), and Dennis Jones of the IMB's Global Research Department. Jones and the Coopers are proficient Spanish-speakers. James Slack, while not fluent in Spanish, has conducted research for years in Spanish-speaking countries, and has a functioning knowledge of the language, and understands well the history and culture.
[341] The final report was Slack, Jones, R. Cooper, and D. Cooper, "Church Planting Movement Assessment of the Two Baptist Conventions," 17 December 2002.
[342] Ibid, 18
[343] Ibid, 1
[344] Ibid.
[345] Ibid.

Church Growth Components of the Cuban Church Planting Movement

As seen in Chapters 2 and 3, Cuban Baptists rather quickly developed highly institutional structures. This historic structure of the churches, conventions, and institutions was a product of the Southern and American Baptist influences from decades past. As the crisis of the 1990s unfolded, many of these traditional structures were stretched beyond their capacity to respond to the massive influx of new believers and others interested in the Gospel. The traditional categories of preaching points, missions, and churches had to adapt to accommodate the emergence of the *casa culto* and *casa de oración* phenomenon. The traditional church pastors and convention leaders did an admirable job of making many of the needed adjustments, but other changes were slow to emerge.

The church growth categories monitored over the last years included the numbers of traditional churches, missions, house churches, houses of prayer, membership, Sunday School enrollment, baptisms, ordained pastors, lay missionaries, and professions of faith. The information included in these statistics provides the reader an idea of the movement's scope. The data is a combination of both Eastern and Western Baptist Conventions' statistics from 1990 to 2010.[346]

Growth of Traditional or Historic Churches

Cubans have begun a move to change the terminology from "Traditional Church" to "Historic Church," in order to change the Cuban Baptist mentality. The term "Traditional Church" can be viewed in the Cuban context as a pejorative term meaning "backward" or "stagnant."[347] (For the purpose of this book the term will be used interchangeably) Traditional, or historic, churches are those recognized by the denomination and reported to the Department of Religious Affairs of the PCC as "officially recognized" convention churches. These traditional churches then come under the responsibility of the national convention and, by law, are required to have a convention-recognized pastor responsible for the ministry and actions of that local church.

Early in Cuban Baptist life, evidence exists of a number of Baptist churches being organized in members' homes, theaters, hotels, and other non-traditional places. As the decades passed, the work became increasingly institutional. As they grew, the Baptist conven-

---

[346]These numbers were compiled from the annual statistical reports from the Eastern and Western Conventions.
[347]Daniel González Garcia, *Modelo Cubano de Reinocrecimiento: Una Iglesia Sistemica* (A Cuban Model for Kingdom Growth: A Systemic Church) (Havana: Western Baptist Convention Mission Board, 2008), 22-23.

tions began to require more and more extra biblical requirements for a group of believers to become a convention-recognized church. For example, Baptists of both conventions came to require a convention-recognized church to have its own land, building, and convention-recognized departments. The majority of these traditional churches included an attached parsonage to house the pastor and his family.

The following numbers reflect the growth in traditional churches in the years prior to and during the emergence of the Cuban CPM. In 1905, both conventions were formed with a combined total of 20 churches. By 1960, they had grown to 210 churches. Thus, in the first fifty-five years, the conventions planted 190 churches. This represented an average growth of 3.45 new churches a year during this period. By 1990, the number of churches increased to a total of 238. Therefore, in the first thirty years of the Cuban Revolution, 1960-1990 the conventions grew by only twenty-eight churches. On average, that was a little less than one church per year. This demonstrated the suffocating effects of the Revolution on the growth of Cuban Baptists.[348]

From 1990 to 2000, the conventions recognized 153 additional churches, reaching a total of 391. This averaged an annual growth of 15.3 new churches during the decade of the 1990s. During these years, Cuban Baptists planted 4.4 times as many churches per year than at any point in their history. From 2000 to 2010, the conventions reached 792 churches by recognizing an additional 401 churches during the first ten years of the twenty-first century.

This growth reflected an average of 40.1 new churches per year among Cuban Baptists. Clearly, Cuban Baptists were experiencing the majority of their growth of traditional churches in this twenty year period (see Graph 1 below).

---

[348]This reflects the effects of the legal and illegal migration of leaders and members to the United States, as well as being the result of constant harassment by the Communist system.

Traditional Churches 1905-2010

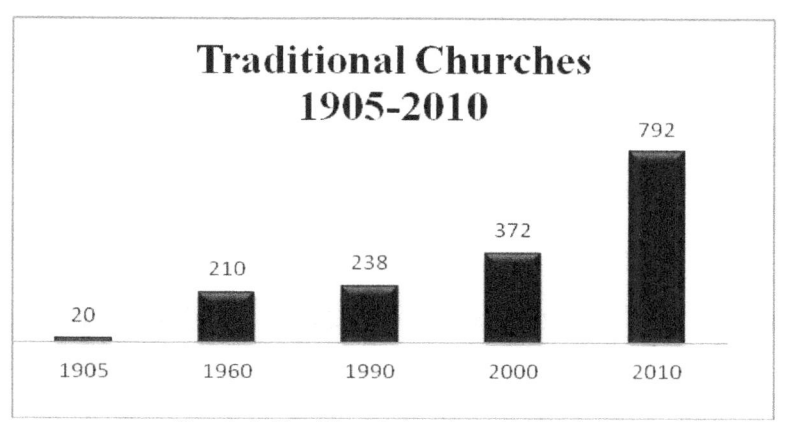

Year	Churches
1905	20
1960	210
1990	238
2000	372
2010	792

Graph 1: Traditional churches 1905-2010

**Growth of Traditional Churches 1990-2010
From a CPM Perspective**

From a Cuban Baptist perspective, the growth of traditional churches, from 1990 to 2010, had been unprecedented. As can be seen in Graph 2, Cuban Baptists received 554 new churches into their conventions during these twenty years (1990-2010). That was more than 2.92 times the number of churches started in the first eighty-five years of the Cuban Baptist Conventions' history! The increase of only the traditional churches--as seen within both conventions combined from 1990 through 2010--was a picture of incremental, steady, and healthy growth.

By the end of 2003, the total number of churches reached 488, which meant the 238 total churches, in 1990, had doubled in just thirteen years. From the first doubling of 476, in 2003, the total number of traditional churches has not come close to doubling again, reaching only 792 by 2010. On the other hand, if one looks at the total number of churches over the ten years of 2000 to 2010, they have increased the pace at which traditional churches were being recognized by the conventions as the 391 churches recognized by 2000 did double, in 2010, reaching 792.

Looking at only the growth of traditional churches reflected a strong picture of growth and a significant increase in church planting, but the growth of traditional churches alone did not reach the level to qualify as a CPM. For the Cuban reality to be understood, one had to also consider the other expressions of church life in the Cuban Baptist experience (see Graph 2 below).

Traditional Churches 1990-2010

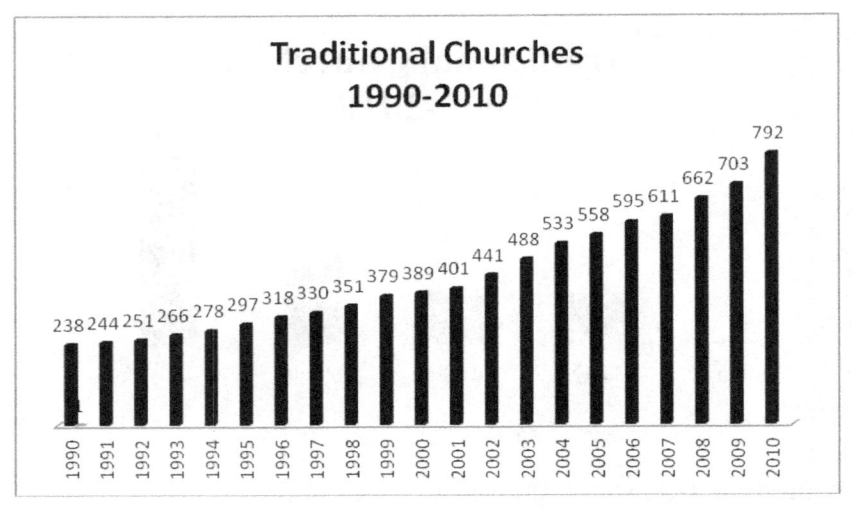

Graph bars: 238, 244, 251, 266, 278, 297, 318, 330, 351, 379, 389, 401, 441, 488, 533, 558, 595, 611, 662, 703, 792 (years 1990 through 2010)

Graph 2: Traditional churches 1990-2010

Growth of Missions 1995-2010
From a CPM Perspective

Historically, a mission was the vehicle through which a Bible study or preaching point would develop to become a convention-recognized church. As new outreach groups were formed in new communities, they were established under the auspices of a traditional church, or using Cuban Baptists' terminology, of a "mother church." A mission could be started by members of a local church, missionaries of that church, or even seminary students assigned to the mother church for that purpose.

A mission was considered by the convention and the Cuban government to be the responsibility of the pastor of the local mother church. In the vast majority of the cases, the actual leadership of the missions was comprised of faithful laymen or seminary students operating under the direction of the mother church's pastor. Often, the mother church assumed the financial responsibility for the mission, and the offerings of the mission were counted as a part of the mother church's budget. This pattern persists today.

As with traditional churches, the number of missions grew dramatically from 1995 to 2010.[349] The number of missions in the two

---

[349] In order not to skew the data, this writer chose 1995 as the beginning year for reporting the number of missions. The Western Convention did not start reporting the number of missions in its Annual Statistical Report until 1992, when 58 were reported. In 1993, they reported 94; in 1994, 142; and in 1995, 147. The Eastern Convention did not report the number of missions in their Annual Statistical Report until 1995, when they reported 206. To show the numbers as starting in 1992 would have given a false impression, since the other statistics in this report are combined totals from the

conventions doubled, from 353 in 1995, to 706 sometime during 1999, reaching a total of 1,185 missions by the end of that same year. However, the number of missions doubled only once during the period of 1995 through 2010. The number of missions came close to doubling again in 2010 reaching a total of 1,346. Still, the doubling of missions during these years represented very healthy growth.

It must be remembered that, during this same period, 495 of the missions were converted into convention-recognized churches. If these 495 were included in the count of missions, the total number of missions for that period would have reached 1,841, easily representing a second doubling. It is obvious that the rate missions matured and became recognized churches increased during the period, 1995 through 2010. These missions served to nurture and sustain the increased growth experienced by both conventions during these fifteen years (see Graph 3 below).

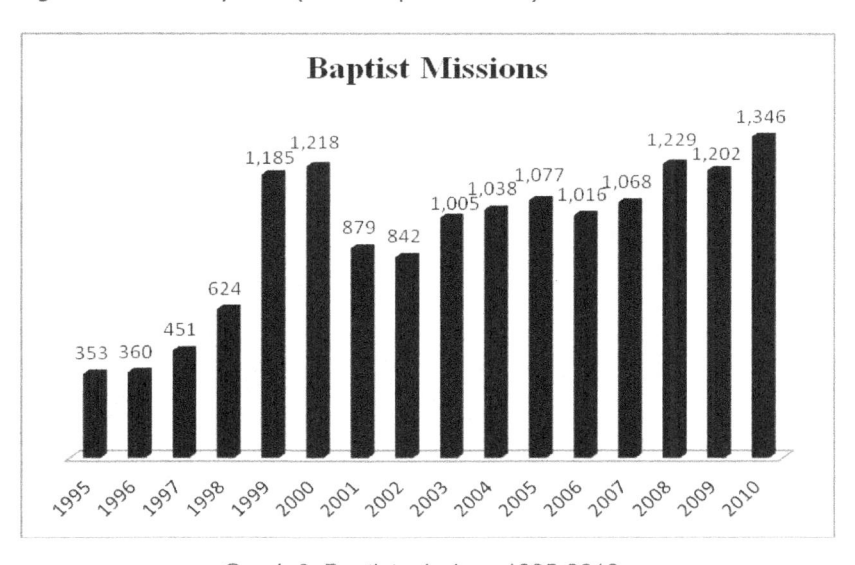

Baptist Missions

Year	Count
1995	353
1996	360
1997	451
1998	624
1999	1,185
2000	1,218
2001	879
2002	842
2003	1,005
2004	1,038
2005	1,077
2006	1,016
2007	1,068
2008	1,229
2009	1,202
2010	1,346

Graph 3: Baptist missions 1995-2010

Emergence of House Churches/Houses of Prayer 1995-2010 from a CPM Perspective

As stated previously, the emergence of the house church phenomenon occurred due to a combination of factors. The economic, social, political, and spiritual crisis of the "Special Period" caused

---

two conventions. Although both the Eastern and Western Conventions were starting missions during these years, they simply were not reported and, therefore, that data was not available to this researcher.

Cubans to flock to the existing traditional churches. These churches found it impossible to accommodate this influx of seekers. The economic crisis led to a transportation crisis where church members and others interested in attending church could not travel the distance required for lack of accessible public or private transportation.

Following repeated complaints to the authorities, Dr. Carneado, of the Office of Religious Affairs of the Communist Party, rather than authorize the repair of existing church buildings or the construction of new churches, made the historic suggestion that believers worship at home. The first year *casas culto* were recorded in the annual statistics of the Western Baptist Convention was 1993; 237 were reported. In 1994, the Convention reported 278 and, in 1995, 563 *casas culto*.

Initially, the government either did not recognize that *casas culto* were being started, or they simply ignored the fact. In 1993, the government insisted that the Conventions register the *casas culto* with the Department of Associations of the Ministry of Justice. For the most part, the Conventions and local churches chose not register their house churches, though those that were registered during this period continued to function without intervention. To encourage the proliferation of these groups, the Conventions just changed the name of the newly formed groups to *casas de oración* and continued to plant these new groups. From 1995 onward, the *casas culto* and *casas de oración* numbers were combined in the reporting.

The Eastern Baptist Convention did not begin reporting the number of *casas culto* or *casas de oración* until 1995, when they reported 806. Clearly, they had been planting these groups since the declaration by Dr. Carneado, in 1992, but chose not to report those numbers publicly until 1995.[350]

It must be stated that the number of house churches and houses of prayer reported by the conventions were only those the churches choose to report. The government periodically sought to close or restrict the growth of the number of house churches in Cuba.

---

[350] The reason that Graph 4, "House Churches and Houses of Prayer," does not begin to record the totals until 1995 is to not skew the numbers. Though the Western Baptist Convention did begin recording the numbers of groups, in 1993, the Eastern Baptist Convention did not begin until 1995.

An example of the restrcitions related to house churches is expressed in the account below:

> Prisoner of conscience the Reverend Orson Vila Santoyo, a Pentecostal minister belonging to the Assembly of God Evangelical Pentecostal Church, was arrested in May, 1995 in Camagüey and sentenced after a summary trial the same day to 23 months' imprisonment, later reduced on appeal to 18 months, for 'disobedience' and holding 'illegal meetings'. The charges related to his refusal to close down a *casa culto* (house church) which he had been operating in his home since 1991. The authorities had that month ordered the closure of 85 of the 101 house churches in Camagüey province. While freedom of religion is guaranteed in the Cuban Constitution, as revised in 1992, religious activities, particularly those relating to freedom of expression and assembly and proselytism, are tightly restricted by law.[351]

The 1,369 total number of house churches and houses of prayer reported in 1995 was impressive. The number of traditional churches reported that same year was 297. The potential for the doubling of the 297 churches in 1995, when considered in the light of the 353 missions and 1,369 house churches and houses of prayer, which totaled 1,722 ecclesiastical-type units translated into 5.8 times the doubling potential of the total churches that year (1995).

The existence of this number of ecclesiastical-type units validated the existence of a CPM among Cuban Baptists. One can see how the emergence of these house churches and houses of prayer fed the growth of the number of missions and traditional churches. The total number of convention-recognized churches did not rise at the same rate (see Graph 4 below).

---

[351]Quote from "Annual Report for Cuba, 1996," Amnesty International Report 1996, [on-line]; accessed 4 February 2010; available from http://www. amnestyusa.org/annualreport.php?id=ar&yr=1996&c=CU; Internet. See also López, "Draconian New Restrictions," Internet.

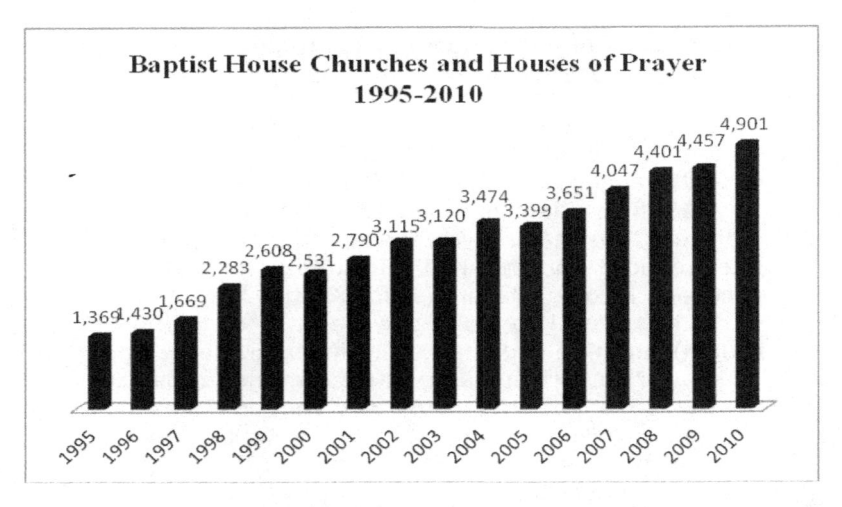

Baptist House Churches and Houses of Prayer 1995-2010

Year	Value
1995	1,369
1996	1,430
1997	1,669
1998	2,283
1999	2,608
2000	2,531
2001	2,790
2002	3,115
2003	3,120
2004	3,474
2005	3,399
2006	3,651
2007	4,047
2008	4,401
2009	4,457
2010	4,901

Graph 4: Baptist house churches and houses of prayer 1995-2010

Growth of Church Membership
1990-2010

Following the analysis of the phenomenal growth in the combined numbers of traditional churches, missions, house churches, and houses of prayer, one could logically assume that the number of official church members would also have multiplied. However, data provided by the conventions did not demonstrate the same level of growth.

Official Baptist church membership, in 1990, was reported at 13,358. That number doubled sometime, in 1997, at 26,716, eventually reaching 29,144 by the end of that year. The number of official members did not double again. By 2010, the conventions reported a total of 53,425 members.

A significant issue was related to church membership. The reported membership usually included only baptized members of traditional churches and the missions associated with those churches. The number did not include those who were regularly worshiping in the house churches or houses of prayer. The discrepancy arose from the way the conventions related to the house churches and houses of prayer.

If one looked at the average members per church, the situation appeared healthy. Church membership in 1990 was 13,453, which was an average of fifty-seven members per church in 238 churches.

Note the statistics below:

1. In 1995, the membership was 23,698, an average of eighty members in 297 churches.
2. In 2000, church membership was 33,205, in 391 churches, or eighty-five members per church.
3. In 2005, the membership grew to 42,815 in 558 churches, an average of seventy-seven members per church.
4. By 2010, the membership had grown to 53,425 in **792 churches**, which translated to **sixty-seven** members per church.

From a casual review of the data, it appeared that the average members per church remained fairly high throughout the movement, but this was only part of the picture. It must be remembered that these numbers were collected from the traditional churches, and reflected the mother church membership and, in most cases, their respective missions' membership. Historically, the baptism of new believers in traditional churches and missions had been administered by the ordained pastor of the mother church and, therefore, counted by the mother church.

For the most part, the local leaders of the *casas culto* and missions were not ordained as "convention-recognized pastors" and, therefore, were not allowed by the mother church or the conventions to administer the Lord's Supper or to baptize new believers. It is important to note that, even though the mother churches and the conventions did not recognize these leaders as pastors, the local congregations did. What is known, based upon on-site interviews, is that between 2005 and 2010, more and more of these house church and mission leaders began to be called "pastor" by their congregations. In a number of places, the pastor of the mother church, responsible for the mission or house church allowed the missionary or a church deacon to administer baptism and the Lord's Supper, alone, or together with the mother church pastor.

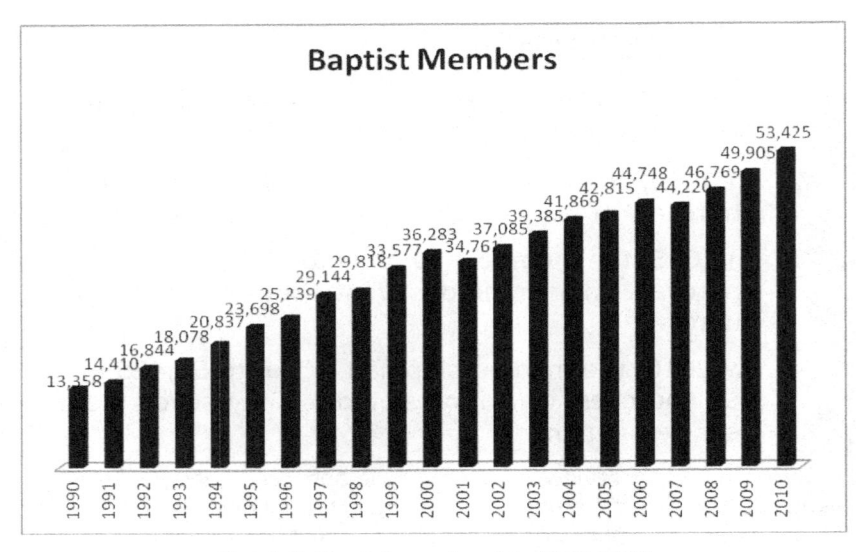

Graph 5: Baptist membership 1990-2010

Comparison of Church Membership And Sunday School Attendance

According to church growth research, professions of faith, baptisms, and the resultant church membership have had a direct relationship with ongoing Bible study. The IMB's global research department found, "Historically, Sunday School attendance was a major pool out of which a majority of the professions of faith, baptisms and membership in local churches emerge."[352] In the Cuban CPM, it was clear that the relationship of Sunday School attendance to overall church membership was very positive:

1. In 1990, 101 percent of membership attended Sunday School.
2. In 1995, 134 percent of membership attended Sunday School.
3. In 2000, 154 percent of membership attended Sunday School.
4. In 2005, 120 percent of membership attended Sunday School.
5. In 2010, 120 percent of membership attended Sunday School.

---

[352]Ibid.

According to the global research department's same report, "Historically, one could expect positive growth to continue as long as the total number of persons in Bible study situations was seventy-five percent and above of the total membership." Clearly, the percentage of individuals attending Sunday School weekly in Cuban churches was well above this norm.

After looking at the percentage of members attending Sunday School, it was important to look at the numerical difference to see how this translated into baptisms:

1. In 1990, 941 more people were in Sunday School than there were members
2. In 1995, 8,061 more were in Sunday School than there were members.
3. In 2000, 17,824 more were in Sunday School than there were members.
4. In 2005, 8,659 more were in Sunday School than there were members.
5. In 2010, 10,955 more were in Sunday School than there were members.

Church Membership and Sunday School Enrollment

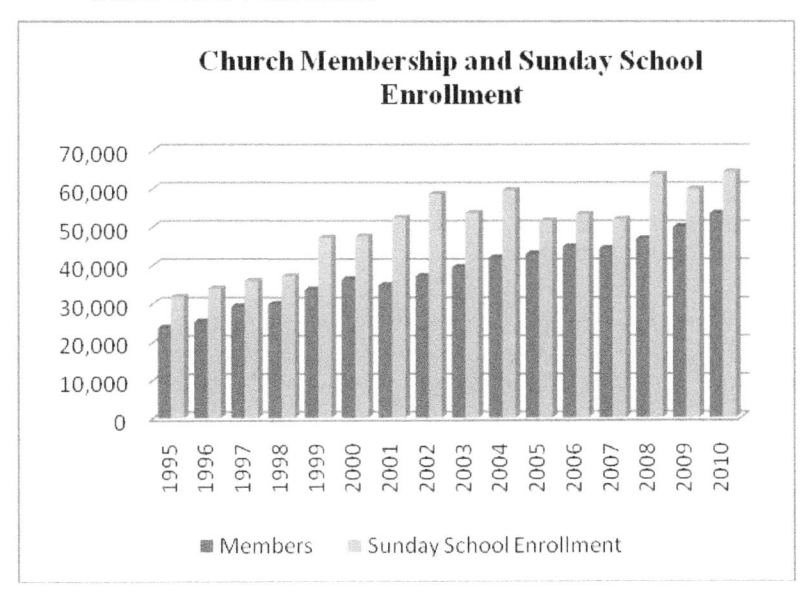

Graph 6: Church membership and Sunday School Enrollment 1995-2010

Growth in Baptisms Among Cuban Baptists

The annual number of baptisms among Cuban Baptists, from 1990 to 2010, has fluctuated from year to year. The number of baptisms per year increased dramatically from 1,054, in 1990, to 6,426 baptisms, in 2010. Although the annual number of baptisms rose and fell, the overall trend was an increase in the number of baptisms (see Graph 7 below).

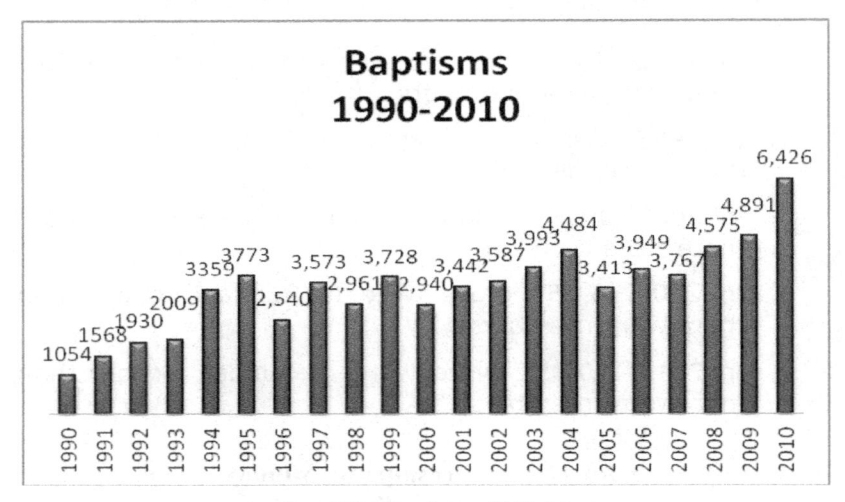

Baptisms 1990-2010

Year	Baptisms
1990	1054
1991	1568
1992	1930
1993	2009
1994	3359
1995	3773
1996	2,540
1997	3,573
1998	2,961
1999	2,940
2000	3,728
2001	3,442
2002	3,587
2003	3,993
2004	4,484
2005	3,413
2006	3,949
2007	3,767
2008	4,575
2009	4,891
2010	6,426

Graph 7: Baptisms 1990-20

As one examines the total number of baptisms in a given year, compared to the number of individuals involved in ongoing Bible study, one has to ask, why were there so many more people in Bible study than were being baptized? Were they just attending to attend, or were they not serious about making a commitment to Christ?

To complicate matters further, the data in the ongoing Bible study shown above showed only people attending Sunday School in traditional churches and missions. This did not include the people studying the Bible regularly in the house church and house of prayer networks. The numbers of people in regular Bible study at that level were simply not reported. As of 2010, there were 4,901 house churches and houses of prayer meeting weekly, but their numbers were not included in church reports. These groups varied in size with some being as small as twelve to fifteen, while others as large as several hundred. As one looked at the discrepancy between the number of people who made professions of faith, and the number who were being baptized, the problem became more understandable.

Differences Between Professions of Faith and Baptisms

An intensely critical issue for the life and health of the Cuban CPM is the stark difference in the number of individuals who professed their faith in Christ, and the number of those baptized into the fellowship of local Baptist churches. Graph 8 clearly shows a marked difference that existed between the annual reporting of professions of faith and baptisms. Several issues need clarification.

First, these numbers came from the conventions' annual statistical reports and, thus, only represented the number of individuals professing faith in the traditional church and evangelistic meetings. This did not include the number of professions of faith made at the house church or house of prayer level. Under the existing recording system, it was simply impossible to trace this to the house church/house of prayer level.

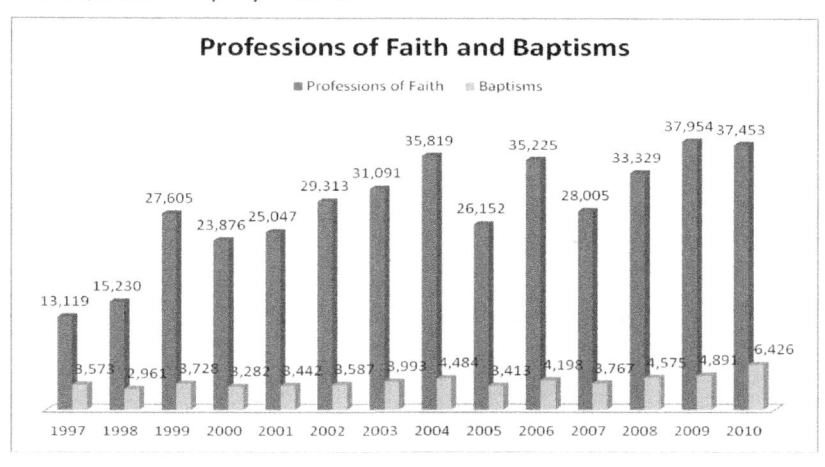

Professions of Faith and Baptisms

■ Professions of Faith　■ Baptisms

Year	Professions of Faith	Baptisms
1997	13,119	3,573
1998	15,230	2,961
1999	27,605	3,728
2000	23,876	3,282
2001	25,047	3,442
2002	29,313	3,587
2003	31,091	3,993
2004	35,819	4,484
2005	26,152	3,413
2006	35,225	4,198
2007	28,005	3,767
2008	33,329	4,575
2009	37,954	4,891
2010	37,453	6,426

Graph 8: Professions of faith and baptisms 1997-2010

Second, this writer heard repeatedly that the numbers of professions of faith needed to be examined cautiously, because no method was available to determine whether the persons professing faith in Christ were truly converted, or whether they may have been moved by emotion, peer pressure, and so forth. While it is true that one cannot be assured that a person who makes a public profession of faith is truly converted, the fact remains that these people made a public profession of faith, which was recorded at the local church/mission level and then reported to the conventions. It is therefore, the local church's responsibility is to follow up on each of these decisions and find the discipleship tools necessary to assimilate as many as possible into the local church.

Traditionally, the only person allowed to baptize a person was the ordained pastor of a local church. Generally speaking, that pastor also taught the new believers' discipleship class. After a year or more of waiting, the church would allow the new convert to be baptized. Much of this practice can be traced back to the local church's fear of perceived communist infiltration. While infiltration had been an issue, the biggest problem fell on the local churches' lack of ability to assimilate this level of growth under their present polity system. The practice of only allowing an ordained local church pastor to baptize, and the extraordinarily long delays in baptizing new believers, compromised the ability of the local churches to take full advantage of the tremendous harvest they were experiencing.

The strict and controlling practices of filtering new believers, that served the churches well during the most difficult years, had become and continue to be a stumbling block during these years of harvest. Some groups of believers have had to wait one or two years for baptism. Church planters were interviewed who were sharing the Gospel and planting churches yet had not been baptized. The issue still must be addressed and the existing model changed if the CPM is to survive, and if the integrity of biblical baptism is to be maintained.

To understand the level of this problem, one only has to review the total number of professions of faith and baptisms over several years (see Graph 9 below).

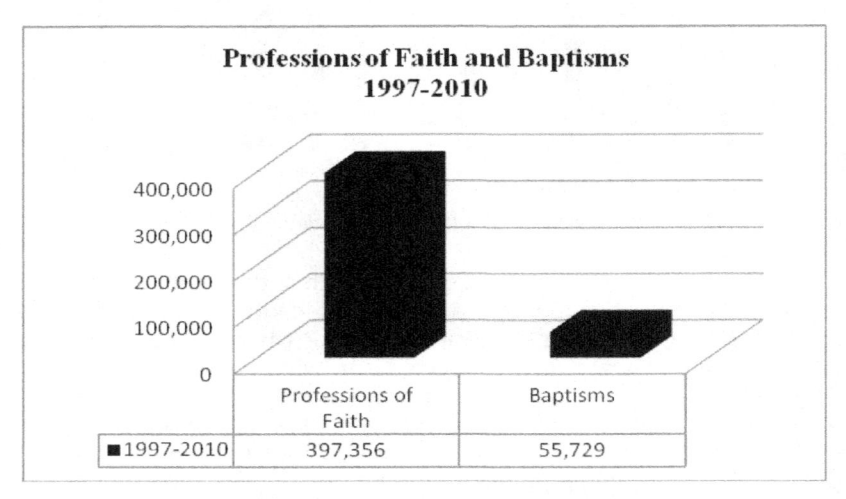

Professions of Faith and Baptisms 1997-2010

	Professions of Faith	Baptisms
■ 1997-2010	397,356	55,729

Graph 9: Professions of faith and baptism totals 1997-2010

From 1997 through 2010, Cuban Baptist churches recorded 397,356 professions of faith, while baptizing only 55,729 people during the same period. This meant Baptists were only able to disciple 14 percent of the new believers to the point of being baptized. This was and continues to be a critical issue. A look at the number of ordained convention pastors will clarify further the reason for this discrepancy.

Growth in the Number of Ordained Pastors

In the Cuban Baptist context, the ordained pastor is the center of the local church and convention system. Usually, this person would have graduated from one of the two established seminaries, following four years of full-time study.[353] While in seminary, the students worked in local churches and missions on the weekends under the supervision of an ordained local church pastor. Following graduation, the convention assigned them to a church, and they were required to serve up to four years before another church called them as pastor. Following one year of pastoral ministry, their church would call an ordination council in which convention leaders and other ordained pastors would intensely question the candidate on a wide range of theological, ecclesiological, ethical, and practical issues before granting ordination.

Following the council review, the local church held a worship service during which the pastor was officially ordained. Once the person was ordained, he became a member of the *Departamento Ministerial* (Ministerial Department), and the convention became responsible for that pastor for life. The convention, therefore, becomes financially responsible for the pastor. Dr. Leoncio Veguilla, one of the most influential leaders in the history of the Western Baptist Convention, describes the relationship between the local church, the pastor, and the convention in the following way:

> The Convention is the owner of all properties. It should insure the good administration of everything it possesses and has handed over to the church for its use. The church is the keeper and defender of the faith; it must preach it, teach it, and obey it. On an administrative level, the church approves members and disciplines them, administers its funds and equipment, but cannot change its doctrine or create it. The pastor and the church owe themselves to the convention of which they form a part. The pastor belongs to the church partially, because he partially belongs to the convention. We have been trying to define these aspects well

---

[353]Among Western Cuban Baptists, the recognized seminary is the *Seminario Teológico Bautista: "Rafael Alberto Ocaña,"* located in the city of Havana. In the Eastern Baptist Convention, the recognized seminary is *Seminario Teológico Bautista de Cuba Oriental*, located in the city of Santiago, Cuba.

in the light of the Bible, theology, and our denominational history.[354]

In the eyes of the historic pastoral leadership, the local church and its pastor owed their existence to the convention. The convention set the rules, and the pastors and churches were to follow those rules. Of course, historically, the principal convention leaders have been pastors. The intention has been to foster convention unity at all costs. This unity has been of vital importance to maintain a united front in the face of contradictions and misunderstandings between the church and the government. The convention functions in a mediating role between the government and the local church and its pastor.

In recent years, due to the extraordinary growth of the work and the desperate need for pastors, a number of laymen have received ordination. These were only ordained following years of faithful service as local church missionaries, or after functioning for years in a pastoral role in a local church or mission, but without the convention's official recognition.

A convention-recognized pastor would have responsibilities that included the traditional church, its missions, *casas culto*, and *casas de oración*. By 2010 there were 451 ordained pastors between the two conventions. That meant, on average, each pastor was responsible for 1.76 traditional churches, 2.98 missions, and 10.86 house churches and houses of prayer. What was the probability that a single pastor could effectively shepherd 15.6 separate ecclesiastical units? For a single pastor to really know the people who were attending these churches was impossible. The truth was these other churches, missions, and house churches were being led by local lay pastors under the supervision of the traditional church pastor or "district pastor." These lay pastors carried out all of the pastoral functions without the convention's recognition of their role.

Complications arose from the fact that not enough convention-recognized pastors were available to serve the existing recognized churches, much less the other levels that fell under their responsibility. The *casas culto* presently are required to register with the government, though the majority does not. At this time, the *casas de oración* are not required to be registered, but must be kept small.[355]

Graph 10 shows the total number of ordained pastors grew significantly, from 1990 to 2010; from 124 to 451. The 124 pastors, in 1990, doubled to 248 sometime during 2005. As of 2010, this

---

[354]Veguilla Cené, *Más de Cien Años*, 68-69.
[355]The Department of Religious Affairs has stated that attendance in the *casas de oración* must be kept to no more than twelve people.

number was well on its way to double again. One can see that, even with the increased number of ordained pastors (451), they have not been able to keep up with the growth in the number of traditional churches (792), much less the total of missions (1,346) and the house church/house of prayer combination (4,901).

In many ways, the growth has occurred in spite of the conventions' inability to produce sufficient numbers of ordained pastors. While the conventions have not been able to produce enough pastors under their systems, God has raised up a sufficient number of leaders through the mobilization of the local church leadership.

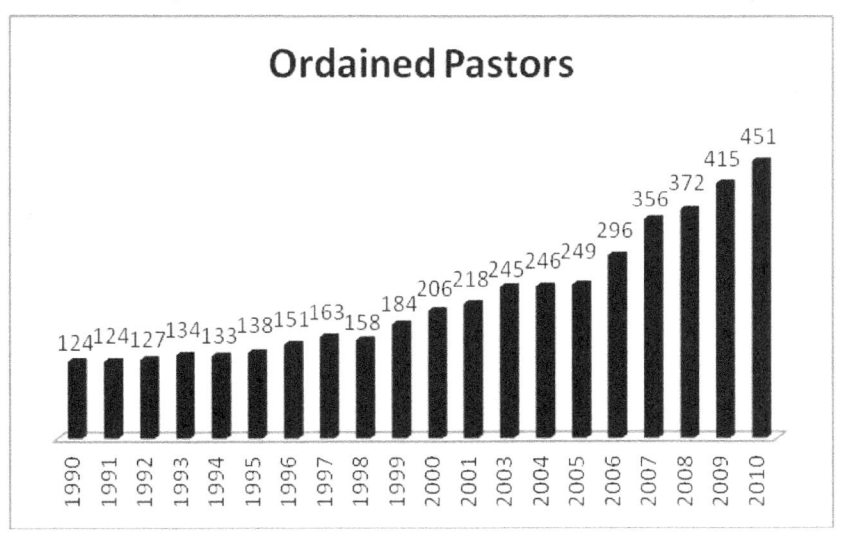

Ordained Pastors

Year	Pastors
1990	124
1991	124
1992	127
1993	134
1994	133
1995	138
1996	151
1997	163
1998	158
1999	184
2000	206
2001	218
2003	245
2004	246
2005	249
2006	296
2007	356
2008	372
2009	415
2010	451

Graph 10: Ordained pastors 1990-2010

Lay missionaries and lay pastors have risen to the task and have served sacrificially to fulfill pastoral functions in the local churches, missions, house churches, and houses of prayer without receiving the recognition of the convention system (see Graph 10 above).

It is obvious that the traditional convention system for recognizing pastoral leadership is insufficient in the light of the extraordinary growth of new churches in Cuba. The fact is that lay pastors and lay missionaries have been the driving force behind the Cuban CPM.

While the trends mentioned above still exist, both conventions are taking steps to address these issues.

Magnitude of the Church Planting Movement Including the Assemblies of God

The CPM among Baptists in Cuba was representative of the movement of God on the island. Not all denominations had experienced the same level of growth.[356] The Assemblies of God is another denomination that had clearly experienced CPM level growth, during the years 1990-2010. As can be seen below in Graph 11, the number of traditional churches among the Assemblies of God in Cuba tripled, from 89 in 1990, to 300 in 1995. They doubled their number of churches, by 2001, reaching 650. They again quadrupled their traditional churches, by 2010, reaching 2,779 by the end of that reporting year. The total number of traditional churches established by 2010 was 3.5 times the growth in the number of the Eastern and Western Baptist traditional churches.

The Assemblies of God experienced even greater growth in the number of house churches. By 1995, they had started 850 house churches in comparison to 1,369 started by Baptists during the same period. Soon AOG would explode in growth, almost doubling numbers in three years, reaching 1,650 in 1998. Three years later, they doubled the number of house churches totaling 3,780 by the end of 2001. They doubled once again by the end of 2010 reaching 7,697.

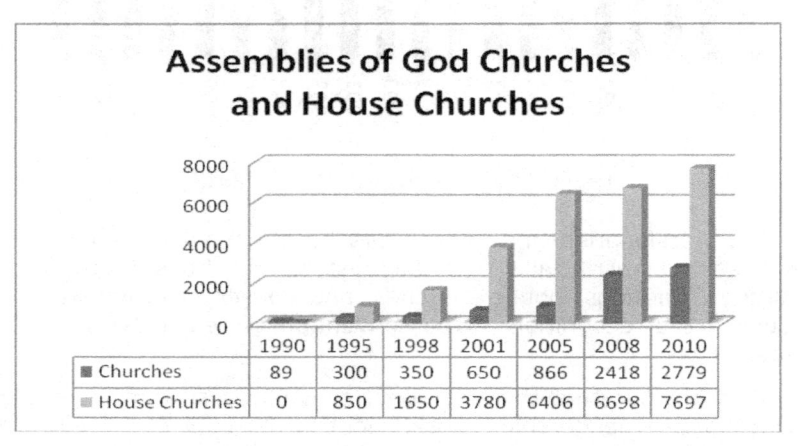

Assemblies of God Churches and House Churches

	1990	1995	1998	2001	2005	2008	2010
Churches	89	300	350	650	866	2418	2779
House Churches	0	850	1650	3780	6406	6698	7697

Graph 11: Assemblies of God Churches and House Churches

---

[356]Unfortunately, this writer did not have access to the church growth statistics for the other denominations in Cuba. The best estimate available--from interviews with Baptist Convention leaders, representatives of the Cuban Council of Churches, and the governmental authorities of the Religious Affairs Department of the Communist Party-- revealed that the largest and fastest-growing groups are in the following order: Assemblies of God, Eastern and Western Baptists, Seventh Day Adventists, and Free Methodists.

The total number of traditional churches and house churches among the Assemblies of God in 2010 was 10,476. This was amazing growth in the light of the difficult social, political, and economic conditions in Cuba. When the Baptist numbers are combined with those of the Assemblies of God, the magnitude of the Cuban CPM becomes clear. By the close of 2010, the two denominations together numbered 17,515 traditional churches, missions, and house churches.

The Assemblies of God also showed remarkable growth in the area of members and adherents. They tripled their membership from 1990 to 1995 growing from 12,000 to 40,000 members. They doubled again by 1998 reaching 85,000 by the end of that year. They doubled their membership again during 2010 reaching 175,754 members. Combined, the denominations numbered 229,179 members.

Unfortunately the two Baptists conventions have not recorded adherents in recent years so that a comparison could be made. Adherents included children of members and those who attended regularly, but had not been baptized. In 2010 the AOG recorded 513,185 such adherents attending their network of churches, and house churches.

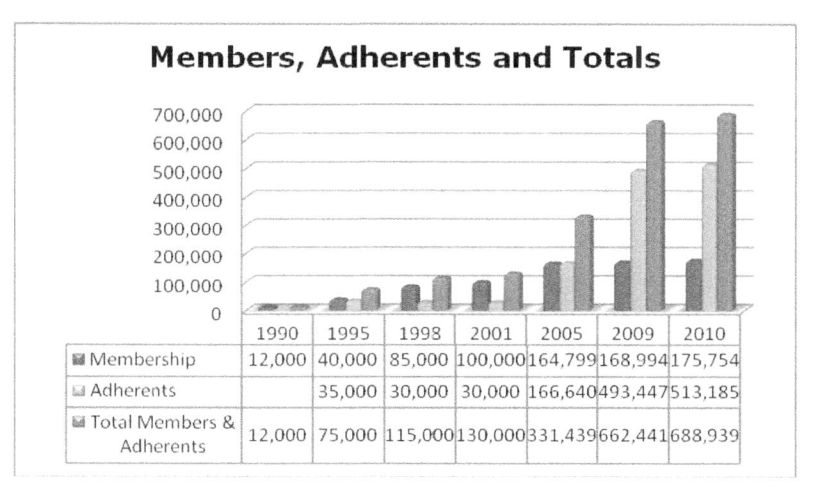

Members, Adherents and Totals

	1990	1995	1998	2001	2005	2009	2010
Membership	12,000	40,000	85,000	100,000	164,799	168,994	175,754
Adherents		35,000	30,000	30,000	166,640	493,447	513,185
Total Members & Adherents	12,000	75,000	115,000	130,000	331,439	662,441	688,939

Graph 12. Assemblies of God Membership, Adherents, and Totals

These numbers make clear that Baptists and the Assemblies of God in Cuba have both experienced a CPM. This raises legitimate questions as to why the Assemblies of God have been able to plant 3,437 more churches and house churches than the Baptists. Additionally, they claim 175,754 members compared to the Baptists' 53,425.

There are a number of possible reasons for the difference in growth seen among the Assemblies of God and Baptists during the years 1990-2010. One reason for the growth of membership in the AOG has been their ability to assimilate those who had made professions of faith into local church membership. Baptists could have added an additional 397,356 members to their churches if they had been able to assimilate the number of those who made professions of faith into local church membership.

In addition to this, the Assemblies of God have been able to provide ministerial training to a large number of leaders. The number of Credentialed and Lay pastors has grown from 200 in 1990 to 7,322 by 2010. It can be reasoned that the AOG have been able to expand the number of new churches in part because they have a large number of leaders. It is probably more accurate to say that they have a large number of leaders due to the multiplication of churches. Whichever is the case they have done a good job of providing training to a large number of existing and future leaders.

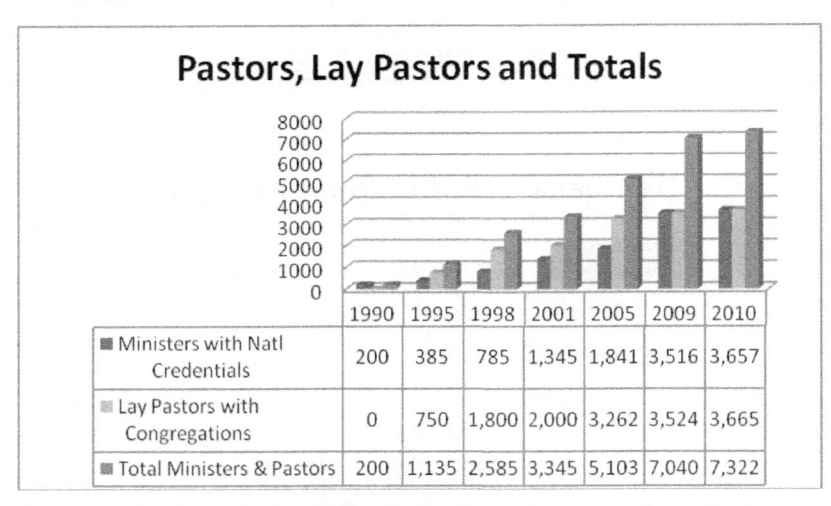

Pastors, Lay Pastors and Totals

	1990	1995	1998	2001	2005	2009	2010
Ministers with Natl Credentials	200	385	785	1,345	1,841	3,516	3,657
Lay Pastors with Congregations	0	750	1,800	2,000	3,262	3,524	3,665
Total Ministers & Pastors	200	1,135	2,585	3,345	5,103	7,040	7,322

Graph 13: Assemblies of God Credentialed Pastors and Lay Pastors

Ministerial Training

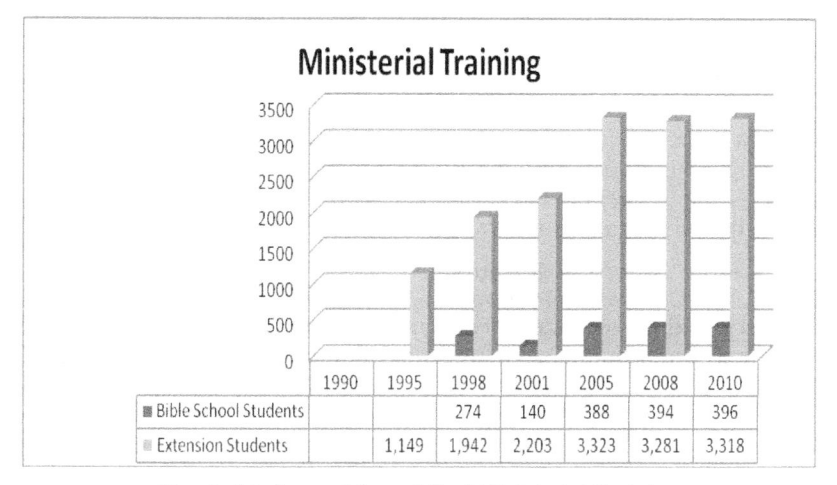

	1990	1995	1998	2001	2005	2008	2010
■ Bible School Students			274	140	388	394	396
■ Extension Students		1,149	1,942	2,203	3,323	3,281	3,318

Graph 14: Assemblies of God Ministerial Training

As stated earlier, a CPM is of necessity a leadership development movement. As can be seen in Graph 14 the AOG have been able to train a large number of leaders who are able to lead and pastor the emerging churches. In 2010 the AOG had a total of 3,714 involved in leadership training. As the years go by they have been able to build a strong base of leaders and have been able to expand the work at a faster pace.

In recent years Baptists have done a good job of expanding their training base. During the first decade of the CPM they were limited to the two residential seminaries located in Havana and Santiago de Cuba. By 2010 there were three seminaries, nine two-year seminary extensions, twenty-five regional lay missionary training schools and eighty-five worship training schools as well as numerous local church seminaries. Even with this increase in training they still have much to do to meet the ever growing need for leaders.

Conclusion

Due to the fall of the Soviet support system and the subsequent economic privations, the Cuban government found it necessary to make drastic changes. They chose to reach a level of peace with the Christian Church so that the world could not use the discrimination against and perceived persecution of Christians as an excuse to continue the economic embargo of Cuba. The government began to make market-driven decisions to draw foreign business investment and foreign tourists with their economic clout.

Changes to the Cuban constitution further lessened the overt pressure on the churches. Multitudes began to flock to the churches seeking answers. The churches were unprepared for the influx of seekers. Though they had prayed for decades for the salvation of their country, God's answer stunned them. This influx of new believers stretched the churches' infrastructure to a breaking point. Dr. Carneado's declaration that they should worship in their homes, rather than seek to build new buildings was providential.

Once the churches got outside their walls and into the people's homes, the CPM was unstoppable. There are some who insist that the government has tried periodically to impede the rapid growth of the church and church planting, but their efforts have proved fruitless. If anything, the restrictions have fueled church growth. Imposed restrictions on the size of home meetings have only served to multiply the number of homes where people gathered for worship.

The Baptist conventions sought to maintain the systems that had served them so well during times of persecution, but found them to be inadequate during a time of great harvest. The local home groups found ways of selecting their own leaders from among their peers, and continued to plant new groups. While the conventions struggled to adapt, the house church networks flourished with local leadership. Although the lay leadership has been frustrated by the lack of traditional pastor and convention recognition, they have still continued to prosper by leaning on the teachings of the New Testament over the teachings of the traditional denominational structure. Remarkably, this lay leadership has been willing to allow the traditional leadership to control ordination. Lay leaders have continued in the faithful service of the local congregations, strengthened and encouraged by the call of God and the testimony of Scripture. The following chapter will analyze some of the CPM church models, as well as obstacles and challenges that the CPM faces.

CHAPTER 7

FINDINGS AND RECOMMENDATIONS FOR THE CUBAN CHURCH PLANTING MOVEMENT

Findings

A primary focus of the research for this book addresses the question: Are Cuban Baptists experiencing a Church Planting Movement, and if so what can be learned from it? The answer to the first part of this question is clear. Statistical analyses of Eastern and Western Baptist Convention growth, coupled with on-site interviews, provide empirical evidence that a CPM emerged in Cuba in the early 1990s and continues today. According to the assessment team, "It was verified by on-site interviews and other kinds of research during the first quarter of 2002 that a Church Planting Movement began to emerge in the Eastern Convention by 1994 and within the Western Baptist Convention by 1993. The CPM had emerged to become a full-fledged reality in 1997. From 1997 to the time of the in-country interviews in 2002, the Church Planting Movement continued to multiply in classical CPM fashion."[357] In addition to this on-site analysis, a study has been conducted of the Cuban Baptist church growth statistics. This research has confirmed the existence of the Cuban CPM.

Baptist work grew from 238 churches in 1990 to, at a minimum, 7,039 traditional churches, missions, house churches, and houses of prayer in 2010.[358] From 1990 to 2010, the number of ecclesiastical-type units had grown 29.57 times larger. The Eastern and Western Baptist Conventions proved to fit Garrison's definition of a "rapid multiplication of indigenous churches planting churches that sweeps through a people group or population segment."[359]

This manifestation of the Holy Spirit took the Cuban churches and the government by surprise. As has been demonstrated, the CPM was built upon strong, historical bedrock. Countless testimonies exist of sacrificial ministry by both national believers and foreign missionaries, which strengthened the solid foundation upon which the Cuban CPM was established.

A key fountain from which the Cuban CPM springs is the spiritual thirst for God among the Cuban people. That desire for God

---

[357]Slack, Jones, Cooper, and Cooper, "Church Planting Movement Assessment," 1.
[358]These numbers only represent what the conventions and local churches have been willing and able to report. Multiple interviews with convention leaders and pastors reveal the existence of many more house churches, houses of prayer, and cells that go unreported.
[359]Garrison, *Redeeming a Lost World*, 21.

can be traced to the very beginnings of Protestant entrance into Cuba in the late 1800s. For a variety of reasons that only God understands, the potential mass turning to Christ did not materialize until the 1990s. Bright days existed in the 1950s, but the doors closed as a result of the Castro-led Revolution. Jeremy Weber of *Christianity Today* offers a concise and helpful outline of the history of the Cuban Church following the Revolution:

> The history of the Cuban Church after the 1959 Revolution can be told in three movements: The 1960s were a decade of persecution; the church declined in size as many Christians left Cuba or left the faith. The 1970s and 1980s were decades of discrimination; the church was consolidated to the faithful few. The 1990s--when Cuba's Soviet support system fell apart--became a decade of revival that continues today.[360]

Cuban Baptists testify unequivocally that God Himself is the author of this movement. The movement is not the result of man-devised plans and strategies. According to González:

> God prepared the way. The majority of Christians in Cuba did not realize during the time the profound significance of the changes made to the Cuban Constitution. . . . We are emotionally touched how the Lord was preparing the legal conditions for what was to come later, that had in fact already begun, but its effects were invisible to us. Of course in making those changes, the government was not planning for the religious growth that was to come in the following years. But God was making it happen!. . Forty years of atheistic teachings decidedly provoked the exact opposite of their design: an insatiable spiritual hunger.[361]

González goes on to name three factors he believes led to the rebirth of religious interest in Cuba:

> First, the "latent interest Cubans have shown over the years for religious issues." The second factor was "the formal elimination, between 1991 and 1992, of the pattern of discrimination that had been applied to believers on the part of the political system, which had unquestioned effects on the portion of the population with religious convictions, by alleviating the tension between religious faith and its socio-political implications." The third factor deals with "the extreme eco-

---

[360] Jeremy Weber, "Cuba for Christ--Ahora," *Christianity Today* 53, no. 7 (2009): 27.
[361] González Muñoz, *Y Vimos Su Gloria*, 136-38.

nomic crisis they suffered which provoked: a paradigm crisis, a crisis of values and an existential crisis, which activated supernatural awareness.[362]

Cuban Baptists have stood their ground in the face of government challenges. In the process, however, they have had to make many adjustments in methodology and polity to accommodate the movement of God within the context of the Cuban political, social, and economic realities.

An IMB research team traveled to Cuba during the first quarter of 2002 to conduct an analysis of the two Cuban Baptist conventions. The task assigned the team was to determine whether a CPM existed among Baptists in Cuba. This exhaustive interview process revealed that a growing CPM occurred within each convention. This research provided a "snapshot in time" of what was happening on the front lines of the CPM, from Pinar del Rio to Guantanamo, during the visit of the researchers.

Even before the CPM study was conducted, a number of key Baptist leaders were aware of the emerging CPM and were struggling with how to integrate it into the existing convention structures without killing one, the other, or even both. In subsequent years, the findings of this research were shared with pastors and convention leaders in a variety of ways. As a result of the research, Cuban Baptist leaders became aware of the existing CPM in their midst and were faced with the challenge of embracing it, fighting against it, or at least making peace with it. Through the CPM study and subsequent research, it became clear that most of those congregating in missions, house churches, and houses of prayer saw themselves as being involved in New Testament churches. They were respectful of the existing convention's polity, but held the conviction that they were participating in churches that were fully functioning.

The existing traditional church pastors and convention leaders were then faced with the dilemma as to what they were going to do with this emerging movement. The statistics made it obvious that the majority of growth among Baptists was taking place at the house church level. That laymen from these house churches were spontaneously starting new house churches was also evident. Over time, Cuban leaders realized that many of these house churches were New Testament churches whether recognized officially or not, and they would continue to multiply with or without formal acceptance.

---

[362]Ibid.

From the time of the research in 2002 to the present, traditional pastors and convention leaders have, positively and peacefully, wrestled with this issue. Some pastors and convention leaders have not been able to accept the development of house churches. The majority of these are now retired or in the last years of their ministries. As the new generation of leaders emerges, most are in agreement with the needed changes. As a result, a number of different models of church have been established by pastoral and convention leadership in an attempt to satisfy the needs of both entities, with the missions and house churches on one side and the traditional churches and conventions on the other.

The investigation for this book revealed that the adjustments in methodology and polity led to the emergence of a variety of expressions of church within the context of the Cuban CPM. This chapter attempts to answer the "what we learned" part of the question raised above by identifying the types of churches that have appeared in the Cuban CPM. While providing a description of the types of churches found within the Cuban CPM, it must be understood that a number of hybrids or variations are present. To introduce every manifestation of church that appears within the Cuban CPM is impossible.

In addition, this chapter will present an analysis of the different church models, indicating the strengths and weaknesses of each one.

Analysis of Church Planting Models in Cuba

The Cuban CPM is unique. Unlike CPMs that have arisen in isolated hostile environments where the Church is forced to survive underground through networks of loosely affiliated house churches, the Cuban CPM emerged and exists in the midst of highly institutional national conventions with strong traditional churches. The vast majorities of house churches within the Cuban CPM are tied to or grew out of, a network of convention-recognized churches. While they have a level of autonomy, these house churches value their relationship to the traditional churches and conventions.

Chapter 6 offered a statistical analysis of the traditional churches, missions, house churches, and houses of prayer. These are the "official categories" used by the two Cuban Baptist conventions to record denominational growth. After their emergence in 1992, the inclusion of house churches and houses of prayer demonstrates that the conventions have been willing to expand their categories beyond just traditional churches and missions to accommodate the growth of the CPM.

Findings And Recommendations For The Cuban Church Planting Movement

Within the CPM, Cuban pastor, Israel Martín Lemos, shares that three primary church models found in the urban setting include the Traditional Model, the Cellular Model or churches having cells, and the House Church Model. He also states, "We are addressing three clearly different church models, but it is important to understand that within these models one can find many variations."[363]

José Enrique Pérez breaks the three primary models down further and shares a six-model system, that expresses a number of different ways Cuban Baptist churches are manifest: (1) Traditional church with a building; (2) Traditional church with a building that heavily uses cell groups to fulfill its functions; (3) Cell churches with a building to support the ministry in the cells; (4) Cell churches with no building; (5) Traditional churches meeting in houses; and (6) House churches under an intentional multiplication model.[364]

Each of these ecclesiastical units manifests the functions of Church through a variety of means.[365] No single church model exists in Cuba. Each manifestation of church has its own strengths and weaknesses. The Cuban CPM has survived and continues to thrive, because the leaders and members of each of these types of churches have learned to appreciate each other and work together toward the mutual end of winning Cuba for Christ. The following is a critical analysis of the different types of Cuban Baptist CPM churches.

Traditional Models

Traditional Church with a Building

Within the Cuban Baptist conventions, the traditional or "historic church" is the easiest ecclesiastical unit to recognize. This model is characterized by its use of a dedicated church building for all its activities. The primary meetings take place within the building with well-planned liturgy. An emphasis is placed on pulpit ministry with well-trained preachers. The worship is unidirectional, as it is led from the platform and directed toward the congregation. The church is generally program-based, including most, if not all, of the

---

[363]"Reflexiones Breves sobre Estratégias para la Plantación de Iglesias en Centros Urbanos (Brief Reflections Concerning Church Planting Strategies for Urban Centers)" (photocopy) (La Habana: Oficina de Publicaciones Seminario Teológico Bautista [R.A. Ocaña]), 2008.
[364]José Enrique Pérez, "Perfil de una Iglesia Cubana (Profile of a Cuban Church)," PowerPoint presentation given during a meeting between the IMB and the Western Baptist Convention Missions Board, September 1, 2007 (Vueltas, Cuba: Junta de Misioenes, Convención Bautista de Cuba Occidental, 2007).
[365]The functions of Church in the profile of a Cuban Church include: Worship, Evangelism, Discipleship, Ministry, and Fellowship. Pérez, *"Perfil de una Iglesia Cubana,"* PowerPoint.

convention's departments and ministries.[366]

Sunday School is the principal place where small group life is experienced. The building is the center of all church activity, and all the functions of church take place within its confines. The church may have cells or small groups, but the emphasis is upon the meetings within the church building. Every traditional church has an ordained pastor who is responsible to the convention and the government for everything that happens as a result of the ministry of that local congregation. The pastor is almost always a seminary graduate.[367]

As was shown previously, buildings offer the church needed visibility and a sense of permanence in the community. Highly trained clergy and worship teams lead dynamic worship services which are very attractive, especially to the professional segments of the Cuban population. Due to their facilities, many of the traditional churches are able to maintain training centers for local church leaders and lay missionaries.

A number of these church buildings and congregations are over one hundred years old, and yet remain strong growing churches. Because of these churches' longstanding presence in their communities, a level of respect is afforded them. Even throughout the years of intense persecution, they never stopped ministering. In these churches, generations of Christians have been able to rear their children, grandchildren, and even great grandchildren to be faithful followers of Jesus Christ. They add a sense of stability to Baptist work that cannot be undervalued.

A major challenge faced by these churches is the difficulty involved in reproducing. The primary method of church planting among these traditional churches is to establish a mission in a different geographic location and duplicate the same traditional system in that place. While they can and do plant churches, the majority of their resources are used to maintain the existing traditional system and infrastructure. Since they cannot build new church buildings, nor in many cases expand their existing facilities, they struggle to make maximum use of their existing facilities. They generally employ a variety of full-time ministry leaders, which has become an economic liability.

---

[366]The official convention departments include: Department of Christian Education, Women's Missionary Union, Men's Missionary Union, Bible Teaching Department including Sunday School and Training Union, Music Department, Stewardship Department, Evangelism Department, Youth Department, History Commission, and Local Missions Department. A list of convention departments and ministries can be found in *Proyecciones 2010* (Projections 2010) (La Habana, Cuba: Editorial Bautista, 2010).

[367]Slack, Jones, Cooper, and Cooper, "Church Planting Movement Assessment," 21 and 52.

An additional weakness is the limited number of seminary-trained leaders that are produced every year. The existing seminary training system only graduates on average 13.77 students a year. It is clear that by using traditional methods, the conventions cannot produce enough seminary-trained pastors for the existing churches, missions, and house churches.

A very practical weakness deals with the inherent institutional barriers, which make it difficult for visitors or new believers to acclimatize. A distinct Baptist culture exists with its own terminology and a myriad of traditions that are difficult for outsiders to understand. When new people attend church, they have to be reoriented to function within an institutional church culture. This can be a challenge for individuals who have grown up in an atheistic anti-church system.

Some of these churches have continued to grow during the past twenty years. Under different political circumstances, some could have become "megachurches."[368] Due to government restrictions and economic realities, these churches are forced to discover alternative ways to expand their ministries. Some do this through the use of house churches and houses of prayer. This shift has come since they now understand the legitimacy of the new models and how they are being used to reach the lost.

Traditional Church with a Building that Uses House Churches and Houses of Prayer to Fulfill its Functions

These churches are much the same as those discussed above. The major difference lies in the emphasis of the church: congregational life is not centered on in-church activities, but upon outreach which takes place in house churches and houses of prayer.

The church continues to maintain the traditional structure and ministries within the existing building--an approach to which many Cubans have become accustomed--but adds the outreach component through house churches and houses of prayer. The leadership in these outreach groups are laymen who are trained within the local church and in lay missionary training centers.

---

[368]Hartford Institute for Religion Research, "Megachurches" [on-line]; available from http://hirr.hartsem.edu/megachurch/megachurches.html; accessed July 7, 2010; Internet. "The term megachurch is the name given to a cluster of very large, Protestant congregations, that share several distinctive characteristics. These churches generally have: (1) 2,000 or more in attendance at weekly worship, (2) a charismatic, authoritative senior minister, (3) a very active seven day a week congregational community, (4) a multitude of social and outreach ministries, and (5) a complex differentiated organizational structure."

This type of lay leadership is very effective and easily reproducible. Evangelism and discipleship take place in the community through the house churches and houses of prayer. At the same time, the house church groups are able to come together for corporate worship. This gathering together gives them a sense of being a part of a larger Christian community and adds to their identification with the traditional Baptist Conventions.

The traditional churches serve as an umbrella of protection for the outreach groups. As discussed previously the government restricts these home-based groups. By remaining under the umbrella of a traditional church, the pastor and the convention function as a buffer between these groups and the government.

The weaknesses of this type of church include the inability to recognize that the house churches are valid New Testament churches and need to be respected as such. The lay pastoral leadership has not been "officially" recognized by the traditional churches and, therefore, these lay pastors are not allowed to offer the ordinances of baptism and the Lord's Supper at the house church level. Members either have to travel to the mother church to observe the ordinances or wait for the traditional church pastor to come to them, which can take months or, in some cases, years.

Additionally, the lack of reproducibility is a liability. Even though it reaps the benefits of the house churches, the traditional church generally seeks to plant other traditional churches instead of expanding its network of house churches. When any of these house churches are organized as convention-recognized churches, they must find a convention-ordained pastor willing to be responsible for their existence and ministry.

Because of the perception that it would add to their already extremely heavy workloads, many of the existing traditional church pastors are reluctant to recognize these house churches. Their lack of willingness to recognize the lay pastoral leadership that is already functioning at the house church level is a crucial impediment.

Cellular Models

Cell-type Churches with a Building to Support the Ministry of the Cells

These models of church have come into existence, due to the particular challenges raised within urban centers. As already noted, many existing churches are unable to purchase land and expand their facilities, so this cell and/or house church relationship has evolved. These are not pure cell-church models in the strictest sense, but the emphasis is upon the ministry of the cells or house churches. The major difference between these models and the traditional church with a building that uses house churches and houses of prayer is that ministry in the house church and cells is primary, and the building is auxiliary when it comes to the functions of church. The building is only used for training and celebration services. The functions of the church take place in the cells or house churches.

The major strength of this model is that it enables the church to multiply its effectiveness through the use of functional cells or house churches for outreach and discipleship. Evangelism, personal discipleship, Bible study, and prayer take place within the cells or house churches. Large celebration services are held in the church building so that the cells or house churches can experience a sense of being a part of a larger Christian community.

In one emergent model, every five house churches join together to support financially a district pastor. This provides a way for the work to be self-supporting and continue to multiply without outside financial assistance. The house churches meet once a week in their homes, and once a week as a combined group at the district level. Additionally, the house church leaders meet once a week in the building for contextualized training. Since the five house churches pool their resources, they can pay for a full-time lay missionary (pastor), as well as afford to print their own evangelism, discipleship, worship, and training materials.

In a separate model, church leadership functions in a pyramid system--or what César D. Castellanos calls the "Jethro Model."[369] The leadership at the top of the pyramid sets the church's priorities and strategies. They train the cell group leaders in what to teach, thus creating uniformity in the discipleship and teaching.

According to Israel Martín Lemos, in the Cuban context, these types of churches have proven to be much more effective than the traditional model:

> It is undeniable that in comparison to the traditional church model, the cell or house church structure we have witnessed in the Cuban urban centers has experienced a much higher growth rate and at the same time is more open to starting and recognizing new churches. Without a doubt, taking the ministry to the people in their own context has proven much more fruitful than bringing them to our church buildings.[370]

---

[369]For an in-depth discussion of this model, see Joel Comiskey, *Groups of 12* (Houston: Touch Publications, 1999). See also César D. Castellanos, *La Llave de la Multiplicación* (The Key to Multiplication) Hollywood, FL: G-12 Editores, 2004.
[370]Martín Lemos, "Reflexiones Breves," 3.

The benefit of these models is that they take the Church to the people with an intentional "go and make disciples" emphasis, rather that asking the people to come to a church building with the traditional "come and hear" mentality that prevails within building centered churches.

Since the government will close any "convention-recognized house churches" meeting within two kilometers of another church or house church, the "mother church" serves as an umbrella of protection for the house church network. As the government focuses on the mother church with the building, the house churches continue to proliferate under the protection of their "mother church."

While a number of strengths exist for these models, there are some weaknesses. One potential area is the model that combines house churches in order to pay for a full-time worker thus weakening the local house church leadership. This system fosters dependency on a person who floats between the groups.

The primary weakness of the pyramid model is found in the leadership role at the top of the pyramid. An exceptionally gifted leader or leadership team is required to keep up with the needs of all the cells. According to Martín:

> The persons who are at the top of the pyramid have special gifts with interpersonal relationships, leadership, preaching, administration, teaching, etc. If a problem arises with the upper leadership, the entire structure suffers greatly. We believe that the development and growth of the Lord's Church should not depend on personalities and exceptional human abilities.[371]

An additional weakness deals with reproducibility. While the structure is easily reproducible, the charismatic upper leadership is not. Men with the gift mix necessary to administer these growing cell networks effectively are hard to come by. Another problem is in the area of ecclesiology. In some of the Cuban cell church models, the cells are considered only a part of the larger church, but are not considered autonomous churches.

The cells depend on the upper leadership for strategic direction and training materials, as well as for the administration of the ordinances. The lay leadership within the cells can only teach what they are taught, limiting the cells' ability to act autonomously under the Holy Spirit's leadership. According to the CPM definition, while cells can be an integral part of CPMs, they do have inherent limitations

---

[371]Ibid, 3-4.

that intentionally reproducing house churches do not possess. These cells have the potential to become autonomous local churches, depending on the vision of the individual cell members and their leadership. This is not to say that all cell groups meet all the characteristics of New Testament churches. Some do and some do not. The issue is one of intentionality. These cell groups are not being planted with the purpose of becoming fully functioning New Testament churches. Though more fruitful than traditional churches, they could be exponentially more effective if they were intentionally planted with the purpose of becoming reproducing churches.

Traditionally, cells from a cell church look back to the cell church leadership for direction. The focus of house churches on the other hand, is outward toward the lost community. The traditional churches and church buildings that are a part of these networks could be described more accurately as associational offices that relate to multiple house churches. The building services these churches rather than these churches serving the building.

**Cell Church Without
a Permanent Building**

These cell churches function well within urban apartment complexes. These stand-alone cells meet for evangelism, discipleship, Bible study, and prayer. The cells meet together only periodically for corporate celebration either in common areas between buildings, in a building borrowed from a sister church, or during mass baptism services held at the beach or alongside a river.

These cell churches have a number of strengths. First, they are easily reproducible. They do not have to pay rent or pay for the upkeep of expensive facilities. These groups are led by lay leaders who are able to mentor future generations of cell leaders through on-the-job training. This kind of training is functional in nature, allowing members of the group to witness how cells are planted and how they function. As participants in the process, these growing leaders learn everything they need to know to start their own reproducing groups.

The cells enjoy functional worship services that can be adapted to the group. The primary method of Bible study is participatory with a high level of interaction. Their small size helps them to be highly mobile. This is important within a country where the State persecutes or discriminates against the Church. When the authorities begin to harass a cell, it can move to another location without disrupting the life of the cell. These cell groups have a loose connection to a "mother church," but in general function with a high level of autonomy.

The primary weakness of these cell churches is the lack of identity as a Church. Often, the "mother church" controls the leadership and is hesitant to recognize the cells as churches for fear of losing control. Another potential weakness is the lack of denominational identity. While some do not see denominational identity as being important, for Cuban Baptists, the issue is critical.

This denominational identity helps the cells to maintain their doctrinal orthodoxy. For individuals to "contaminate" the doctrine of the cells is more difficult if they have a strong connection to the denominational community. In the area of stewardship, if the cells have no denominational identity, the Convention's cooperative program is undermined. This cooperative program helps to support the Convention's production of evangelism, discipleship, and training material, as well as supporting the Convention's theological training and missions ministries.

House Church Models

Traditional House Church

The first house church model is paradoxically called a "traditional house church." The house church concept is not traditional in Cuba, but the structures of these churches follow that of the historic churches.

In this model, the traditional church is located in a house versus a dedicated church building. A variety of manifestations exist for this type of church. The church can meet in an individual's residence or apartment. Additionally, it might meet in other settings such as a patio, garage, rooftop, under a tin or thatched roof, or even under a tree. While the location varies, the style of service is very traditional with organized liturgy.

The group meets together for worship and preaching, and then breaks into small groups for Sunday School. The younger children may be in one house, while the primary school-aged children meet in another. The adolescents meet in a third location and the adults in a fourth. Depending on the size of the church, they gather in a small or large number of houses or apartments. They have been known virtually to take over neighborhoods and/or apartment complexes. The pastor can either be an ordained convention pastor, layman, or lay missionary.

This type of church is reproducible, and is numbered among the convention-recognized churches. The leadership is most often comprised of local laymen or lay missionaries. Many times, the leader is the owner of the house where the church meets. This type of house church does have an ordained convention-recognized pastor responsible for the ministry.

The conventions have a number of what they call "district pastors." These "district pastors" are convention-recognized pastors with a traditional church in a building who serve as "pastors" for multiple traditional churches, missions, and house churches. They are "pastor" in name only, as the lay pastor or lay missionary is the person who is resident and implements all of the practical pastoral functions.

While this "mother church" pastor is not the resident pastor, he is responsible before the government and the convention for the activities of the church. This convention-recognized pastor oversees the ministry of the lay pastor, which can be helpful since the traditional church pastor can serve as a mentor and counselor for the house church pastor. Additionally, the convention-recognized pastor serves as the go-between for the house church leader and government authorities and Convention leadership. Because the house church is located in a neighborhood or apartment complex, it is much more accessible to the community.

One challenge that arises is when the house church grows large and comes under government scrutiny. These groups regularly receive pressure from the government to limit the size of meetings or to disband altogether if a number of government requirements are not met.[372]

Another weakness is inherent with being a convention-recognized church, even though it meets in a house. According to Martín:

> We have seen many attempts to develop house churches in Cuba. In a number of occasions, multiple congregations that are meeting in homes have adopted a liturgical system and ministries very similar to a traditional church; therefore they have in essence converted the house into a type of "temple." Undoubtedly, when this has occurred, the church loses its dynamism and rhythm of growth and reproduction.[373]

Martín's concern deals with the physical limitations of growing large churches in small homes. For the church to expand, the homeowners often tear out walls, or build outside roofs or other structures to accommodate the growing crowds. This is a real challenge for the families that house these types of churches. Over time, families tend to struggle with the stress caused by a lack of privacy.

---

[372]While practically it is a hindrance to the individual house church, experience proves that these churches are more fruitful if they multiply by starting new works rather than growing a large congregation.
[373]Martín Lemos, "Reflexiones Breves," 4.

The important issue is that the house church need grow only large enough to fulfill the functions of the church. The core of these house churches is the body of Christ encouraging and praying for one another, studying the Scripture and worshiping together, making disciples of the lost in their neighborhood, and assisting each other in daily living. The house church need only be large enough to where it can multiply by propagating other churches like itself.

House Churches Under an Intentional Multiplication Model

This model of house church is growing in Cuba and appears to be the majority of the *casas culto* and many of the *casas de oración*. These are autonomous groups, which from their inception view themselves as churches. Their structure is much more functional and contextualized than the traditional house churches. Reproducing house churches have a different dynamic than does the traditional house church. According to Daniel González:

> We call them house churches (*iglesias caseras*) and not churches that meet in houses (*iglesia en casa*), because the house is not only the place where the people meet, but it also deals with the dynamics of the meeting. It is a family style church, built around the family, more than a church that maintains a traditional liturgy within a home that inevitably leads to institutionalization.[374]

The leadership in these churches is composed of functioning lay pastors and does not depend on the pyramid leadership structure of cell churches.

House churches begun with the purpose of reproducing are more likely to reproduce. This type of church becomes systemic in the community. Individuals come to Christ, are discipled, and learn to worship in very intimate settings. The church is not just a part of their lives. They do not have to go to church. Being the Church is who they are. A much higher level of mutual accountability exists among members, due to the intimate fellowship fostered in house churches. When addressing the reproducing house churches, Martín declares:

> I believe that these house churches have the highest potential because of their strong biblical and contextual base, coupled with their simple structure which is dy-

---

[374]González García, *Modelo Cubano de Reinocrecimiento*, 23.

namic and highly reproducible.[375]

He adds an important element for the Cuban context when he states, "They are capable of surviving whatever persecution that arises."[376]

As government persecution mounts, this type of house church is highly mobile and can relocate with facility. As these house churches are planted, the DNA of the new disciples, leaders, and house churches begins to be reproduced in the following generations. Members of these churches learn to pray, worship, study the Bible, evangelize, make disciples, and reproduce as a natural part of who they are.

Both the government and the Baptist conventions have struggled to accept this model. The government will not recognize a church that is not recognized by the denomination. Even though a majority of the house churches and many of the houses of prayer are, from a scriptural standpoint, fully functioning New Testament churches, the conventions--for a variety of reasons--are reticent to recognize them as such.

First, the government has instituted laws prohibiting the establishment of house churches within two kilometers of an existing church or other house church. According to López, "Services that have not been authorized are banned, while those organizing approved services must submit the names of and signed approval from all owners of the house, days and times when services are held and the number of worshipers. The full name and place of residence of the pastor and details on their theological education must be given. No more than one church of any denomination can exist within two kilometers (1.25 miles) of each other."[377] Christian Solidarity Worldwide reports:

> Directive 43 and Resolution 46 require all such home meetings to be registered and once authorization is granted, the legislation plainly states that the authorities will supervise the operation of meetings. . . Rooms within the house that have not been approved may not be used by the house church, nor may the church members meet on a roof, a common practice in Cuba both because of the heat and because of the shortage of space. Authorities may also dictate how many people may meet in any given house church--which will

---

[375]Martín Lemos, "Reflexiones Breves," 4.
[376]Ibid.
[377]López, "Cuba: Draconian New Restrictions; Internet.

effectively put a stop to any church growth.[378]

Due to concern over government encroachment into the activities of the house churches and the Baptist conviction of the separation of church and state, a majority of house churches have refused to register. Some of these house churches choose to remain under the umbrella of a mother church, while others do not. Those which remain under the umbrella of the mother church have a higher probability of avoiding direct conflict with existing Cuban law. Those which choose to reproduce on their own have more conflict with the government, but also experience a higher level of autonomy and reproducibility.

The second reason why the conventions are reluctant to recognize these groups as churches deals with the pastor of the mother church and his vision and willingness to take on the responsibility before the government; to be the recognized pastor of multiple congregations. The workload of an average Cuban Baptist pastor is tremendous. As stated in Chapter 6, the average convention pastor is responsible for 1.76 traditional churches, 2.98 missions, and 10.86 house churches and houses of prayer.[379] This fact translates into every pastor being responsible for 15.6 ecclesiastical units.

All of the house church's functional pastors are laymen or lay missionaries. While many of them work under the supervision of a traditional church pastor, they still maintain a level of autonomy. A number of traditional church pastors fear losing control of the work due to its magnitude.

A third reason for slow assimilation of house churches is an issue of ecclesiology. Some pastors believe that the only churches that can be recognized must meet all the traditional convention requirements to qualify as a church: a dedicated house of worship, and a number of functioning convention departments, as well as a convention-ordained pastor who is a graduate of the convention seminary. They hold the conviction that the heritage passed down to them is sacred and should be followed to the letter. Any variation from traditional practice would be an insult to their spiritual fathers. This struggle is not unique to Baptists.[380]

---

[378]Ibid., 1-3.
[379]In addition to the pastoral responsibilities, the vast majority of convention-recognized pastors serves in denominational positions; teaching in the theological education system (Seminary, Seminary Extension, Lay Missionary Training Schools).
[380]Martín Lemos, "Reflexiones Breves," 4-5. Other denominations in Cuba deal with the same issues. Martín shares his experience with other denominations in the following way: "As a part of interdenominational leadership with Evangelism Explosion we have been in contact with a large number of church leaders who have begun phenomenal movements of house churches, in which humble people have been able to receive Christ, enjoy the fellowship of their brothers, exercise their gifts and reproduce themselves; but have then come under the strong pressure of established denomina-

When discussing the house church movement among Baptists, Martín makes the following comments:

> Among Baptists there have been constant attempts to establish the house church model. For a number of reasons there was not an understanding that these were in fact true churches (due to the traditional conditioning, or steps imposed by the convention authorities concerning the ordinances and ordination), however, in practice they have functioned with a large degree of autonomy and have established many other house churches, even though regretfully, they have almost always had to submit themselves to an institutional church with a building or fixed meeting place, which has served to limit their potential. However, as one of a number of Baptist leaders who have lived and experienced both the traditional model and the house church model, and have understood in the light of the Bible and the undeniable scriptural support that exists for the house church model (as well as its extraordinary growth benefits), we are giving our lives to establish this model.[381]

Hope for the Future

While there are still obstacles to overcome, the pastors and convention leaders have made great strides. An example of this can be seen in the writings and teachings of Alberto González. As the Western Convention President from 2002-2007, González made a tremendous impact on Baptist work by championing the New Testament concepts of church and church leadership. An example of this can be seen in his book, *Y Vimos Su Gloria* (And We Have Seen His Glory), in which he insightfully shares what the essence of the church in Cuba should be:

> It is more healthy to accept that a church exists in a geographic location as soon as a group of people have responded positively to the preaching of the gospel, accepting Jesus Christ as their personal Lord and Savior, without regard to the place where they meet, the number who attend or the level of knowledge they have attained at that moment. This last element will follow, in accordance with the express plan of the

---

tions (who place an emphasis upon maintaining their institutions) to limit many such initiatives and force them to adopt traditional models of church in order to be considered 'legitimate'."
[381]Ibid., 5.

Great Commission. From the moment that a group of people experience conversion, they are believers that God has "called apart," and need to be worked with to grow and develop; but they are a church. To call them a mission, a *casa culto* or *casa de oración* is to denigrate and disclaim the essence of who they are and introduce a foreign element, that instead of helping them, confuses their understanding of all that has happened in their lives and what God now expects from them. We understand the reasons why we began to use these various terms (mission, *casa culto*, *casa de oración*) due to our unique circumstances, but we should never undermine the true concept of what God has established for the community of believers.[382]

González continues saying:

> As you go, make disciples . . . baptizing them . . . teaching them . . . A more effective method does not exist. A church, even when the members do not know everything, or have not changed their lifestyles completely, nor having been able to form all the burdensome organizational requirements, convention departments and commitments that we have come to believe in following two thousand years of Christianity. According to our interpretation and denominational methods, some churches in the New Testament would not fulfill the convention requirements to be recognized as a church.[383]

As time has passed, an ever-growing number of pastors have embraced the New Testament concept of Church. During meetings with both Eastern and Western Cuban Baptist leaders, it became clear the time had come to make the adjustments needed to take full advantage of the present CPM. During a "Kingdom Growth Conference" in late 2009, both the Eastern and Western Baptist Conventions' leadership expressed their commitment to changing some of the traditional patterns that have become impediments to the growth of the CPM. They stated first that they would begin to recognize the true nature of house churches; second, they would allow these house churches to recognize their own leaders; and, third, that they would allow these leaders to baptize and administer the Lord's Supper.[384] If the conventions and pastors are able to make

---

[382]González Muñoz, *Y Vimos Su Gloria*, 179.
[383]Ibid.
[384]According to on-site interviews during a Kingdom Growth Conference held in the Western Cuban Baptist camp in Yumuri, Matanzas, on November 23-December 4, 2009, for both Eastern and Western Convention leadership, which were confirmed

this paradigm shift, bright days lie ahead for the Cuban CPM.

Conclusion

This author sees an analysis of different models of church in the Cuban CPM as necessary, in part due to the misconception that a CPM can only be a house church movement. Research clearly demonstrates that many different types of churches exist within the Cuban CPM, and each has a legitimate role to play; some models are clearly more effective in reaching the lost of Cuba.

Traditional churches offer the work a sense of historic Baptist identity, provide facilities for mass gatherings the government will not permit outside of existing church buildings, and facilitate training for local church leaders, house church leaders, lay missionaries, and seminary extensions. Traditional churches have strong pastoral leadership with correspondingly powerful preaching ministries. While they offer these advantages, they are by far a minority of the existing churches. At present, only 792 convention-recognized churches exist between the two conventions, which are 11 percent of the total number of churches, missions, house churches, and houses of prayer. It also needs to be said that many of these convention-recognized churches meet, not in dedicated church buildings, but in private homes, apartments, patios, etc.[385]

Cell church hybrids and house churches offer a different set of benefits. They take the ministry of evangelism and discipleship outside the confines of church buildings and into the community. Their leadership is easily reproducible and makes discipleship extremely personal. Cell and home-based ministries have a distinct advantage in urban areas. Cell churches can easily proliferate in the high rise apartment buildings, while house churches are more effective in the urban neighborhoods.

Greater difficulty exists to ascertain the number of cells and house churches that exist. The following is an attempt to reconcile the convention statistics with what is actually happening in the

---

during on-site interviews in a number of cities in Eastern and Western Cuba during that same visit, both the Eastern and Western Baptist Conventions were in the process of making crucial decisions that could potentially lead to an explosive expansion of the Cuban CPM. The IMB participants during this event who conducted the interviews and on-site visits include: Dr. and Mrs. Jerry Rankin, President of the IMB and his wife; Dr. Terry Lassiter, Affinity Leader for the Americas; Adam Hammond, Cluster Leader for the Middle America-Caribbean Cluster; Dr. James Slack, Church Growth Analyst; and IMB missionaries to Cuba, Dr. and Mrs. Roy (Dirce) Cooper, Dr. And Mrs. Joe (Yvonne) Bruce, and Dr. Kurt Urbanek.

[385]González Muñoz, *Y Vimos Su Gloria*, 187. According to Gónzalez, at this time, half of the convention-recognized churches in the Western Baptist Convention meet in houses. In 2008, 273 convention-recognized churches existed, of which 136 met in private homes, apartments, or patios. This writer has not been able to trace the number in the Eastern Cuban Baptist convention-recognized churches that meet in homes.

cities and rural areas of Cuba.

In 2010, the conventions reported 1,346 missions, which is 19 percent of the total number of ecclesiastical units. Multiple personal interviews confirm that, for all practical purposes, every one of these is, in fact, a church. The only difference between them and convention-recognized churches is the act of recognition by the convention.

To complicate the situation further, the cells that are part of the cell-type churches are not reported in the conventions' annual statistical reports. At this time it is impossible to ascertain the numbers of cells that compose these urban cell networks. Truth is, the Cuban Baptist Conventions' do not know these numbers. While additional IMB missionaries and researchers have visited many of these networks and can confirm their existence, they cannot say definitively how many cell-type groups exist at present. To know that this author has visited some of these groups on multiple occasions over the past fifteen years, and they continue to function is important. They do not simply appear for a time and then disappear.

The intentionally reproducing house churches have the highest potential for reproduction. The conventions reported 4,901 of these types of churches at the end of 2010. This includes the *casas culto*, as well as the *casas de oración*. The vast majority of the *casas culto* can be considered churches. A large number of the *casas de oración* are in fact churches, while others are churches-in-formation. Due to the changes in nomenclature and the dynamic nature of these groups, it is simply not possible to state exactly how many of these *casas de oración* meet all of the qualifications to be considered New Testament churches. Of the 7,039 ecclesiastical units in the Cuban CPM, 70 percent are house churches and houses of prayer. The inability of the conventions to identify the numbers that exist reinforce the position that the CPM among Baptists is larger than being reported.

The leadership within these *casas culto* and *casas de oración* is easily reproducible and the worship services kept simple, allowing the involvement of the greatest number of members. The DNA planted in these churches keeps them doctrinally sound through a commitment to follow God's Word as the final authority for faith and practice,[386] and the building of intimate nurturing relationships,[387] as well as the commonly held commitment to the Apostolic Mission of Christ's Great Commission.[388]

---

[386]The authority of Scripture as seen in 2 Tim 3:16-17; and 2 Pet 1: 20-21.
[387]The Great Commandment of love as seen in Matt 22: 36-40.
[388]The Great Commission as seen in Matt 28: 18-20.

These types of churches can be planted easily in both urban and rural settings. They tend to follow networks of family relationships, planting churches as they go. An important need is to intentionally involve these house church leaders in ongoing theological training through a lay missionary training school or seminary extension. This would enable the leaders to remain sound doctrinally and to find encouragement from others who minister in the same context.

As demonstrated, each of these manifestations of church offers benefits to the work. Each adds elements to the expansion of the Kingdom of God that the others cannot because of their distinct structures. While these are positive signs for the future of the Cuban CPM, areas of great concern still exist. A number of obstacles have to be overcome and challenges confronted if the CPM is to continue and expand.

CHAPTER 8

OBSTACLES TO OVERCOME AND CHALLENGES TO CONFRONT

In a number of ways, the Cuban CPM has emerged and thrives in spite of highly controlling institutional practices in both conventions. The challenge is exacerbated by the fact that some of these very practices were beneficial to the conventions during times of intense persecution. These practices initially became rallying points and sources of identity.

Out of necessity, convention and local church leaders built walls around themselves to protect their families and the work. The removal of these now unneeded protective barriers has been a challenge. In the words of Alberto González:

> Those who prayed and waited for this growth in their respective churches ignored the fact that when something like this occurs, it inevitably provokes many changes in the life of the church and its members. During times of persecution or discrimination, the church raises fraternal and doctrinal systems of protection against the external adversary who surrounds them. These defense mechanisms, which do help them to survive and in some ways to grow in the midst of the trials, have the tendency to become so rigid that they have difficulty responding when the situation changes and the Holy Spirit begins to move people towards the faith. A process of genuine growth inevitably provokes a spiritual revolution inside the churches. This spiritual renewal affects the established traditional structures. As a result the brothers resist any type of change and want everything to remain the same, the traditional practices, schedules, programs and methods of work. They become the largest hindrance to the renewal! They want everything to stay the same and view any change of methodology as a threat to the core of the gospel.[389]

Practices that historically gave churches a sense of unity and identity have now become impediments to the future of the work. A similar pattern can be seen in the Jerusalem Council in Acts 15. As the early Church expanded, some just wanted things to remain the same. The early Church found it necessary to make adjustments in

---

[389]González Muñoz, *Y Vimos Su Gloria*, 182.

order to stay in line with the proliferation of the Gospel through the movement of the Holy Spirit.

The Eastern and Western Conventions' highly institutional history and Presbyterian or even Episcopal-style polity threatens the future of the CPM. The conventions' historic extra-biblical traditions dealing with persons who profess their faith in Christ and the subsequent extended waiting periods for new believers to be baptized threaten the doctrinal soundness of Baptist practice in Cuba. Change is happening among Cuban Baptist leaders, but some still continue to foster these obstacles.

Obstacles to Be Overcome

The list of obstacles that need to be addressed include: the conventions' lack of recognition of the various models of church within the Cuban CPM, their need for an enlarged understanding of the place of lay leadership in these churches, the return to a biblical administration of the ordinances, and assimilation of new believers into the life of the local church.

Lack of Full Recognition of Multiple Models of Church

With the emergence of the CPM in the 1990s, Cuban Baptists were forced to wrestle with their concept of church. While the teaching in the seminaries and from the pulpit concerning the nature of Church has been biblical and sound,[390] the practice has not always been in agreement with the teaching.[391] As the Cuban CPM emerged, models of church continued to evolve. In the late 1980s, the existing works included only traditional churches and missions. In the early 1990s, the *casas culto* emerged followed by *casas de*

---

[390] Jonathan E. Sharp, "A Qualitative Study of Selected Aspects of Ecclesiology Within the Baptist Convention of Western Cuba" (Ph.D. diss., New Orleans Baptist Theological Seminary, 2009), 60. Historically, Baptists have included the following four elements in their definition of Church: (1) A gathering of local baptized believers, (2) meeting under the Lordship of Christ for worship, (3) observing the ordinances of baptism and the Lord's Supper, and (4) seeking to extend the Gospel message. A common definition of church among Cuban Baptists can be found in: H. E. Dana, *Manual de Eclesiología* (Manual of Ecclesiology) (El Paso Tex: Casa Bautista de Publicaciones, 1987), 93. "A church is the local body of believers, having been baptized following their making a profession of faith in Christ, voluntarily congregating for the promotion of the redeeming purposes of God for humanity."
[391] Ibid., 61-62. Sharp offers the definition of church given by a long-time pastor and professor of the seminary who is seen as a representative of the "older generation" of Baptist leaders: "He defined the church as 'a group of people, believers in Jesus Christ, who have been baptized by immersion by a pastor who is ordained according to the Bible'." The emphasis leaves its scriptural base when he states that "the true church is formed only by those who are baptized by immersion by *rightly ordained ministers*" (italics added by the writer). Much of the missionary influence within the Western Baptist Convention came from a strong Landmarkist tradition.

oración. Soon after, there followed a number of variations or hybrids using a combination of existing buildings, apartments, houses, patios, garages, roofs, and so forth. As these manifestations of church emerged and evolved, the conventions continued to view the work through the traditional church/mission pattern. They had difficulty seeing house churches and cell churches with their variations as legitimate churches.

While the conventions did begin the official recognition of churches at an unprecedented rate, they were still limiting the number given recognition. These limitations existed for a variety of different reasons. First, some remaining pastors and convention leaders are reticent to organize a church that does not own its own building.[392] These same leaders require a new church to have a determined number of members,[393] functioning convention ministries, and departments. A second issue deals with leadership. Pastors and convention leaders will not recognize a church until it has a convention-ordained pastor. Third, many pastors do not want to lose church members and leaders to new church starts. They do not mind if their members minister in missions and house churches, but they want them in the mother church for Sunday worship. Fourth, some pastors simply do not want to be responsible for multiple churches. The Cuban government and national conventions--as an issue of control--require a convention-recognized pastor to be responsible for each convention-recognized church. While the conventions are recognizing more new churches than at any time in history, the reality is that an abundance of other groups exist that

---

[392]James Slack, "Strategies for Church Development," in *Missiology: An Introduction to the Foundations, History, and Strategies of World Missions*, ed. John Mark Terry, Ebbie Smith, and Justice Anderson (Nashville: Broadman and Holman, 1998), 504. "Some church leaders and agencies recognize a group as being a church only when it owns its own property--land and building. Some conventions and unions will not recognize as a church a group that meets in borrowed or rented facilities. No record exists of a New Testament church owning its own land or having its own building until at least a century after the Lord's death. During New Testament times, churches were housed within homes, under trees, by rivers, in synagogues, in the temple, and elsewhere (see Rom 16:5; 1 Cor 16:19; Col 4:15). As persecution came, first from the Judaizers and later from the Romans, churches met in the catacombs (underground tombs), caves, secretly in homes, in fields, and other places. Would anyone question that these groups were any less 'church' than those that owned a piece of property with a nice building on the Appian Way?" See Justo González, *The Story of Christianity*, vol. 1, *The Early Church to the Dawn of the Reformation* (San Francisco: HarperCollins Publishers, 1984), 125: "At first, Christians gathered for worship in private homes. Then they gathered in the catacombs and cemeteries. By the third century there were structures set aside for worship. The oldest church that archeologists have discovered is that of Dura-Europos, which dates from about A.D. 250. This is a fairly small room, decorated with very simple murals."

[393]Slack, "Strategies for Church Development," 503. "In most cases the motives for requiring larger numbers in order to be recognized as a church have been honest—to provide a healthier, well-founded new church that has strength in numbers. There is not biblical justification for this qualification, and there is certainly no church growth and developmental justification for such a requirement."

demonstrate all the New Testament characteristics of a church, but do not have convention recognition.

With the emergence of the rapidly growing house church phenomenon, Baptists have been forced to reevaluate their traditional definitions and structures of church in the light of Scripture and the realities of the Cuban CPM. It has become necessary for the conventions and churches to develop new structures that allow Christ's Church to permeate every level of society. Daniel González, pastor of the McCall Baptist Church and director of the foreign mission arm of the Western Cuban Baptist Mission Board, calls for "a search for and implementation of new strategies and the generation of a massive movement among evangelical churches in Cuba that will result in the saturation of every community in Cuba with churches."[394]

The plea is for the recognition of the multiple forms of church currently within the Cuban CPM and for the development of contextualized models that will allow these churches to multiply without undue convention and government intervention. While understandably difficult, the pastors and convention leaders need to empower the multiplication of churches. They need to develop a biblical house church ecclesiology. Currently, the churches that are being organized, although they meet in a variety of settings, are to a degree still being held to the same structural standards of the traditional convention churches of the past instead of accepting the forms of Church as they have emerged.

The rise of the house church phenomenon occurred due to the confluence of the unique spiritual, social, political, and economic circumstances surrounding the "Special Period." If those factors had not come together as they did, little possibility exists that the house church movement would have emerged. Convention leaders accepted the house churches presence with the fact that, in the light of the extraordinary growth, they had no other option.

Due to the forging of better relations with the government in the last five years and the resulting permissions given for the remodeling and reconstruction of a number of traditional church buildings in Cuba, a push is underway among some that focuses the attention once again on the primacy of the church building. According to Daniel González, "Almost simultaneously with the emergence of the house church movement in Cuba, in the beginning of the 1990s, the megachurch influence appeared (a North American variant of the church growth movement) that tampered with the evolution of the *criollo* (Latin American or Indigenous) model."[395] A high level of concern exists that the house church phenomenon will not survive a change in the current Cuban political

---

[394]González García, *Modelo Cubano de Reinocrecimiento*, 5.
[395]Ibid., 11.

system. If the doors open to an influx of funds from the outside, accompanied by the ability to purchase land and build church buildings, the present CPM will be in grave danger.

Possible Solutions for Recognition

Devise a Way to Recognize House and Cell Groups as Churches

The reasons why the conventions are reluctant to open the doors for all the new churches in light of government pressure is understandable. At the same time, the conventions must devise a way to recognize these groups as churches with the ability to choose their own lay pastoral leadership. They need to allow these churches to authorize their leaders to baptize new believers and to administer the Lord's Supper at the house church level. They can do so without requiring them to be organized as "convention-recognized" churches with all the excess baggage which this brings. This is essential for the future of the CPM.

Develop House Church Networks

In Cuba, it has been strategically important to connect house churches together in networks as opposed to planting them to function and multiply in isolation from the rest of the body of Christ. A need exists for mutual accountability and shared vision. Every house church does not necessarily have resident all of the gifts or needed competencies to thrive in isolation from the rest of the body. A network of house churches can have a number of gifted "trainers" who can be available to encourage, teach, and equip leaders and members of the network. There may be specific needs for instruction in the areas of evangelism, discipleship, teaching, exhortation, mercy, and so forth. Further, the house church network can track the individual health of churches within the network through simple tools of church growth analysis, such as an adaptation of the principles found in Christian Schwartz's book, *Natural Church Development*.[396] Once needs are identified, these "trainers" are able to bring the desired instruction to the individual leader, house church, or network. The teaching in the lay missionary training schools can be adapted to meet the actual needs of the house church leaders.

---

[396]Schwartz, *Natural Church Development*. In this publication, Schwartz includes tools for measuring the health of a local church. The eight characteristics emphasized include: (1) Empowering Leadership; (2) Gift-Oriented Ministry; (3) Passionate Spirituality; (4) Functional Structures; (5) Inspiring Worship; (6) Holistic Small Groups; (7) Need-Oriented Evangelism; and (8) Loving Relationships. The one element missing is "Reproduction." Schwartz states that reproduction should be assumed. This writer's assessment is that healthy organisms reproduce. This element should be intentionally included.

Maintain Corporate Identity

The other vital issue is that of celebration in the corporate community. A strong need exists for corporate identity, especially in Latin America. José Enrique Pérez indicates that "Cubans meet well together during the week in small groups (House Churches) but they like on Sunday to meet in a church building where they can see more brothers and can worship God together."[397] It is important that the community needs be met while maintaining the genius of house church multiplication.

Recognize the Role of Lay Leaders

Throughout Cuban Baptist history, laymen have played key roles in the establishment and expansion of the Church. During the 1880s, Adela Fales, and Alberto and Minnie Díaz, along with members of the Getsemaní Church, were effective evangelists and church planters. During the 1960s when pastors were either in prison or serving in UMAP, laymen played a vital role in the survival of Baptist work. From the beginning of the Cuban CPM in the early 1990s, lay leaders have been at the forefront of growth.

Alberto González has written:

> It is imperative that we rediscover the true biblical concept of Church--including the concepts of leadership--to be willing to accept that in order to prevent a backlash that will stop what could be an exponential multiplication of New Testament style churches. . . . If it happens, it will probably be the laymen who will be used, in the same way it happened during the early days of Christianity. Accepting the biblical pattern of New Testament Church and applying it to the thousands of groups that have proliferated these past few years, will lead to an even greater level of growth.[398]

These laymen are the ones who sacrificially opened their homes, apartments or patios to their neighbors for prayer meetings and church services. They have paid the price of harassment by some local authorities and at times being misunderstood by their own pastors and convention leadership.

From a scriptural standpoint, the Baptist conventions have overemphasized the role of the ordained convention pastor to the point that the lay member of a local church is precluded from the pastorate with rare exceptions. Alberto González states:

---

[397]José Enrique Pérez, personal e-mail to the writer, 24 March 2004.
[398]González Muñoz, *Y Vimos Su Gloria*, 187.

In spite of our insistence in faithfulness to the Bible, Western Cuban Baptists as with other evangelicals have adopted the term "*laico*" (layman) to differentiate those who are not professional clergy, acting as if there is a differentiation. That does not come from the New Testament, which teaches that all are "a chosen people, a royal priesthood, a holy nation, a people (*laós*) belonging to God, that you may declare the praises of him who called you out of darkness into his wonderful light (1 Peter 2:9)."[399]

He continues, "The truth is that the activity of laymen and women can be considered the principal factor for the survival of the Church during the difficult times and being responsible for the growth in these later years."[400] He further states:

It is significant that in the hour of growth, while some ordained pastors supported the expansion, others backed away, and all the while a multitude of lay missionaries stepped to the forefront opening new works and leading missions, house churches and houses of prayer. Again, the "laós" of God became the principal protagonist of the movement of the Holy Spirit and the growth of the churches. . . . A great number of lay missionaries–both male and female–have arisen in these last years to plant a majority of the new churches. They, more than the pastors, have worked in the planting and training the majority of the new groups that have formed. Some of the missionaries have planted several churches and have worked sacrificially and valiantly. In spite of their lay missionary roots we have witnessed that some of these same men once recognized officially as pastors, and are ordained, rarely continue the church planting ministry with the same momentum and do not reproduce in the new churches–once their church is officially recognized–the same development system that formed them.[401]

When examining Cuban Baptists' church growth statistics, one finds in 2010 that there were 451 convention-ordained pastors and

---

[399] Ibid.
[400] Ibid. "During 1965 and 1966, when the Western Convention lost in all 81 workers, having 88 churches and 22 missions, how did the work survive? The answer is found in the '*laós*' of God."
[401] Ibid., 188. "We have to look into this phenomenon because it has the same effect on the theological education which is academically focused at its highest levels. For some sad reason, when students move deeper in their studies, some begin to lose interest and the missionary fervor that burned in their hearts. Should not the opposite be true?"

1,419 lay missionaries. These missionaries are either convention mission board missionaries or traditional local church missionaries. Each of these missionaries comes from a local church and is directly accountable to local church pastors. These are only the missionaries the local churches choose to report. With 792 traditional churches, 1,346 missions, and 4,901 house churches and houses of prayer--not to mention the vast number of unreported cells, it is obvious that many more lay leaders are functioning than the local churches report to the conventions. These leaders need to be recognized, empowered, and offered further training.

Recognize and Train Lay Leaders

Each local church needs to select its own leadership and empower them to administer the ordinances. These leaders are already functioning as pastors even without the denominations' recognition. This will remove a huge burden from the existing convention-recognized pastors, which will allow them to concentrate on the training of these house church leaders.

The training of these lay pastors can be provided in a variety of ways. First, each house church, house of prayer, and cell leader needs to have at least one apprentice. This apprentice, or shadow pastor, walks alongside the lay pastor, learning on the job. As the group multiplies, this shadow pastor then takes over the original group or the group that is newly formed.

The second level of training occurs through the local church seminary. These classes are generally held in a local church that has a building. This practitioner-oriented training is for local church leaders, lay missionaries, and evangelists. The person receives the training and then immediately applies it in his ministry setting. This allows for a constant feedback loop to reinforce the training. During the class, the person reports on the practical application of what he has learned, providing opportunity for needed feedback from the class and trainers.

The third level of training is for lay missionaries and house church leaders. This training is very practical in nature, but goes deeper than the local church seminary. While the local church seminary reinforces and strengthens the ministries of the local church, as well as outreach ministries, the lay missionary/house church leader training focuses on missionary outreach. This training includes evangelism, discipleship, church planting, small group dynamics, preaching, Bible study methods, simple hermeneutics, worship, Christian doctrine, and so forth. Shaped by the actual needs on the field, the instruction can be offered in a local church that has a building, a camp, or other accessible venue.

The fourth and fifth levels deal with higher theological education. This includes the first two years of seminary, known as the basics (*Los Básicos*), and the third and fourth-year studies, which are called specialties (*Especialidades*).[402] The first two years are for lay pastors and those who desire to continue with the third and fourth years. The specialties are primarily for those who aspire to full-time vocational ministry, and for those who serve as the trainers in the seminaries, extensions, and regional training schools.

Need for a Biblical Administration of the Ordinances and Timely Assimilation of New Believers

Discrepancy of Baptisms

One of the primary concerns in the Cuban CPM is the disparity between the number of people who openly profess their faith in Jesus Christ and those who reach the point of believers' baptism. From 1997 through 2010, Cuban Baptist churches recorded 396,196 professions of faith, while baptizing only 56,585 people during the same period. This means Baptists discipled 14 percent to the point of being baptized. This indicates that the total number of professions of faith is a staggering 878 professions of faith per pastor. This does not include those who profess their faith in Christ, but remain unreported. If this issue is not addressed, the CPM will fragment or die.

There needs to be a return to the biblical pattern of believer's baptism, in which a person is baptized, based upon his/her profession of faith in Jesus Christ. The practice of forcing a new believer to wait for a year or more to be baptized is not biblical and is doctrinally dangerous. According to the IMB, Church Planting Movement study team, a great deal of frustration was encountered concerning delayed baptism.[403] Some groups must wait for months or even years for an ordained pastor to administer baptism. Out of frustration, members of these groups will either be baptized outside the system, or worse, come to believe that baptism is irrelevant.

Delayed Administration of the Lord's Supper

The same issue exists with the administration of the Lord's Supper. In the Cuban Baptist system, only an ordained pastor can

---

[402]At this time, the third and fourth-year specialties are offered in the following areas: Theology and Pastoral Care, Evangelism and Missions, Music and Worship, Christian Education, Youth Ministry, and Christian Counseling. As of 2010, there were three residential seminaries (Havana, Santa Clara, Santiago de Cuba), nine two-year extensions (seven in the west and two in the east), twenty-five regional training centers, and eighty-five music schools across Cuba.

[403]Slack, Jones, Cooper, and Cooper, "Church Planting Movement Assessment," 50.

administer the Lord's Table. It has become an ordinance of the clergy instead of an ordinance of the local church. As a result of the lack of ordained pastors, a problem exists in getting the ordinance to the people. Between traditional churches, missions, and house churches, 7,039 ecclesiastical units exist, but only 451 ordained pastors. This author has talked to church members who have not partaken of the Lord's Supper in a year or more.

Cuban Baptists need to return the ordinance to the local church and allow the local church to decide who will administer the Lord's Supper. The need is to return to the biblical pattern.

Timely Assimilation of New Believers

This is a critical issue for Cuban Baptists. Surprisingly, it is not an issue of discipleship. According to the IMB CPM Study team, the level of discipleship in Cuba is phenomenal. They state:

> Based upon Church Growth Strategy Studies, surveys, and other types of inquiries among other Baptist Conventions and their churches in various countries, none compare with the comprehensive and committed discipleship program and activities of Baptists in Cuba. Among those interviewed, at least 88% of the pastors and 84% of the members said they had been discipled after they accepted Christ as their Lord and Savior.[404]

The report continues, "It can be said of Cuba, no Convention or churches disciple their believers as much and as thoroughly as do those in Cuba."[405] The issue is one of being able to baptize new believers in a timely fashion and to then follow up with thorough discipleship. This author has interviewed effective church planters in Cuba who have not been baptized. They are aware of their need to obey the Scripture, but are waiting for their convention-ordained pastor to baptize them.

The issues of church recognition, lay pastoral leadership, and the timely administration of the ordinances have been discussed for years, and finally movement has occurred in these critical areas. During the annual "Kingdom Growth Conference" held from November 23-December 4, 2009, pastors and leaders from both the Eastern and Western Baptist Conventions testified that the time had come for change. They shared unanimously that it was time to recognize the right of the missions and house churches to choose their own lay pastoral leadership and to administer the ordinances

---

[404]Ibid., 48.
[405]Ibid.

of baptism and the Lord's Supper.[406] It remains to be seen how the changes will be implemented, but on-site interviews made clear that a number of house church networks already exist with recognized lay pastoral leadership administering the ordinances with the blessing of the local mother church pastors.

While Cuban Baptists are in the process of overcoming these obstacles that threaten the CPM, a number of additional challenges need to be addressed for the movement to be able to continue and flourish. These include the challenge of unhealthy dependency, the religion of Santería, urbanization, and the need to share the Cuban CPM vision with others.

Challenges to Confront

As stated above the challenges that need to be confronted include: unhealthy dependency, the religion of Santería, urbanization, and the challenge of sharing the CPM vision with others. The study turns to a discussion of these obstacles and challenges.

Challenge of Unhealthy Dependency

From the founding of the first Baptist church in Cuba in 1886 until the entrance of U.S. mission agencies in 1898, Baptist work in Cuba was led by Cubans. With the entrance of U.S. missionary agencies the control of the work was taken over by these missionaries until they left or were expelled following the Castro led Revolution. Baptist work has been in the hands of Cuban leadership from the onset of the Revolution until now. With the governmental changes in recent years, the conventions and churches have more access to outside contacts and resources than they have in decades. The temptation is to compromise their autonomy by following after outside funding for pastors, missionaries, churches, and so forth. This pattern is already emerging.

The challenge is what this author calls "Caribbean Indigenaity." A common refrain among Cubans is, "*Vivimos por la Fe* (We Live by Faith)." Faith in Spanish is spelled **FE**. The play on words comes from the **F** standing for Family (*familia*) and the **E** standing for those who live in the Exterior (*extranjero*). To be able to survive financially in Cuba, many people have come to depend upon economic assistance from family who have left Cuba and then send remittances back to support them. The monthly quota of government-subsidized food is sufficient for about one half of what a fami-

---

[406]Audiotaped reporting during a Kingdom Growth Conference held in the Western Cuban Baptist camp in Yumuri, Matanzas on November 23-December 4, 2009, for both Eastern and Western Convention leadership.

ly needs to survive.[407] Most Cubans depend on someone from the outside to send money, clothing, electronics, and so forth.

The churches are no different. For churches to pay their pastors, repair church buildings, print evangelism and training materials, provide theological education, and plant churches in the struggling economy is very difficult. If someone from the outside comes into the church with funding, it is easier to let these outsiders pay.

A growing pattern in Cuba is for church members to leave their low-paying jobs with the State to work full-time for the church as long as someone from the outside is willing to pay for it. In so doing, strong relational evangelism opportunities are lost in the workplace.[408] The spiritual initiative for Christian service is being replaced by an economic motivation. Those who have been ministering effectively as bivocational lay ministers now become dependent on outside individuals or organizations for their daily needs.[409]

As time passes there are increasing numbers of outside churches and organizations that desire to enter Cuba and help. While there is a need for assistance, it must be understood that not all outside support is helpful. Outside groups and individuals need to learn from the errors committed in Romania and the former Soviet Union following the fall of Communism. Well meaning groups flooded in to help by paying pastor's salaries and building church buildings and importing western evangelism, discipleship and leadership training programs. While there was a time of growth as the people embraced the western relationships and resources the results were short-lived. Now, many of these buildings stand virtually empty and pastors are without funding as the interest of their western benefactors has waned. As groups look to work in Cuba they must be sure that the help that is brought empowers Cubans in the ministry and does not create unhealthy dependency.[410]

---

[407]For an excellent discussion of the present economic situation in Cuba and the unique ways that the Cuban people have learned to resolve their economic problems, see Ben Corbett, *This is Cuba: An Outlaw Culture Survives* (Cambridge, MA: Westview Press, 2004).
[408]Cuban doctors, teachers, engineers, professional musicians, and others are leaving their jobs in droves to become full-time paid missionaries. Many of the church planting and ministry jobs that were being done effectively bi-vocationally are now being done by Cuban workers paid from the outside.
[409]This author has been present when word was received that an outside donor or organization was no longer willing or able to send the salary support that they had promised. He has seen the tears and felt the anxiety of families who left their jobs and, at times, homes to work "full-time" in the ministry and now have no way to provide for their families.
[410]During a conversation with a former President of one of the conventions he shared with this author, "Everyone who comes wants to train pastors. It is like we have never done anything and need for them to come in and tell us how to evangelize, disciple and

Challenge of the Santería Religion

While in-depth research into the *Santería* religion is outside the scope of this book, an investigation of the *Santería* worldview and the development of strategies to evangelize the followers of Santería are of vital importance to the future of Kingdom work in Cuba and in Latin America. In his book, *Santería: The Beliefs and Rituals of a Growing Religion in America*, Miguel De la Torre speaks of the proliferation of Santería in the Americas: "Although it is impossible to document the exact number of *orisha*[411] worshipers, some scholars estimate that about one hundred million are identified with the religion of Santería in the Americas, . . ."[412] Cuban culture is saturated with spiritism. According to De la Torre, "Today, as in the days of slavery, it is probably the most practiced religion in Cuba."[413]

Jualynne Dodson identifies, ". . . at least seven sacred lifestyles or religions in Cuba that evolved indigenously from information absorbed within the island's early colonial environment."[414] She identifies these as follows: ". . . the *reglas congo*, consisting of different traditions that adhere to Kongo-derived rules of practice: Regla de Ocha/Lecumí; Vudú; Espiritismo; Regla de Ifá; Abakuá/Ñañigo; and Regla Arará."[415]

One of the challenges that arise is the *Santeros*'[416] use of "house temple" as a center of their worship. As Baptists continue to use the term "house church," they need to take this phenomenon into consideration. Although a clear differentiation exists between a

---

pastor our churches. With the number of volunteers wanting to travel to Cuba, the day is coming when it will be rare to see a Cuban pastor preaching in a Cuban church."

[411] An Orisha (also spelled Orisa and Orixá) is a spirit which reflects one of the manifestations of *Olodumare* (God) in the Yoruba religious system.

[412] De la Torre, *Santería*, xiv. The rest of this quote says: ". . . of which anywhere between half a million and five million are located in the United States. If this is true, there may be more practitioners of Santería than some of the mainline U.S. Protestant denominations."

[413] Ibid., xi.

[414] Jualynne E. Dodson, *Sacred Spaces and Religious Traditions in Oriente Cuba* (Albuquerque, NM: University on New Mexico Press, 2008), 15.

[415] Ibid., 15-16. Dodson adds: "An additional set of ritual practices, Muertéra Bembé de Sao, may come to be considered an uban religion, as it appears to contain rituals that can be connected to the colonial experiences that were foundational behaviors for most traditions, and we found that it continues in contemporary Oriente." According to noted Cuban Baptist scholar Veguilla, "There are five forms of syncretism in Cuba. These five forms of syncretism include: Pure African Religion, Santería or Regla de Ocha, Brujería, Conguería or Regla de Palo, Ñañiguismo or Abakuá, and Spiritism." See Leoncio Veguilla Cené, "Cinco Formas de Sincretismo Religioso en Cuba (Five Forms of Religious Syncretism in Cuba)" (Th.M. thesis, Seminario Teológico Bautista "R.A. Ocaña," 1997), 7.

[416] A *Santero* is a follower of Santería.

"house church" and a "Santería house temple" in the hearts and minds of Baptists, they need ensure that no confusion exists in the minds of the lost who need to come to Christ.

Another challenge is the *Santeros'* use of "oral tradition" in the propagation of their beliefs. Evangelicals in general and Baptists in particular are using evangelism methods such as "Chronological Bible Storying," which employ oral methodologies in evangelism, discipleship, and leadership training among oral communicators. Therefore, it is important the methods of Santería be understood so as not to increase the problem of syncretism; this is of vital importance!

The most fruitful Evangelical evangelism methodology in Cuba among *Santeros* is persistent prayer. In recent years, a number of Santería centers have been converted into churches as a result of their leaders and members coming to Christ. In every case, Christian believers had engaged in fasting and prayer vigils on behalf of those involved in *Santería*. Additionally, missionaries have witnessed *Santeros* convicted through dreams. As a result of the dreams, they have sought out Christians and come to Christ.

Another methodology used in reaching *Santeros* is the reading of the Bible. A number of Santería priests have come to Christ through the reading of Scripture. They then seek Christian fellowship to help them with discipleship and in transforming their Santería centers into churches.

While a number of *Santeros* are turning to Christ in Cuba, a great need in this area is still present. During his years as a missionary, this author has yet to encounter any contextualized strategies used by other missionaries to reach the followers of these spiritist religions in the Americas. A concerted effort needs to occur on the part of national conventions, churches, and missions agencies to confront this issue proactively.

Challenge of Urbanization

The Phenomenon of Urbanization

Urbanization is a global phenomenon. Mission agencies, national conventions, and churches on every continent confront this reality. Cuba is no exception. Urban centers in Cuba continue to be a tremendous challenge. According to Daniel González, quoting data received from the Office of National Statistics (*Oficina Nacional de Estadísticas*):

> The present level of urbanization in Cuba is 76%. There are currently 6,993 townships in Cuba, of which 591 are considered urban. This means that 76% of the

Cuban population is located in 8% of the townships. In the 27 cities (with a population over 40,000) one will find nearly 50% of the Cuban population. As a result, nearly 50% of the Cuban population can be found in only 4% of the townships.[417]

According to NationMaster.com, Cuba has a population of 11,423,952 people with 8,508,397 living in urban areas.[418] A large part of the urbanization in Cuba is due to the government relocation of citizens from the arable land during the years following the Revolutionary takeover in 1959. A number of those were returned to the rural areas during the "Special Period" where they are being housed in multi-level Russian-style block buildings.

Daniel González laments, "it is in these same urban settlements where there have been the least number of churches planted in the last 20 years."[419] Both conventions have voiced the need to focus their church planting efforts on the urban centers. According to the Eastern Baptist Convention leadership, one issue is the churches in the urban centers, for whatever reason, feel more comfortable planting churches in the rural areas. A major reason cited was the urban church members have a burden to evangelize, disciple, and plant churches among family members who live in rural areas.[420]

González, a member of the Western Cuban Baptist Missions Board concurs, stating that urban churches have a tendency to overlook their "Jerusalem," feeling that missions begin with their "Judea" (or outlying areas). According to González, one reason for this is that:

> Many of those who feel called to serve as missionaries are in truth frustrated laymen who feel called to serve as pastors but have been denied that opportunity within the present convention system. Since they cannot exercise their call locally they reach out into rural areas, away from the "mother church," to plant a church

---

[417]González Garcia, *Modelo Cubano de Reinocrecimiento*, 10; and "Cuba People 2010," *2010 CIA World Factbook* [on-line]; accessed 13 July 2010; available from http://www.theodora.com/wfbcurrent/ cuba/cuba_people.html; Internet.
[418]According to NationMaster.com, "Cuban People Stats" [on-line]; accessed 13 July 2010; available from http://www.nationmaster.com/country/cu-cuba/peo-people; Internet.
[419]Clarification needs to be given that González is speaking of the planting of convention-recognized churches in the urban areas. Research needs to be conducted to determine the actual number of house churches, houses of prayer, and cell churches in urban centers.
[420]International Mission Board, "Eastern Cuban Baptist Leadership Consultation," Ft. Lauderdale, FL: The Forum, November 11, 2007; audio recording.

or churches, and serve there as lay pastors.[421]

Recommendations

In the face of this challenge, local churches and conventions must embrace their responsibilities to reach Cuba's urban centers. Eastern and Western Cuban Baptists have made major strides through the "CUBA 2010" initiative. The vision expressed in this initiative calls for Cuban Evangelicals to win one million Cubans to personal faith in Christ through the planting of 100,000 new house churches by the end of 2010--a church within walking distance of every Cuban.[422] As a result of this vision, Cuban Baptists have begun to recognize a variety of models of Church as being legitimate New Testament churches.[423] As of 2009, nine different Evangelical groups in Cuba had joined the "CUBA 2010" initiative. Cuban Baptists understand the need to mobilize the entire body of Great Commission Christians to fulfill the vision of winning Cuba for Christ.

The national conventions and local churches need to take full advantage of the house church and cell church models that are intentionally reproducing and functioning well in Cuba's urban areas. These cell and home-based ministries have a distinct advantage in urban centers. Cell churches can easily proliferate in the high-rise apartment buildings, while house churches are more effective in the urban neighborhoods. While the intentionally reproducing house churches have the highest potential, each model can be strategically important.

Churches that do have buildings can use them to house training centers for evangelists, lay missionaries, and lay pastors. For the urban strategies to work, local churches and conventions need to empower the local lay leadership so these churches can function as close to the New Testament example as possible.

The Challenge of Sharing the CPM Vision

The Cuban Church has a great deal to share. Cuban Christians have a passion for missions and a desire to go as missionaries to reach the peoples of the world. In recent years, pastors and convention leaders have been able to travel to other countries on

---

[421]Daniel González García, "*Estrategias de Siembra de Iglesias en Centros Urbanos en Cuba* (Strategies for Church Planting in Cuban Urban Centers)," Tms [photocopy] (La Habana, Cuba: Junta de Misiones, Convención Bautista de Cuba Occidental, 2008), 2.
[422]Caribbean Itinerant Team, *50 Days of Prayer for Cuba* (Sunrise, FL: International Mission Board, 2008), 1. See *Cuba 2010* (Havana, Cuba: Junta de Misiones, 2008). The vision is not just one million professions of faith. The call is for "One million disciples integrated into local churches in all parts of Cuba by 2010."
[423]Pérez, "Perfil de una Iglesia Cubana," PowerPoint.

short-term trips to share what God is doing in Cuba. Due to the unique nature of the Cuban CPM, Cuban Baptists can help other Baptist conventions and churches to embrace CPM-fostering methodologies.

As Cuban Baptists continue to search for ways to collaborate in global evangelization, the IMB and other mission organizations need to cooperate with them in this endeavor. The IMB has participated in World Missions Conferences and taught cross-cultural missions courses and workshops in the seminaries and other training venues. Southwestern Baptist Theological Seminary has worked closely with the IMB to send professors to train those who teach missions in the residential seminaries and regional training centers. Many other projects are underway to further Cuban Baptists missions sending possibilities. In the area of CPM vision casting, plans are underway to take Cuban Baptist trainers to other countries to share what God has done in Cuba.

Conclusion

A key for working within a traditional church/convention context is to pray for and seek out "pastors of peace." Jesus spoke of locating a "person of peace" when entering into a new area, establishing a base of operations in that person's home, and reaching out to the community. Similarly, it is important to seek out those leaders who share a passion for evangelism, discipleship, and church planting, but who do not necessarily have the missiological understanding of CPM-fostering methodologies. These individuals are the positive "gatekeepers" who can influence other local church and denominational leaders to initiate reproducible strategies that will promote CPMs. The process can be longer than trying to start from scratch, but the potential is much greater.

In a majority of traditional settings, the missionary or national church planter who desires to implement CPM methods may encounter stiff resistance from the existing church and denomination. Many of the target peoples have been influenced by the concept of church that is culturally prevailing. In Latin America, North America, and Europe, the prevailing concept of church includes a building. This centuries-old belief will not simply defer to a new concept or form of church. This is a major reason that CPMs have not been realized with more frequency within traditional church environments. Because Cuban Baptists have been a part of a CPM in the midst of a church/convention environment, they have the authority to speak concerning the process they have experienced in embracing the movement. They can be instrumental in helping others in traditional environments to embrace CPM-fostering methodologies.

CHAPTER 9

LAST THINGS

Within the context of Cuban Baptist history, this book describes and analyzes the CPM among Eastern and Western Cuban Baptists that emerged in the early 1990s and continues to this day. This endeavor has been aided by previous research concerning the emergence of Baptist ministry in Cuba in the late 1880s. Additional research related to the development of Baptist work and the involvement of Southern and American Baptist missionaries in that process has proven helpful. Contemporary Cuban authors, Baptists, and others have recently begun to evaluate what God is doing in Cuba and establishing strategies to deal with the extraordinary growth. What follows is a summary of the major Cuban realities that served as a background from which the Cuban CPM emerged.

Overview

As shown in Chapter 2, by the late 1800s, Roman Catholicism was the unquestioned and unrivaled religious presence in Cuba. As Baptists and other Evangelicals entered Cuba, they met with strong Catholic resistance. The origins of Baptist work in Cuba was traced to 1883 and the return to Cuba of Alberto Díaz and the subsequent establishment of the Getsemaní Church as a Reformed Church on April 10, 1883. With the assistance of Reverend Wood, from Key West, and the financial support of the Florida Baptist Convention and the Home Mission Board of the Southern Baptist Convention, Díaz then reorganized this church on January 26, 1886, as the first Baptist church founded in Cuba.

Although Cuban Baptists did receive financial support from the United States, and encouragement from outside leaders, the Baptist ministry in Cuba remained under the direction of Cubans from its beginnings in 1883 until the United States military intervention in 1898. From 1898 to 1959, Baptist work in the West remained under the control of Southern Baptist home missionaries, while American Baptist missionaries directed the work in the East.

Effects of the Americanization
of Cuban Work

While Evangelical work in general and Baptist work in particular was started by Cubans, they made the choice early on to depend on outside resources for the growth of the ministry. Under the circumstances it was understandable, but it came with a price. The indigenous nature of the work was lost as Cuban Baptists came to rely heavily upon North American personnel and finances to solidify the work and expand the ministry. Following the United States military intervention in 1898, national leadership was disenfranchised as the North American missionaries took over. A number of established leaders were lost to Baptists as a direct result of the Americanization of the work.

While much of the Cuban leadership was not pleased with the Americanization of the ministry, they did not have the economic resources to compete with the influx of foreign missionaries and their financial backing.[424] Since the United States mission organizations paid the Cuban Baptist leaders' salaries, bought properties, and constructed church and school buildings, they assumed control over these resources. Cuban leaders were relegated to secondary positions, and even when the nationals assumed leadership, the missionaries had the final word in major decisions.

During these years, Baptist work became highly institutionalized. They built a system that resulted in economic dependency, which endured until the misunderstandings between the churches and the Revolution provoked the exodus of American missionaries. The positive results of the American missionary presence was that, despite their controlling influence, they did build a strong denominational structure, established institutions, and developed a large number of capable national leaders.

Effects of the Purchase of Properties and the Building of U.S. Style Church Buildings

The United States missionaries quickly began buying strategic properties and constructing buildings to house the churches and institutions. While in the formative years this gave Baptist work a much-needed sense of permanency, in later years, it would prove to be an impediment to growth. The idea that a local church required its own building to be considered a true church can be seen as early as 1904, when Daniel, then superintendent of the HMB work in western Cuba, is quoted as saying, ". . . no unhoused church could be regarded as a permanent institution."[425]

During the present CPM, these church structures serve effectively as training centers for the preparation of house church leaders in support of the ever-growing house church movement. In recent years, these buildings have also provided an umbrella protecting the emerging house church movement from the countless difficulties they face while trying to become officially recognized. The problem occurs when a local church feels that a United States-

---

[424]The Cuban refrain is "*El que paga manda*" (He who pays, dictates).
[425]Daniel, "Church Buildings for Cuba," 2, cited in Greer, "1886-1916," 192-93.

style building is necessary to be recognized as a church. This erroneous concept impedes growth and, in future years, has the potential of halting the Cuban house church movement.

At present, it is impossible for Cuban Baptists to purchase properties for new church construction. If the conventions required groups to wait for the purchase of land or for the construction of new buildings in order to recognize new churches, the movement would quickly stagnate. Nothing is inherently wrong with a church owning land and having a nice building. These are tools a church can use to benefit the local body of Christ and the Kingdom of God. The problem arises when a group of believers is required to own land and a building to be considered a church, which for all practical purposes would eliminate the possibility for a multiplication of indigenous churches planting churches. To provide adequate finances for the purchase of land and buildings, while at the same time maintaining the multiplication necessary to sustain a CPM, is impossible. Energy will inevitably be diverted toward fund raising and to the practical struggles inherent in building programs and away from evangelism and church planting.

Effects of North American Missionary Influence on the Two Conventions

Both the Eastern and Western Baptist Conventions were organized in 1905 with United States missionaries directing the work. As stated earlier, while the missionaries were controlling, they did build enduring relationships and worked with the existing strong national leadership to mentor future generations of Baptist leaders. McCall espoused sound missiological principles when he outlined the foundational teachings that shaped Baptist work in Western Cuba. First, if Cuba were won to Christ, it would be won by Cubans.[426] Second, if Cuba were won to Christ, the effort would be led by Cubans. Third, if Cuba were won to Christ, the effort should be financed by Cubans.[427]

At the same time, the ABHMS taught that the work of the missionaries should be auxiliary and that the responsibility for the

---

[426]Acosta García, *1898-1960*, 107. Acosta, from the perspective of the Eastern Baptist Convention, makes the same point. "The missionaries of the ABHMS, with their leader being the superintendent, also considered evangelization as primarily the work of the local church, and even though the missionaries were involved in evangelistic activities, they promoted that the evangelization of Cuba be done by Cubans." Robert Routledge, the ABHMS superintendent, is quoted as saying, "The ABHMS acts as counselor in the planning of the work, and helps materially when possible, but the work of evangelization is carried entirely by the Cubans." Robert Routledge, *Annual Report of the Board*, 1921, cited in Acosta García, *1898-1960*, 107.

[427]Acosta García, *1898-1960*, 105-06. Acosta points out that Routledge pushed for the Eastern Baptist Convention to take ever-increasing responsibility for convention and pastoral self-support.

evangelization of Cuba lay with the Cubans. Even though the Southern and American Baptist missionaries did not fully practice what they taught, the missionaries did invest their lives in the preparation of indigenous leadership who were very capable of taking over the work as soon as the United States missionaries exited.

Both the ABHMS and the HMB significantly impacted the doctrinal and ecclesiastical formation of their respective conventions. Inevitably, many of the structures, traditions, and practices of both the Western and Eastern Conventions were shaped and solidified under the leadership of missionaries from Southern Baptist and American Baptist backgrounds. Some of the traditions and practices helped to keep these conventions grounded doctrinally and structurally during very difficult years, allowing them to survive the onslaught of the Revolution's atheistic philosophy. To some degree, the highly institutional structure of the conventions allowed them to protect the local churches during times of confrontation with this ideology.

Additionally, the structure helped the conventions maintain some degree of control over the pastors and, thus protect the overall work. The strict training at the seminaries, as a requirement for ordination, allowed the conventions to prepare ministers who maintained the convention's doctrinal integrity and, at the same time, filter out those who could cause disruption to the unity of the conventions. Over time, convention unity came to mean uniformity. Each pastor was, from the conventions' and government's perspective, legally responsible for whatever happened in the churches and missions to which they were assigned. The conventions sought to ensure that none of the pastors would compromise the work.

Some traditions, while they helped the conventions during times of trial and persecution, have not served them well in the present climate of unprecedented growth. One of the main issues deals with baptism and church membership. The pastors and churches tried to control who was baptized in order to control the voting membership of the church. They feared that infiltrators would work their way into the churches to disrupt the unity and compromise the local church's ministry. During the time of exceptional growth, the churches were afraid of the influx of new believers, feeling that by using the congregational polity of the local church, these newcomers potentially could outnumber the existing members and take over the churches and their properties.

Effects of Cuban Baptist's Highly Institutional Structure

Another example of the paradoxical nature of Baptist work in Cuba can be found in the requirements for the foundation of Baptist churches and the administration of Church ordinances. Before the organization of the first Baptist church in Cuba, a Baptist church in the United States counseled Díaz that the only guide for the founding of a church should be the New Testament. Even so, it appears that Díaz either chose to accept, or was led to accept, Southern Baptist traditional practices as the norm for Baptist work. Although ordained in Key West on December 13, 1885, Díaz found it necessary to wait until Wood, an ordained Baptist minister from Díaz's mother church, came to conduct the first "Baptist baptisms" in Cuba, on January 20, 1886. This practice of waiting for an ordained minister from a "mother church" to officiate baptisms can, therefore, be traced back to the very first Baptist baptisms and Baptist church organization in Cuba.

While the mother-church concept proved helpful during the formative years of the conventions, and especially during the years of persecution, it has produced mixed results during the emergence of the CPM. The mother-church concept and the fact that only ordained Baptist ministers have been allowed to baptize new believers and administer the Lord's Supper, introduced some inherent limitations. The limitations of the mother-church model depend primarily on the vision of church leadership. Mother churches with leadership that have a missionary vision can serve as a true asset to the work. At the same time leadership without a missionary vision can impede the beginning and expansion of the CPM.

Effects of Cuban Receptivity to the Gospel and Baptists' Inability to Assimilate the Resulting Growth

From the beginning of Baptist work in Cuba, the Cuban people proved to be very receptive to the Gospel. Early on, Cuban Baptists demonstrated a strong desire to evangelize their own countrymen and to minister to human needs. Over the years, many Cubans have responded to the call for salvation. Both Baptist conventions have found it difficult to assimilate the numbers of those who professed their faith into their churches.

Throughout the years, a large disparity has existed between the number of Cubans who professed faith in Christ, and the number eventually baptized and assimilated into the lives and ministries of the local churches. This trend can be seen early in Baptist life. For example, following the smallpox epidemic in 1887, Getsemaní Baptist Church, and her two sister churches in Havana, reported eight thousand professions of faith. Of the eight thousand professions of faith, only eight hundred were baptized. This means they only assimilated 10 percent of those who professed faith in Christ into church membership. While eight hundred baptisms was a tremendous increase from previous years, it still was only a small sample of those indicating they had become Christians. This same trend exists to this day.[428] The practice of delayed baptism and slow acceptance by Baptists of new converts can be traced to the earliest days of Baptist work in Cuba, as seen by comments made by Moseley, the head of the American Baptist work in eastern Cuba, in a letter dated March 15, 1900:

> The people gladly hear the gospel; our preaching halls are crowded at every service. The Cubans, however, have no idea of spiritual religion; they are nominally Catholics, but care very little for their religion. . . . We could receive and baptize hundreds of them who are disgusted with Romanism, but who know nothing of real heart religion. . . . It would be easy to baptize many and get a newspaper reputation at home, but we are trying to go slowly, realizing that we are doing foundation work, and that the future of our work in this island depends largely upon the beginnings we are now making.[429]

Another paradox becomes evident when one examines the conventions' practices of discipleship in relationship to baptism. While Cuban Baptists have demonstrated wise insight concerning the need for foundational discipleship, they have been unable to formulate a system of discipleship whereby they retain large numbers of Cubans who have made public professions of faith. Their desire to produce disciples who are truly committed is noble and correct, but they have not been able to make the necessary adjustments to conserve the extraordinary results of their evangelistic efforts. A large factor has been that in many cases, the ordained pastor has been the only person teaching the new believers classes. For example, for Díaz and the two other pastors in Havana to disciple eight thousand new believers was impossible; although it is impressive that they were able to orient eight hundred new believers to the place where they could be baptized.

It is evident that a need exists to empower the body of Christ to allow local church members to take on the task of discipling the masses. Historically, the pastors have not been willing to give up

---

[428]An exception to this seems to be in the ministry of O'Hallorán in eastern Cuba. He held evangelistic meetings, won and promptly baptized new converts, and immediately organized the churches and ordained the leadership.
[429]Greer, "1886-1916," 99-100.

control of new member discipleship. While those who finally complete the discipleship classes have a high degree of biblical and doctrinal knowledge, the churches have lost 85 to 90 percent of new believers in the process.

The Effects of Strong Lay Leadership

From the earliest years of Baptist work in Cuba, laymen have played an indispensable role in evangelism, church planting and local church leadership. This was never more clearly evident than during the imprisonment of the pastors and the sending of the seminary students and young leaders to UMAP. As other denominations lost churches due to the early trials of the Revolution, Baptist laymen demonstrated through their service the long held Baptist belief in the priesthood of all believers. This strong lay base would prove invaluable in the coming CPM. Laymen are crucial in the founding and leading of the house church networks as well as providing leadership in the multiple traditional churches and missions who do not have ordained convention-recognized pastors.

The Effects of the Revolution

As discussed in Chapter 4, in the 1960s, Cuban Baptists were confronted with the brutal reality of Communism. With the philosophical onslaught of dialectic materialism and scientific athiesm, Cuban Baptists struggled to maintain their identity and independence of worship and evangelism. During and following the imprisonment of Baptist leaders and subsequent internment of Baptist young people in UMAP, Baptists fled the country in mass. Baptist lay leaders, along with the pastors who did not suffer imprisonment, struggled to keep the churches open and ministering.

During the 1970s and 1980s, Baptists -- as well as other Christians -- suffered extreme discrimination but continued to minister faithfully. Their key Scripture passage during this period was Psalms 126:5-6, "Those who sow in tears shall reap in joy. He who continually goes forth weeping, bearing seed for sowing, shall doubtless come again with rejoicing, bringing his sheaves with him." Though results were sparse, Baptists remained faithful, ministering, and praying for the day God would pour out His Spirit upon Cuba.

The Emergence and Growth of the CPM

By the 1990s, Baptists and the Assemblies of God were growing consistently, though incrementally. With the collapse of the Soviet Union, Cuban society faced its greatest crisis. With the crashing economy came hunger, disease, and privations of every kind. The fullness of God's time had come for the Cuban people. The Communist system had sought to remove God from their consciousness but had failed to put anything in His place. As the social, political, and economic struggles escalated, the Cuban people were awakened to their spiritual needs. They began to flock spontaneously to the churches. This movement of the Holy Spirit took Baptists and the government by surprise. Even though Baptists had prayed fervently for this type of awakening, they were not prepared when it arrived. As a result of the overflow of people, shockingly, the conventions received permission from government authorities to meet for prayer and worship in their homes. The resulting exponential growth of the Cuban Evangelical Church has become a part of the history of the mighty acts of God in Cuba.

Through church growth statistics, documented interviews, and through an on-site professional IMB research team, this book clearly demonstrates that a Cuban CPM emerged in the early to mid-1990s and continues to this date. As demonstrated in Chapter 6, from 1990 to 2010, Baptists grew from 238 churches with no reported missions to 792 reported churches, 1,346 missions, and 4,901 house churches and houses of prayer. This represents a growth from 238 to 7,039 ecclesiastical units in **twenty** years. This is unprecedented growth for Cuba.

On top of that, by 2010, the Assemblies of God denomination had grown from 89 churches in 1990 to 2,779 churches and 7,697 house churches. The Assemblies of God grew from 89 to 10,476 ecclesiastical units during the **years 1990-2010**. This does not take into consideration the growth of other denominations, including the Free Methodists whose data was unavailable to this author, but whose growth has been empirically observed.

Chapters 7 and 8 introduced the complexities and resultant discussions concerning the emergence of the CPM within the Cuban Baptist Conventions. In light of their historic, almost Episcopal polity, the two Baptist conventions have struggled with the growth of the house church phenomenon. In recent years, dialog has increased among Baptist leaders in both conventions on how to deal with and navigate this new CPM reality without killing it or splitting the existing conventions. They have struggled to develop acceptable forms of church that will enable them to recognize the house churches and houses of prayer along with their non-seminary graduate lay pastors without ostracizing the traditional Baptist leaders on one side, nor alienating the house church movement on the other.

As shared in chapter 7, a breakthrough in these dialogs among the Eastern and Western Baptist Convention leadership came during the Kingdom Growth Conference held at the Yumurí Baptist

Camp in Matanzas, Cuba, on November 23-December 4, 2009. In attendance were the Executive Committees of both the Eastern and Western Baptist Conventions, along with pastors and lay missionaries.

During these historic meetings, convention-ordained pastors and lay pastors/lay missionaries shared multiple testimonies concerning what God was doing in both Western and Eastern Cuba. At the conclusion of the conference, convention leaders and pastors declared that they knew this growth was of the Lord, and they had to change their polity if they were to witness the continuation of this incredible movement of God. Leadership from both conventions expressed their commitment to changing some of the traditional patterns that have become impediments to the growth of the CPM. They stated first that they would begin to recognize the true nature of house churches; second, that they would allow these house churches to recognize their own leaders; and third, that they would allow these leaders to baptize and administer the Lord's Supper. If the conventions and pastors are able to make this paradigm shift, bright days lie ahead for the Cuban CPM, and especially for the lost persons in Cuba.

Challenges remain ahead for the CPM to continue. Not only do the polity issues need to be addressed, but an intentional emphasis needs to be placed on reaching the urban centers in Cuba. They need to develop contextualized strategies to reach the millions of followers of *Santería*. Cuban Baptists need to make their leaders cognizant of the inherent dangers of unhealthy dependency on outside sources for pastoral salaries and the possible future purchase of land and construction of church buildings. *The Lord has freed Cuban Baptists from the confines of the church buildings, and for the sake of the lost of Cuba, they dare not return.*

Additional Needed Research

This study was limited to the combined results of the CPM among the Eastern and Western Baptist Conventions. Research that includes the other Evangelical denominations is needed. This would give a true global picture of what God is doing within the Cuban CPM.

An investigation of the reasons behind the disparity in the growth between the Eastern Baptist Convention and the Western Baptist Convention would be beneficial. The Eastern Convention has easily doubled the growth of the Western Convention. It would be helpful if the reasons for this disparity were identified and the results applied to the work in Cuba and possibly elsewhere.

By its very nature, a CPM is a leadership development movement. The rapid multiplication of churches requires a corresponding multiplication of functional leaders. Both the Western and Eastern Baptist Conventions have made great strides in the area of leadership development. At present, three seminaries, nine two-year extensions, and twenty-five lay missionary training schools exist between the conventions. The area of worship leader training has experienced great advances as well. At this time there are eighty-five lay music training schools across the country. There are also projects under way to expand the availability of training through the proliferation of local church seminaries. These local church seminaries will allow Cuban Baptists to train their own local leaders as well as the house church leaders needed in their area. Research needs to be conducted to evaluate the effectiveness of these models of leadership training.

There are numerous training programs being introduced from outside Cuba, with mixed results. Additional research is needed into the types of leadership development best suited for undergirding a growing CPM. An examination of the role of indigenous training versus training programs imported from the outside should be conducted. There is also a need to investigate the best delivery systems for training (i.e. residential programs, extension programs, guided learning programs, video delivery systems, one-on-one mentoring or a combination of the above).[430] A final area of theological education that needs evaluation is the effects of upper level theological training upon pastors and convention leaders during a CPM.[431]

It would be of great service to the Kingdom of God if research were conducted and contextualized strategies considered to reach the millions of *Santería* followers in Cuba and the 100,000,000 or more in the Americas. This is the largest socio-religious people group segment in the Americas. It is the largest stand-alone social group outside of urban dwellers in the Americas. A void remains in strategies that are contextually appropriate and effective to evangelize the *Santería* peoples, and to plant reproducing churches among them.

---

[430]Robert Banks, Reenvisioning Theological Education: Exploring a Missional Alternative to Current Models (Grand Rapids: Eerdmans, 1999); Mark Young, "Planning Theological Education in Missions Settings," in With and Eye on the Future: Development and Mission in the 21st Century, ed. Duane H. Elmer and Lois McKinney (Monrovia, CA: MARC, 1996), 69-86; Ralph D. Winter, ed., Theological Education by Extension (South Pasadena, CA: William Carey, 1969).
[431]It has been observed that, as pastors and convention leaders enter masters and doctoral level studies, ministry on the local level suffers. Research is needed to evaluate the value of such studies during periods of extraordinary growth.

Future Usefulness of This Study

This book can serve as a starting point for the potential research projects listed above. This author is already gathering the previous research on Cuban Baptist history and development to aid in future research. While a number of books cover segments of this history, this book attempts to tie them together into a meaningful narrative that shows how Baptist work was founded, developed, attacked, survived, and now thrives.

This research will be especially beneficial to those who work in traditional church contexts. Hopefully, they will be able to see how they can place themselves in a position to experience a CPM. *While it is clear that a CPM is the sovereign work of the Holy Spirit, there is no reason that Christ followers cannot do all they can to place themselves in a position to experience a similar moving of the Holy Spirit.*

Cuban Christians' passion for prayer, evangelism, discipleship, church planting, and leadership training is contagious. When discussing the phenomenon of revival, Richard Owens Roberts speaks of Revival as "an extraordinary movement of the Holy Spirit producing extraordinary results."[432] He goes on to say, "*On these precious occasions God Himself has stepped into the stream of history and done a work so mighty and wonderful that thereafter the mere retelling of God's acts is sufficient to excite expectation and longing in the hearts of the faithful.*"[433]

As Baptist leadership shares the powerful testimony of the extraordinary movement of the Holy Spirit in the Cuban CPM, others will sense God's hand and, in turn, will seek His face. The prayer of all Cuban Christians is that others might experience the same powerful moving of the Holy Spirit that they are living out.

---

[432]Richard Owen Roberts, *Revival* (Wheaton, IL: Richard Owen Roberts Publishers, 1993), 16.
[433]Ibid., 19.

Bibliography

Books

Acosta García, Roy. *Historia y Teología de la Convención Bautista de Cuba Oriental 1898-1960* (History and Theology of the Eastern Baptist Convention of Cuba 1898-1960). Vol. 1. Santiago de Cuba: privately printed, 2000.

_____. *Historia y Teología de la Convención Bautista de Cuba Oriental 1959-1980* (History and Theology of the Eastern Baptist Convention of Cuba 1959-1980). Vol. 2. Santiago de Cuba: privately printed, 2004.

_____. *Historia y Teología de la Convención Bautista de Cuba Oriental* (History and Theology of the Eastern Baptist Convention of Cuba). Vol. 3. Santiago de Cuba: privately printed, 2005.

Alamino, Carlos. Tras las Huellas del Llamado (In the Footsteps of God's Call). Camagüey: privately printed, 2005.

Allen, Roland. *Missionary Methods: St. Paul's or Ours?*. Grand Rapids: Eerdmans, 1962.

_____. *Missionary Principles*. Grand Rapids: Eerdmans, 1964.

_____. *The Spontaneous Expansion of the Church: And the Causes Which Hinder It*. Grand Rapids: Eerdmans, 1962; reprint, Eugene, OR: Wipf & Stock, 1997.

Anderson, Justice. *An Evangelical Saga: Baptists and Their Precursers in Latin America*. Longwood, FL: Xulon Press, 2005.

_____. *Historia de los Bautistas: Sus Comienzos y Desarrollo en Asia, Africa y America Latina* (History of Baptists: Their Beginnings and Development in Asia, Africa and Latin America). Vol. 3. El Paso: Casa Bautista de Publicaciones, 1990.

Banks, Robert. *Reenvisioning Theological Education: Exploring a Missional Alternative to Current Models*. Grand Rapids: Eerdmans, 1999.

Barnett, Mike, and Dan Morgan. "Biblical and Historical Foundations for Church Planting Movements." In *Church Planting Movements in North America*, ed. Daniel R. Sánchez, 59-94. Fort Worth: Church Starting Network, 2007.

Barrett, David B., ed. World Christian Encyclopedia. Nairobi: Oxford University Press, 1992.

Barrett, David B., George T. Kurian, and Todd M. Johnson. *World Christian Encyclopedia*. Vol 1. New York: Oxford University Press, 2001.

Batista, Fulgencio. *The Growth and Decline of the Cuban Republic*. New York: Devin-Adair Co., 1964.

Berges, Juana, and Reinerio Arce. *40 Años de Testimonio Evangélico en Cuba* (40 Years of Evangelical Testimony in Cuba). Inglaterra: Consejo de Iglesias de Cuba, n.d.

Brierley, Peter, ed. *World Churches Handbook*. London: Christian Research, 1997.

Canizares, Raul. *Cuban Santería: Walking in the Night*. Rochester, VT: Destiny Books, 1999.

Caribbean Itinerant Team. *50 Days of Prayer for Cuba*. Sunrise FL: International Mission Board, 2008.

Carlton, Bruce. *Amazing Grace: Lessons on Church Planting Movements from Cambodia*. Chennai, India: Mission Educational Books, 2000.

Caudill, Herbert. *Meet the Youth of Cuba*. Atlanta: Home Mission Board of the Southern Baptist Convention, 1942.

_____. *On Freedom's Edge: Ten Years Under Communism in Cuba*. Atlanta: Home Mission Board of the Southern Baptist Convention, 1975.

Conferencia de Obispos Católicos de Cuba. *El Papa Habla a los Cubanos* (The Pope Speaks to the Cubans). México: Offset Multicolor, 1988.

Corbett, Ben. *This is Cuba: An Outlaw Culture Survives*. Cambridge, MA: Westview Press, 2004.

Corder, Lloyd. "Baptists in Cuba." In *Encyclopedia of Southern Baptists*, ed. Norman Wade Cox, 339-42. Nashville: Broadman, 1948.

Corse, Theron. *Protestants, Revolution and the Cuba-U.S. Bond*. Gainesville: University Press of Florida, 2007.

Cuba 2010. Havana, Cuba: Junta de Misiones, 2008.

Dana, H. E. *Manual de Eclesiología* (Manual of Ecclesiology). El Paso, TX: Casa Bautista de Publicaciones, 1987.

Davis, J. Merle. *The Cuban Church in a Sugar Economy*. New York: Academy Press, 1942.

De la Torre, Miguel A. *Santería: The Beliefs and Rituals of a Growing Religion in America*. Grand Rapids: Eerdmans, 2004.

Dodson, Jualynne E. *Sacred Spaces and Religious Traditions in Oritente Cuba*. Albuquerque, NM: University on New Mexico Press, 2008.

Evangelical Christian Humanitarian Outreach for Cuba. *The Evangelical Revival and the Protestant Church in Cuba*. Miami: Eco-Cuba, 1999.

Fite, Clifton Edgar. *In Castro's Clutches*. Chicago: Moody Press, 1969.

Fitts, Bob, Sr. *Saturation Church Planting: Multiplying Congregations through House Churches*. 2nd ed. Colorado Springs: DAWN, 1994.

Garnett, Christine. *Through a Cuban Window*. Atlanta: Home Mission Board of the Southern Baptist Convention, 1954.

Garrison, David. *Church Planting Movements*. Richmond, VA: International Mission Board Southern Baptist Convention, 2000.

_____. *Church Planting Movements: How God is Redeeming a Lost World* (Movimientos de Plantación de Iglesias: Cómo Dios está Redimiendo al Mundo Perdido). Bangalore, India: WIGTake Resources, 2004.

González García, Daniel. *Modelo Cubano de Reinocrecimiento: Una Iglesia Sistemica* (A Cuban Model for Kingdom Growth: A Systemic Church). La Habana: Western Baptist Convention Mission Board, 2008.

Gonzáles Muñoz, Alberto I. *Dios No Entra en Mi Oficina* (God Does Not Enter My Office). La Habana, Cuba: Editorial Bautista, 2003.

_____. *Y Vimos Su Gloria: Documento Histórico de la Convención Bautista de Cuba Occidental 1959-2006* (And We Saw His Glory: Historic Document of the Western Baptist Convention of Cuba 1959-2006). La Habana, Cuba: Editorial Bautista, 2007.

Gravette, Andy. *Cuba*. London: New Holland Publishers, 2000.

Gupta, Paul R., and Sherwood G. Lingenfelter. *Breaking Tradition to Accomplish Vision Training Leaders for a Church-Planting Movement: A Case from India*. Winona Lake, IN: BMH Books, 2006.

Hageman, Alice, and Philip Wheaton, eds. *Religion in Cuba Today: A New Church for a New Society*. New York: Association Press, 1971.

Johnstone, Patrick. *Operation World: Pray for the World*. Singapore: Alby Commercial Enterprises, 1993.

Kirk, John. *Between God and Party: Religion and Politics in Revolutionary Cuba*. Tampa: University of South Florida Press, 1989.

Lara, José Bell, ed. *Cuba in the 1990's*. Translated by Lisa Makarchuk. La Habana: Editorial José Martí, 1999.

Lasher, George William. *The Gospel in Cuba: The Story of Alberto Diáz a Marvel of Modern Missions*. Cincinnati: George E. Stevens, 1893.

Lawrence, Una Roberts. *Cuba for Christ.* Atlanta: Home Mission Board of the Southern Baptist Convention, 1926.

_____., ed. *Cuba: Leader's Resource Book.* Atlanta: Home Mission Board of the Southern Baptist Convention, 1942.

López Muñoz, Agustín. *Apóstol Bautista en la Perla Antilliana: Biografía del Dr. Moisés Nathanael McCall* (Baptist Apostle in the Pearl of the Antilles: A Biography of Moses Nathanael McCall). La Habana: Editorial Federación Lealtad Cristo, 1945.

Luis, William. *Culture and Customs of Cuba.* Westport, CT: Greenwood Press, 2001.

Maroney, Jimmy K., and James B. Slack, eds. *Handbook for Effective Church Planting.* Richmond, VA: Foreign Mission Board, 1987.

McCall, M. N. *A Baptist Generation in Cuba.* Atlanta: Home Mission Board of the Southern Baptist Convention, 1942.

McGavran, Donald. *Bridges of God.* London: World Dominion, 1955; reprint, Eugene, OR: Wipf and Stock, 2005.

_____. *Effective Evangelism: A Theological Mandate.* Phillipsburg, NJ: Presbyterian and Reformed Publishing, 1988.

_____. *Understanding Church Growth.* 3rd ed. Grand Rapids: Eerdmans, 1990.

Memoria Anual: Informes y Estadísticas 2001 (Annual Memory: Reports and Statistics 2001). Guantanamo, Cuba: Ediciones Ministerio Misionero SINAÍ, 2001.

Memoria Anual: Informes y Estadísticas 2002 (Annual Memory: Reports and Statistics 2002). Guantanamo, Cuba: Ediciones Ministerio Misionero SINAÍ, 2002.

Memoria Anual: Informes y Estadísticas 2003 (Annual Memory: Reports and Statistics 2003). Guantanamo, Cuba: Ediciones Ministerio Misionero SINAÍ, 2003.

Memoria Anual: Informes y Estadísticas 2004 (Annual Memory: Reports and Statistics 2004). Guantanamo, Cuba: Ediciones Ministerio Misionero SINAÍ, 2004.

Memoria Anual: Informes y Estadísticas 2005 (Annual Memory: Reports and Statistics 2005). Guantanamo, Cuba: Ediciones Ministerio Misionero SINAÍ, 2005.

Memoria Anual: Informes y Estadísticas 2006 (Annual Memory: Reports and Statistics 2006). Guantanamo, Cuba: Ediciones Ministerio Misionero SINAÍ, 2006.

Memoria Anual: Libro Anual de Informes y Estadísticas 1988 (Annual Memory: Annual Book of Reports and Statistics 1988). La Habana, Cuba: Editorial Bautista, 1989.

Memoria Anual: Libro Anual de Informes y Estadísticas 1989 (Annual Memory: Annual Book of Reports and Statistics 1989). La Habana, Cuba: Editorial Bautista, 1990.

Memoria Anual: Libro Anual de Informes y Estadísticas 1990 (Annual Memory: Annual Book of Reports and Statistics 1990). La Habana, Cuba: Editorial Bautista, 1991.

Memoria Anual: Libro Anual de Informes y Estadísticas 1991 (Annual Memory: Annual Book of Reports and Statistics 1991). La Habana, Cuba: Editorial Bautista, 1992.

Memoria Anual: Libro Anual de Informes y Estadísticas 1992 (Annual Memory: Annual Book of Reports and Statistics 1992). La Habana, Cuba: Editorial Bautista, 1993.

Memoria Anual: Libro Anual de Informes y Estadísticas 1993 (Annual Memory: Annual Book of Reports and Statistics 1993). La Habana, Cuba: Editorial Bautista, 1994.

Memoria Anual: Libro Anual de Informes y Estadísticas 1994 (Annual Memory: Annual Book of Reports and Statistics *1994*). La Habana, Cuba: Editorial Bautista, 1995.

Memoria Anual: Libro Anual de Informes y Estadísticas 1995 (Annual Memory: Annual Book of Reports and Statistics 1995). La Habana, Cuba: Editorial Bautista, 1996.

Memoria Anual: Libro Anual de Informes y Estadísticas 1996 (Annual Memory: Annual Book of Reports and Statistics 1996). La Habana, Cuba: Editorial Bautista, 1997.

Memoria Anual: Libro Anual de Informes y Estadísticas 1997 (Annual Memory: Annual Book of Reports and Statistics 1997). La Habana, Cuba: Editorial Bautista, 1998.

Memoria Anual: Libro Anual de Informes y Estadísticas 1998 (Annual Memory: Annual Book of Reports and Statistics 1998). La Habana, Cuba: Editorial Bautista, 1999.

Memoria Anual: Libro Anual de Informes y Estadísticas 1999 (Annual Memory: Annual Book of Reports and Statistics 1999). La Habana, Cuba: Editorial Bautista, 2000.

Memoria Anual: Libro Anual de Informes y Estadísticas 2000 (Annual Memory: Annual Book of Reports and Statistics 2000). La Habana, Cuba: Editorial Bautista, 2001.

Memoria Anual: Libro Anual de Informes y Estadísticas 2001 (Annual Memory: Annual Book of Reports and Statistics 2001). La Habana, Cuba: Editorial Bautista, 2002.

Memoria Anual: Libro Anual de Informes y Estadísticas 2002 (Annual Memory: Annual Book of Reports and Statistics 2002). La Habana, Cuba: Editorial Bautista, 2003.

Memoria Anual: Libro Anual de Informes y Estadísticas 2003 (Annual Memory: Annual Book of Reports and Statistics 2003). La Habana, Cuba: Editorial Bautista, 2004.

Memoria Anual: Libro Anual de Informes y Estadísticas 2004 (Annual Memory: Annual Book of Reports and Statistics 2004). La Habana, Cuba: Editorial Bautista, 2005.

Memoria Anual: Libro Anual de Informes y Estadísticas 2005 (Annual Memory: Annual Book of Reports and Statistics 2005). La Habana, Cuba: Editorial Bautista, 2006.

Memoria Anual: Libro Anual de Informes y Estadísticas 2006 (Annual Memory: Annual Book of Reports and Statistics 2006). La Habana, Cuba: Editorial Bautista, 2007.

Memoria Anual: Libro Anual de Informes y Estadísticas 2007 (Annual Memory: Annual Book of Reports and Statistics 2007). La Habana, Cuba: Editorial Bautista, 2008.

Memoria Anual: Libro Anual de Informes y Estadísticas 2008 (Annual Memory: Annual Book of Reports and Statistics 2008). La Habana, Cuba: Editorial Bautista, 2009.

Memoria Anual: Libro Anual de Informes y Estadísticas 2009 (Annual Memory: Annual Book of Reports and Statistics 2009). La Habana, Cuba: Editorial Bautista, 2010.

Memoria Anual: Libro Anual de Informes y Estadísticas 2010 (Annual Memory: Annual Book of Reports and Statistics 2010). La Habana, Cuba: Editorial Bautista, 2011.

Murphy, Edward F. "Follow Through Evangelism in Latin America." In *Mobilizing for Saturation Evangelism*, ed. Clyde W. Taylor and Wade T. Coggins, 150. Wheaton IL: Evangelical Information Services, 1970.

Newton, Louie D. *Amazing Grace: The Life of M. N. McCall Missionary to Cuba*. Atlanta: Home Mission Board of the Southern Baptist Convention, 1948.

Office of Overseas Operations. *Something New Under the Sun*. Richmond, VA: International Mission Board, 1999.

Open Doors. *Cuba for Christ: The Amazing Revival*. Kent, England: Sovereign World, 1999.

Orr, J. Edwin. *The Re-study of Revival and Revivalism*. Pasadena, CA: School of World Mission, 1981.

Pérez, Louis A., Jr. *Cuba: Between Reform and Revolution*. New York: Oxford Press, 1995.

Pipes, Richard. *Communism: A History*. New York: Modern Library, 2001.

Pool, Rose Goodwin. *Light of Yumurí*. Atlanta: Home Mission Board of the Southern Baptist Convention, 1954.

Proyecciones 2010 (Projections 2010). La Habana, Cuba: Editorial Bautista, 2010.

Ramos, Marcos Antonio. *Panorama del Protestantismo en Cuba* (Panorama of Protestantism in Cuba). San José, Costa Rica: Editorial Caribe, 1986.

_____. *Protestantism and Revolution in Cuba*. Miami: University of Miami, North-South Center for the Research Institute for Cuban Studies, 1989.

Reza, H. T. *After the Storm, the Rainbow*. Kansas City: Nazarene Publishing House, 1994.

Roberts, Richard Owen. *Revival*. Wheaton, IL: Richard Owen Roberts Publishers, 1993.

Rodríguez, Alfredo, S. *La Obra Bautista en Cuba Occidental* (The Baptist Work In Western Cuba). La Habana, Cuba: Imprenta Bautista, 1930.

Sánchez, Daniel R. *Church Planting Movements in North America*. Fort Worth: Church Starting Network, 2007.

Sandoval, Mercedes Cros. *Worldview, the Orishas, and Santería*. Gainesville, FL: University Press of Florida, 2006.

Schwarz, Christian A. *Natural Church Development: A Guide to Eight Essential Questions for Healthy Churches*. Carol Stream, IL: ChurchSmart Resources, 1996.

SI-Mar, S. A., ed. *Fidel y La Religión: Conversaciones con Fredi Betto* (Fidel and Religion: Conversations with Fredi Betto). 2nd ed. La Habana: SI-Mar, S.A., 1997.

Simmons, Geoff. *Cuba: From Conquistador to Castro*. New York: St. Martin's Press, 1996.

Simson, Wolfgang. *Houses that Change the World: The Return of the House Churches.* London: OM Publishing, 2001.

Slack, James B. "Assessments of Church Planting Movements." In *Church Planting Movements in North America*, ed. Daniel R. Sánchez, 263-72. Fort Worth: Church Starting Network, 2007.

Slack, James. "Strategies for Church Development." In *Missiology: An Introduction to the Foundations, History, and Strategies of World Missions*, ed. John Mark Terry, Ebbie Smith, and Justice Anderson, 498-514. Nashville: Broadman and Holman, 1998.

Smith, Ebbie C. *Growing Healthy Churches: New Directions for Church Growth in the 21st Century.* Forward Stephen A. Macchia. Fort Worth, Texas: Church Starting Network, 2003.

Snowden, Mark, ed. *Toward a Church Planting Movement.* Richmond: International Mission Board, 1998.

Southern Baptist Convention. *Baptist Faith and Message.* Nashville: LifeWay, 2000.
Sujov, A.D. *Las Raíces de la Religión* (The Roots of Religion). La Habana: Editorial de Ciencias Sociales, 1972.

Treto, Raúl Gómez. *The Church and Socialism in Cuba.* New York: Orbis Books, 1988.

Van Rheenen, Gailyn. *Communicating Christ in Animistic Contexts.* Grand Rapids: Baker Book House, 1991.

Veguilla Cené, Leoncio. *Más de Cien Años de Obra Bautistia en Cuba Occidental 1882-1996* (More Than One Hundred Years of Baptist Work in Western Cuba 1882-1996). La Habana, Cuba: Oficina de Publicaciones de Seminario Teológico Bautista "R.A. Ocaña," 1997.

_____. *Teologia Sistematica: Personas y Temas de la Teologia.* Habana: Oficina de Publicaciones Seminario Teológico Bautista "R.A. Ocaña," 1997.

Wagner, C. Peter. *Church Planting for a Greater Harvest.* Ventura, CA: Regal Books, 1990.

_____. *Frontiers in Missionary Strategy.* Chicago: Moody Press, 1971.

_____. *Strategies for Church Growth.* Ventura, CA: Regal Books, 1987.

Warren, Rick. *The Purpose Driven Church: Growth Without Compromising Your Message & Mission.* Grand Rapids: Zondervan, 1995.

Wingeir-Rayo, Philip. *Cuban Methodism: The Untold Story of Survival and Revival.* Lawrenceville, GA: Dolphins & Orchids Publishing, 2004.

Yaremko, Jason M. *U.S. Protestant Missions in Cuba: From Independence to Castro.* Gainesville: University Press of Florida, 2000.

Young, Mark. "Planning Theological Education in Missions Settings." In *With and Eye on the Future: Development and Mission in the 21st Century*, ed. Duane H. Elmer and Lois McKinney, 69-86. Monrovia, CA: MARC, 1996.

Theses

Greer, Harold Edward. "History of Southern Baptist Mission Work in Cuba from its Beginnings to 1896." Th.M. thesis, University of Alabama, 1963.

Veguilla Cené, Leoncio. "Cinco Formas de Sincretismo Religioso en Cuba (Five Forms of Religious Syncretism in Cuba)." Th.M. thesis, Seminario Teológico Bautista "R.A. Ocaña," 1997.

Dissertations

Delgado, Primitivo. "The History of Southern Baptist Missions in Cuba to 1945." Ph.D. diss., Southern Baptist Theological Seminary, 1947.

Esqueda, Octavio. "Theological Higher Education in Cuba: A Case Study of the Eastern Baptist Theological Seminary." Ph.D. diss., University of North Texas, 2003.

Fowlkes, Dane Winstead. "Developing a Church Planting Movement in India." Ph.D. diss., University of Free State, 2004.

Greer, Harold Edward. "History of Southern Baptist Mission Work in Cuba, 1886-1916." Ph.D. diss., University of Alabama, 1965.

Moldovan, John. "Romanian Baptists Under Marxism-Leninism: A Study of the Impact of Communist Persecution on Evangelism, 1945-1990." Ph.D. diss., Southwestern Baptist Theological Seminary, 1994.

Rosado, Caleb. "Sect and Party: Religion Under Revolution in Cuba." Ph.D. diss., Northwestern University, 1985.

Sharp, Jonathan E. "A Qualitative Study of Selected Aspects of Ecclesiology Within the Baptist Convention of Western Cuba." Ph.D. diss., New Orleans Baptist Theological Seminary, 2009.

Articles

Anderson, Justice C. "What Kind of Church: Building a Biblical Ecclesiology for Culturally Relevant Church Planting, 1999." Tms [photocopy]. International Centre for Excellence in Leadership, Richmond, VA.

Azcuy, Hugo. "Los cambios de la constitución cubana (The Changes to the Cuban Constitution)." In *Cuadernos de Nuestra América* (Notebooks from Our America), no. 20, La Habana, 1993.

Barrientos, Alberto. "El Uso del Templo (The Use of the Church Building)." ¡La Marcha! Internacional 17 (Julio-Diciembre 1970): 6-8.

"Biography of Díaz." *Christian Index* 66 (December 19, 1889), 6.

Brawner, Jeff. "An Examination of Nine Key Issues Concerning CPM." *Journal of Evangelism and Missions* 6 (Spring 2007): 3-13.

Burrows, N. N. "The Havana Church." *Christian Index* 69 (March 31, 1892): 6.

Byrd, Mark. "People Movements vs. Church Planting Movements." *Journal of Evangelism and Missions* 7 (Spring 2007): 15-27.

Caudill, Margorie. "Cuba's Crucial Hour" (late January 1959).

Cooper, Loyd. "Baptists in Cuba." *Encyclopedia of Southern Baptists* (1958): 339-42.

Daniel, Charles David. "Church Buildings for Cuba." *Christian Index* 84 (July 21, 1904): 2

Garrison, David. "Global Church Planting: Something is Happening." *Journal of Evangelism and Missions* 4 (2004): 77-87.

Gonzáles Muñoz, Alberto I. "*Terroristas en Barajas* (Terrorists in Madrid's Barajas International Airport)." *Editorial Bautista*, La Habana, Cuba, 1998, 9.

Graham, William C. "Church Planting and the Larger Church." *Journal of Evangelism and Missions* 4 (2004): 15-21.

Greer, Harold. "Baptists in Western Cuba: from the Wars of Independence to Revolution." *Cuban Studies* 19 (1989): 61-77.

Hendricks, Shawn. "Baptist Churches Overseas Top 100,000." *Commission Magazine*, 2006, 12-13.

Joerg, Gertrude. "The Cuban Mission." *Christian Index* 90 (June 30, 1892): 5.

Jones, J. William. "Sketch of Rev. A. J. Díaz, 'The Apostle of Cuba'." *Seminary Magazine* 9, April 1896, 350.

Kennedy, John. "Cuba's Next Revolution: How Christians and Reshaping Castro's Communist Stronghold." *Christianity Today* 42, no. 1 (1998): 19-25.

King, H. M. "Origin of Cuban Work." *Our Home Field* 1 (March 1889): 6.

"Letter, Cova, n.d." *Christian Index* 69 (December 8, 1892): 5.

"Letter, Parker, Guantánamo, November 2, 1898." *Christian Index* 78 (November 24, 1898): 1.

"Letter, Wood, Havana, January 23, 1886." *Christian Index* 64 (February 14, 1886): 4.

"Letter, Wood, Havana, January 26, 1886." *Christian Index* 64 (February 25, 1886): 4.

Lovelace, Hoyt. "Is Church Planting Movement Methodology Viable?: An Examination of Selected Controversies Associated with the CPM Strategy." *Journal of Evangelism and Missions* 6 (Spring 2007): 45-58.

May, Stan. "Ecclesiology: The Missing Ingredient in Modern Missions." *Journal of Evangelism and Missions* 4 (2004): 89-102.

Meador, Clyde. "The Left Side of the Graph." *Journal of Evangelism and Missions* 6 (Spring 2007): 59-63.

Montgomery, R. B. "Letter, Brooklyn, February 23, 1893." *Our Home Field* 5 (March 1893): 5.

O'Brien, William R. "Executive Vice President Report." Richmond, VA: Report to the Board of Trustees, Foreign Mission Board, Feb. 13, 1989.

Olasky, Marvin. "No es Fácil: It's not Easy." *World Magazine*, 1 May 2004, 37-49.

"Our Cuban Cemetery." *Christian Index* 65 (June 7, 1888): 1.

"Our Mission Board: Abstract of the Forty-Third Annual Report, 1888." *Christian Index* 65 (May 10, 1888): I-vi.

Padgett, Tim. "Cuba's Chance." *Time Magazine*, 3 March 2008, 34-36.

Phillips, Jere. "Funding New Churches." *Journal of Evangelism and Missions* 4 (2004): 23-38.

Poor, Wally. "Never the Same." *Commission Magazine*, May 1997, 17.

Ramos, Marcos Antonio. "Religion and Religiosity in Cuba: Past, Present and Future." Cuba: Occasional Papers No. 2 (2002): 1-15.

"The Red Cross in Cuba." *Mission Journal* 46 (November 1895): 27-28.

Reese, Robert. "Theological Considerations for Church Planting." *Journal of Evangelism and Missions* 4 (2004): 39-50.

Slack, James B. "Church Planting Movements: A Clarification of the Assessment Process and CPM Definition when Compared to Historical Movements." Tms (photocopy). Richmond, VA: Global Research Department, Evangelism and Church Growth Section, International Mission Board of the Southern Baptist Convention, 12 March 2003.

_____. "Church Planting Movements: Rationale, Research and Realities of Their Existence." *Journal of Evangelism and Missions* 6 (Spring 2007): 29-44.

Speidel, Mary E. "A 'Drop' in the Bucket: Cuba." *Commission Magazine*, May 1997, 6-16.

Speidel, Mary E., Wally Poor, and Betty Poor. "Walking in Victory." *Commission Magazine*, May 1997, 16.

Stroope, Mike W. "One Day . . . Is Today." Richmond, VA: Cooperative Services International Area irector Report to the Board of Trustees, Foreign Mission Board, Oct. 9, 1995.

Telep, Andrew. "With the Blows of the Cross." *Truett Journal of Church and Mission* 3, no. 1 (2005): 67-85.

Tichenor, I. T. "Cuba." *Our Home Field* 1 (August 1888): 2.

_____. "House of Worship in Havana." *Christian Index* 65 (December 6, 1888): 3.

_____. "A Second Visit to Cuba." *Our Home Field* 1 (December 1888): 6.

_____. "Visit to Cuba." *Christian Index* 65 (February 9, 1888): 2-3.

"W. F. Wood to I. T. Tichenor, Key West, 22 July 1885." *Christian Index* 63 (August 6, 1885): 5.

Weber, Jeremy. "Cuba For Christ–Ahora." *Christianity Today* 53, no. 7 (2009): 20-28.

Wilkes, Steve. "Missiological Misgivings?" *Journal of Evangelism and Missions* 6 (Spring 2007): 1-2.

Willis, Avery. "Senior Vice President Report." Ridgecrest, NC: Report to the Board of Trustees, Foreign Mission Board, Aug. 14, 1995.

Wood, Rick. "A 'Church-Planting Movement' Within Every People: The Key to Reaching Every People and Every Person." *Missions Frontiers*, May/June 1995.

Unpublished Manuscripts

Dry, Larry W. "Creative Thinking and Paradigms for Ministry, 1999." Tms [photocopy]. Richmond, VA: International Centre for Excellence in Leadership.

González García, Daniel. "*Estrategias de Siembra de Iglesias en Centros Urbanos en Cuba* (Strategies for Church Planting in Cuban Urban Centers)." Tms [photocopy]. La Habana, Cuba: Junta de Misiones, Convención Bautista de Cuba Occidental, 2008.

_____. "Índice de Receptividad del Pueblo Cubano en la Actualidad." Tms [photocopy]. La Habana, Cuba: Junta de Misiones, Convención Bautista de Cuba Occidental, 2008.

Gonzáles Muñoz, Alberto I. "Milagro Espiritual y Soberanía de Dios" (Spiritual Miracle and the Sovereignty of God). Tms [photocopy]. La Habana, Cuba: Editorial Bautista, 2007.

_____. "Movimientos Eclesiásticos: Una Compilación de Materiales Varios para una Visión General de Algunos Movimientos Contemporáneos" (Ecclesiastical Movements: A Compilation of Various Materials for a General Vision of Some Contemporary Movements). MTMs Cuidad de la Habana: Oficina de Publicaciones Seminario Teológico Bautista (R.A. Ocaña), 2004.

_____. "Pastor: Dios Me Habló Hoy" (Pastor: God Spoke to Me Today). La Habana, Cuba: Editorial Bautista, 2007.

Martín Lemos, Israel. "Reflexiones Breves sobre Estratégias para la Plantación de Iglesias en Centros Urbanos (Brief Reflections Concerning Church Planting Strategies for Urban Centers)." Photocopy. La Habana: Oficina de Publicaciones Seminario Teológico Bautista (R.A. Ocaña), 2008.

Myers, Lewis, and James Slack. "To the Edge, 1998." Tms [photocopy]. Richmond, VA: International Mission Board, 1998.

_____. "To the Edge: A Planning Process for People Group Specific Strategy Development." Tms (photocopy). Richmond, VA: International Mission Board, 1999.

Myers, Lewis, James Slack, and Mark Snowden. "Together to the Edge: Planting Churches Strategy Manual." Tms [photocopy]. Richmond, VA: Global Research Department, Evangelism and Church Growth Section, International Mission Board of the Southern Baptist Convention, January 2006.

Nolen, Steve. "Comparison and Contrast of People Movements and Church Planting Movements." Tms [photocopy]. Memphis, TN: Mid-America Baptist Theological Seminary, 2003.

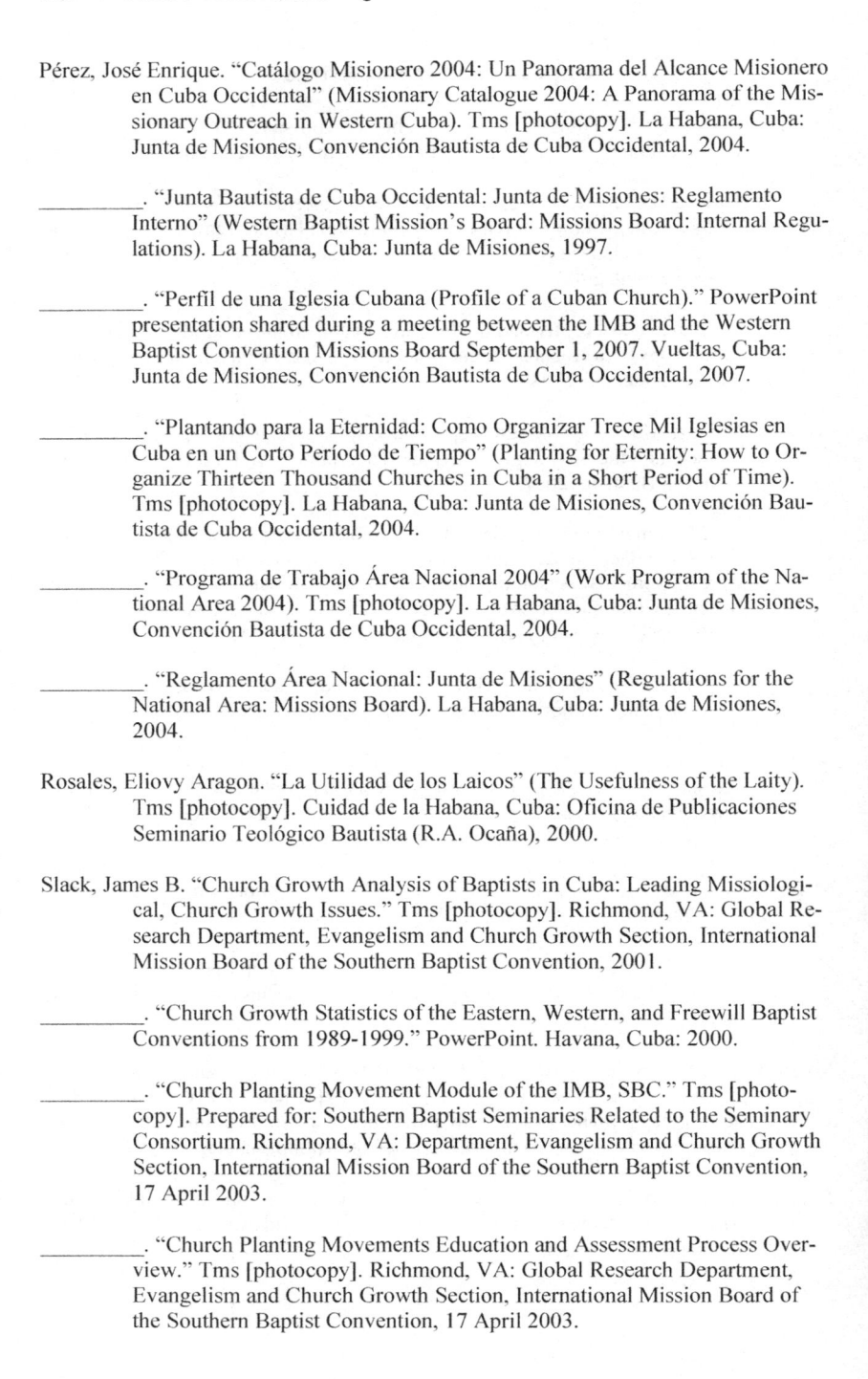

Pérez, José Enrique. "Catálogo Misionero 2004: Un Panorama del Alcance Misionero en Cuba Occidental" (Missionary Catalogue 2004: A Panorama of the Missionary Outreach in Western Cuba). Tms [photocopy]. La Habana, Cuba: Junta de Misiones, Convención Bautista de Cuba Occidental, 2004.

_____. "Junta Bautista de Cuba Occidental: Junta de Misiones: Reglamento Interno" (Western Baptist Mission's Board: Missions Board: Internal Regulations). La Habana, Cuba: Junta de Misiones, 1997.

_____. "Perfil de una Iglesia Cubana (Profile of a Cuban Church)." PowerPoint presentation shared during a meeting between the IMB and the Western Baptist Convention Missions Board September 1, 2007. Vueltas, Cuba: Junta de Misiones, Convención Bautista de Cuba Occidental, 2007.

_____. "Plantando para la Eternidad: Como Organizar Trece Mil Iglesias en Cuba en un Corto Período de Tiempo" (Planting for Eternity: How to Organize Thirteen Thousand Churches in Cuba in a Short Period of Time). Tms [photocopy]. La Habana, Cuba: Junta de Misiones, Convención Bautista de Cuba Occidental, 2004.

_____. "Programa de Trabajo Área Nacional 2004" (Work Program of the National Area 2004). Tms [photocopy]. La Habana, Cuba: Junta de Misiones, Convención Bautista de Cuba Occidental, 2004.

_____. "Reglamento Área Nacional: Junta de Misiones" (Regulations for the National Area: Missions Board). La Habana, Cuba: Junta de Misiones, 2004.

Rosales, Eliovy Aragon. "La Utilidad de los Laicos" (The Usefulness of the Laity). Tms [photocopy]. Cuidad de la Habana, Cuba: Oficina de Publicaciones Seminario Teológico Bautista (R.A. Ocaña), 2000.

Slack, James B. "Church Growth Analysis of Baptists in Cuba: Leading Missiological, Church Growth Issues." Tms [photocopy]. Richmond, VA: Global Research Department, Evangelism and Church Growth Section, International Mission Board of the Southern Baptist Convention, 2001.

_____. "Church Growth Statistics of the Eastern, Western, and Freewill Baptist Conventions from 1989-1999." PowerPoint. Havana, Cuba: 2000.

_____. "Church Planting Movement Module of the IMB, SBC." Tms [photocopy]. Prepared for: Southern Baptist Seminaries Related to the Seminary Consortium. Richmond, VA: Department, Evangelism and Church Growth Section, International Mission Board of the Southern Baptist Convention, 17 April 2003.

_____. "Church Planting Movements Education and Assessment Process Overview." Tms [photocopy]. Richmond, VA: Global Research Department, Evangelism and Church Growth Section, International Mission Board of the Southern Baptist Convention, 17 April 2003.

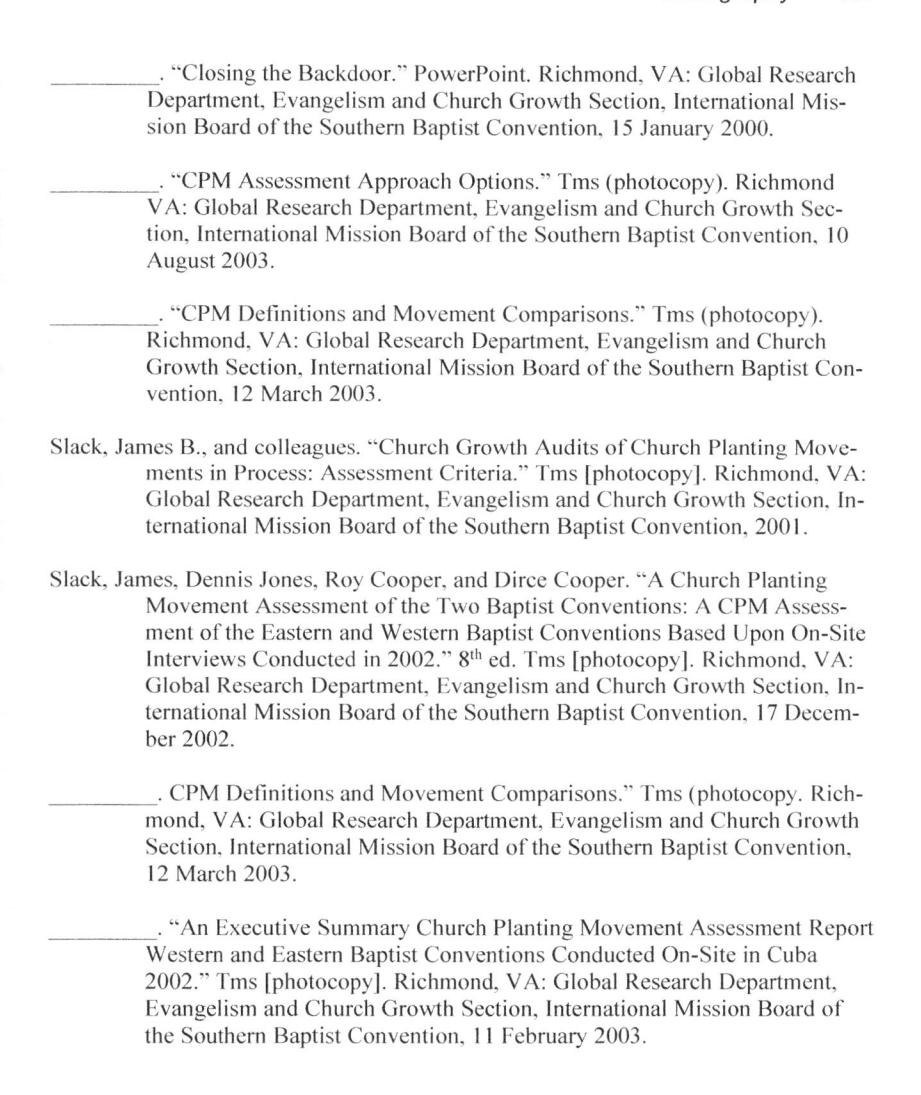

_____. "Closing the Backdoor." PowerPoint. Richmond, VA: Global Research Department, Evangelism and Church Growth Section, International Mission Board of the Southern Baptist Convention, 15 January 2000.

_____. "CPM Assessment Approach Options." Tms (photocopy). Richmond VA: Global Research Department, Evangelism and Church Growth Section, International Mission Board of the Southern Baptist Convention, 10 August 2003.

_____. "CPM Definitions and Movement Comparisons." Tms (photocopy). Richmond, VA: Global Research Department, Evangelism and Church Growth Section, International Mission Board of the Southern Baptist Convention, 12 March 2003.

Slack, James B., and colleagues. "Church Growth Audits of Church Planting Movements in Process: Assessment Criteria." Tms [photocopy]. Richmond, VA: Global Research Department, Evangelism and Church Growth Section, International Mission Board of the Southern Baptist Convention, 2001.

Slack, James, Dennis Jones, Roy Cooper, and Dirce Cooper. "A Church Planting Movement Assessment of the Two Baptist Conventions: A CPM Assessment of the Eastern and Western Baptist Conventions Based Upon On-Site Interviews Conducted in 2002." 8th ed. Tms [photocopy]. Richmond, VA: Global Research Department, Evangelism and Church Growth Section, International Mission Board of the Southern Baptist Convention, 17 December 2002.

_____. CPM Definitions and Movement Comparisons." Tms (photocopy. Richmond, VA: Global Research Department, Evangelism and Church Growth Section, International Mission Board of the Southern Baptist Convention, 12 March 2003.

_____. "An Executive Summary Church Planting Movement Assessment Report Western and Eastern Baptist Conventions Conducted On-Site in Cuba 2002." Tms [photocopy]. Richmond, VA: Global Research Department, Evangelism and Church Growth Section, International Mission Board of the Southern Baptist Convention, 11 February 2003.

Electronic Sources

Acosta García, Roy. Private e-mail to the writer, 7 November 2009.

"Annual Report for Cuba, 1996." Amnesty International Report 1996, [on-line]. Accessed 4 February 2010; available from http://www.amnestyusa.org/annualreport.php?id=ar &yr=1996&c=CU; Internet.

Chambers, Carl. *The Political Weakness of the Church in Cuba* (book on-line). Accessed 2 April 2002; available from www.thepoliticalweaknessofthechurchincuba-carl chambers.htm; Internet.

"Constitution of the Republic of Cuba, 1992" [on-line]. Accessed 7 December 2006; available from http://www.cubanet.org/ref/dis/const_92_e.htm; Internet.

"Cuba People 2010." *2010 CIA World Factbook* [on-line]. Accessed 13 July 2010; available from http://www.theodora.com/wfbcurrent/cuba/cuba_people.html; Internet.

"Evangelicals Come Up for Air." *Christianity Today*, June 1999 [on-line]. Accessed 24 December 2009; available from http://www.christianitytoday.com/ct/1999/june14/9t 723a.html; Internet.

Garrison, David. "Church Planting Movements." *Missions Frontiers Magazine*, April 2000 [on-line]. Accessed 20 October 2009; available from http://www.mission frontiers.org/pdf.2000/02.20000.htm; Internet.

Hartford Institute for Religion Research. "Megachurches" [on-line]. Available from http://hirr.hartsem.edu/megachurch/megachurches.html; accessed July 7, 2010; Internet.

Hurst, Randy. "La Iglesia que se Multiplica." (The Multiplying Church) Enrichment Journal, March 2008 [on-line]. Accessed 10 July 2010; available from http://www.ag.org/enrichmentjournal_sp200803/200803_048_Multiplying. cfm; Internet.

Landers, McBride. "Cuba, Did the Papal Visit Change Anything?" *Christianity Today*, February 1999 [on-line]. Accessed 24 December 2009; available from http://www. christianitytoday.com/ct/1999/february8/9t2018.html; Internet.

López, Lena. "Cuba: Draconian New Restrictions on 'Home Religious Meetings'." *Christian Solidarity Worldwide*, September 15, 2005 [on-line]. Accessed 28 December 2009; available from http://dynamic.CSW.org.uk/article.asp?t=report &id =21; Internet.

Martínez, Ibsen. "Hugo Chavez: The Next Castro?." August 6, 2006; B01 [on-line]. Accessed 24 July 2007; available from http://www. washingtonpost.com/wp-dyn/ content/article/2006/08/04/AR2006080401767pf.html; Internet.

Miles, Nick. "Cuba Faces Political Uncertainty." Washington: BBC News [on-line]. Accessed 1 August 2007; available from http://news.bbc.co.uk/1/hi/world/americas/5236958.stm; Internet.

Missions Frontiers Magazine. April 2000 [on-line]. Accessed 20 October 2009; available from http://www.missionfrontiers.org/pdf/2000/02.20000.htm; Internet.

NationMaster.com. "Cuban People Stats" [on-line]. Accessed 13 July 2010; available from http://www.nationmaster.com/country/cu-cuba/peo-people; Internet.

Open Doors International. "Country Profiles: Cuba" [on-line article]. Accessed 26 July 2007; available from http://www.opendoors.org/content/cubapro.htm; Internet.

Pedraza, Silvia. "The Impact of Pope John Paul II's Visit to Cuba" [on-line article]. Accessed 14 November 2009; available from htpp://lanic.utexas.edu/la/ca/cuba/ asce/cuba8/48pedraza.pdf; Internet.

Vega, Luis. "Hugo Chavez and the Cuban Revolution" (September 24, 2004) [on-line]. Accessed 26 July 2007; available from http://goinside.com/04/9/chavez.html; Internet.

Whoriskey, Peter. "Cubans in Miami Cheer Castro's Illness." *Washington Post*, A08 [on-line]. Accessed 6 August 2006; available from http://www.washingtonpost. com/wp-dyn/content/article/2006/08/01/AR2006080101405.html; Internet.

Wilkerson, Steve. "The Pope's Visit to Cuba" [on-line article]. Accessed 21 December 2009; available on line from http://www.poptel.org.uk/cuba-solidarity.CubaSi-January.PopesVisit.html; Internet.

Wintz, Jack. "The Pope in Cuba: A Call for Freedom" [on-line article]. Accessed 24 December 2009; available from http://www.americancatholic.org/Messenger/Apr 1998/feature1.asp; Internet.

Sources from Home Mission Board Files

Fite, Margaret to Loyd Corder, October 4, 1960. File 3, box "Caudill, Herbert." Herbert Caudill Collection. Atlanta: Home Mission Board of the Southern Baptist Convention Collection.

"Forty-First Annual Report of the Home Mission Board." *Proceedings*, 1886.

Minutes, January 17, 1899, Home Mission Board of the Southern Baptist Convention. Atlanta: Home Mission Board Files.

Minutes, September 10, 1885, Home Mission Board of the Southern Baptist Convention. Atlanta: Home Mission Board Files.

Minutes of the Southern Baptist Convention, 1887. App. B, XXVIII.

Minutes of the Southern Baptist Convention, 1899. App. B, LXXX.

Routledge, Robert. *Annual Report of the Board*, 1921.

Presentations

Gonzáles Muñoz, Alberto I. "50 Años en la Convención Bautista de Cuba Occidental: Estudio de Estadísticas (50 Years in the Western Baptist Convention: Statistical Study)." PowerPoint presentation to the Eastern and Western Cuban Baptist Leaders, along with the IMB. Boca Raton Conference Center, April 1-6, 2001.

Slack, James B. "An Evaluation of the Eastern and Western Baptist Convention in Cuba from 1990-2008 According to Official IMB, SBC, Church Planting Movement Criteria," PowerPoint presentation at the Kingdom Growth Conference at the Baptist Camp, Yumurí Matanzas, Cuba., Matanzas, Cuba, November 23-27, 2009.

_____. "Church Growth Statistics of the Eastern, Western, and Freewill Baptist Conventions from 1989-1999." PowerPoint presentation at the Church Growth Conference, McCall Baptist Church, Baptist World Alliance. Havana, Cuba, July 3-8, 2000.

_____. "Churches and Denominations in Cuba from 1960-1995." PowerPoint presentation at the Church Growth Conference, McCall Baptist Church, Baptist World Alliance. Havana, Cuba, July 3-8, 2000.

_____. "Discipleship Module: Characteristics of New Testament Entry Discipleship." PowerPoint presentation at the Church Growth Conference, McCall Baptist Church, Baptist World Alliance. Havana, Cuba, July 3-8, 2000.

_____. "Five Levels of Leaders." PowerPoint presentation at the Church Growth Conference, McCall Baptist Church, Baptist World Alliance. Havana, Cuba, July 3-8, 2000.

_____. "Primacy of New Church Starts in Reaching the Lost." PowerPoint presentation at the Church Growth Conference, McCall Baptist Church, Baptist World Alliance. Havana, Cuba, July 3-8, 2000.

Miscellaneous

Gonzáles Muñoz, Alberto I. *Leadership Obstacles*. Barbados: Strategy Coordinator Training, 2003; available from Kurt Urbanek, 57 min., DVD.

Martín Lemos, Israel. *Biblical Vision Without Limits*. Barbados: Strategy Coordinator Training, 2003. Available from Kurt Urbanek, 2 hrs., DVD.

_____. *Building a Biblical and Contextualized Strategy*. Barbados: Strategy Coordinator Training, 2003. Available from Kurt Urbanek, 1 hr. 28 min., DVD.

_____. *Preparing for a Positive Transition in the Church*. Barbados: Strategy Coordinator Training, 2003. Available from Kurt Urbanek, 1 hr. 6 min., DVD.

_____. *Testimony of Growth*. Barbados: Strategy Coordinator Training, 2003. Available from Kurt Urbanek, 38 min., DVD.

Made in United States
Orlando, FL
23 June 2025